Research in University Pedagogy

Series Editors
Jean-Marc Labat and Cécile de Hosson

Research in University Pedagogy

Towards a Discipline-based Approach?

Edited by

Stéphanie Bridoux
Nicolas Grenier-Boley
Caroline Leininger-Frézal

WILEY

First published 2023 in Great Britain and the United States by ISTE Ltd and John Wiley & Sons, Inc.

Apart from any fair dealing for the purposes of research or private study, or criticism or review, as permitted under the Copyright, Designs and Patents Act 1988, this publication may only be reproduced, stored or transmitted, in any form or by any means, with the prior permission in writing of the publishers, or in the case of reprographic reproduction in accordance with the terms and licenses issued by the CLA. Enquiries concerning reproduction outside these terms should be sent to the publishers at the undermentioned address:

ISTE Ltd
27-37 St George's Road
London SW19 4EU
UK

www.iste.co.uk

John Wiley & Sons, Inc.
111 River Street
Hoboken, NJ 07030
USA

www.wiley.com

© ISTE Ltd 2023

The rights of Stéphanie Bridoux, Nicolas Grenier-Boley and Caroline Leininger-Frézal to be identified as the authors of this work have been asserted by them in accordance with the Copyright, Designs and Patents Act 1988.

Any opinions, findings, and conclusions or recommendations expressed in this material are those of the author(s), contributor(s) or editor(s) and do not necessarily reflect the views of ISTE Group.

Library of Congress Control Number: 2022948708

British Library Cataloguing-in-Publication Data
A CIP record for this book is available from the British Library
ISBN 978-1-78630-793-4

Contents

Introduction xi
Stéphanie BRIDOUX, Nicolas GRENIER-BOLEY, Caroline LEININGER-FRÉZAL

About the Authors xvii

Part 1. The Links Between University Pedagogy and Didactics 1

Chapter 1. Why and How has Anglophone University Pedagogy Moved Closer to Francophone Subject Didactics? 3
Denis BERTHIAUME

1.1. Introduction. 3
1.2. Some contextual elements: pedagogy versus didactics 5
1.3. English-speaking university pedagogy. 7
1.4. An approach to the disciplinary pedagogical knowledge
of university teachers. 11
    1.4.1. The pedagogical knowledge base of university teachers 12
    1.4.2. Disciplinary specificity in higher education 12
    1.4.3. The personal epistemology of university teachers. 15
1.5. Conclusion 18
1.6. References 19

Chapter 2. Teacher Training at University through the Prism of Disciplines 27
Caroline LEININGER-FRÉZAL

2.1. Introduction. 27
2.2. Difficulties of taking into account disciplines in the training
of higher education teachers. 29
2.3 Resources available for taking into account disciplines
in higher education 33
2.4. How should we take into account disciplines in training
in higher education? 39
2.5. Conclusion 43
2.6. References 44

Chapter 3. Transforming Higher Education and Professional Learning for Academics. 47
Sacha KIFFER and Richard WITTORSKI

3.1. Changes and increasing complexity within university education 48
3.2. The heart of a problem: little recognition and training for teaching. . . 51
3.3. Theoretical framework: competence building practices. 52
    3.3.1. Highly structured learning practices. 54
    3.3.2. Weakly structured learning practices 55
3.4. Methodology: the questionnaire survey 57
3.5. Presentation and discussion of the survey results. 58
    3.5.1. Predominance of autonomous behavior. 58
    3.5.2. Specific training needs. 59
    3.5.3. Commonalities and differences in learning behaviors 61
    3.5.4. Effectiveness of competence-building practices. 62
3.6. Conclusion 63
3.7. References 64

Part 2. The Teaching Practices of University Teachers with a Disciplinary Approach 69

Chapter 4. Academic Territory and Professional Identity: Toward a Differentiation of Teaching Practices at University. 71
Stéphanie BRIDOUX, Nicolas GRENIER-BOLEY, Cécile DE HOSSON,
Rita KHANFOUR-ARMALÉ, Nathalie LEBRUN, Caroline LEININGER-FRÉZAL,
Zoé MESNIL, Céline NIHOUL and Martine DE VLEESCHOUWER

4.1. Introduction. 71

4.2. Academic territory and professional identity: a theoretical
environment to approach the pedagogical practices of lecturers
and researchers 74
4.3. The field survey 76
    4.3.1. Development of a survey tool 76
    4.3.2. Epistemological specificities of the disciplines concerned
    by the survey 77
4.4. Results 81
    4.4.1. Showing the beauty of disciplines 82
    4.4.2. Enhancing the usefulness and legitimacy of disciplines 84
    4.4.3. Drawing on research, even if its results are not directly
    presentable 87
    4.4.4. Staging the research process 90
    4.4.5. Adapting to current students 92
4.5. Returning to the questions of each discipline 98
4.6. Conclusion and implications for university pedagogy 100
4.7. Acknowledgements 102
4.8. References 102

Chapter 5. The Relationship Between Research Activity and the Design of Resources for Teaching – The Case of Mathematics at the University Level 109

Hussein SABRA

5.1. General introduction 109
5.2. The relationship between teaching and research in higher
education 111
    5.2.1. The relationship between teaching and research in
    educational science research 111
    5.2.2. The relationship between teaching and research in
    mathematics and science didactics research 113
    5.2.3. Resources for understanding the relationship between
    research and teaching 115
5.3. The articulation of two approaches: the documentary work
of a university professor in teaching and research institutions ... 116
    5.3.1. The documentational approach to didactics 117
    5.3.2. The complex relationship between teaching and research
    institutions 119
    5.3.3. The documentation work of a university professor,
    explored using pivotal resources 121
5.4. Methodology 123

5.5. Forms of the relationship between research and teaching
in terms of resources 126
    5.5.1. First form: the mobilization of a research resource in
instantiation processes 126
    5.5.2. Second form: a research resource to scaffold learning of
given content 127
    5.5.3. Third form: the form of non-relation in terms of resources 129
    5.5.4. Results and discussions 130
5.6. Conclusions and perspectives 131
5.7. References 132

Part 3. A Sociological Perspective of the Practices of Lecturers and Researchers 137

Chapter 6. Beyond the Disciplinary Approach: Toward a Socio-historical and Critical Reflexivity of its Teaching Practices 139
Stéphanie TRALONGO

6.1. Introduction 139
6.2. The content of the common discursive fund on "higher education
pedagogy" 141
    6.2.1. Recent and growing discourse and practice 141
    6.2.2. Circular and self-referential content 143
    6.2.3. Some areas of traffic 146
6.3. Deconstruction, denaturalization: the political under the obvious 148
    6.3.1. Denaturalizing the chronology 148
    6.3.2. Recomposing democratic functioning 149
    6.3.3. Effects on the perceptions and practices of lecturers
and researchers 151
6.4. Teaching practices in sociology in reverse 153
    6.4.1. Creating a space to express one's practices 153
    6.4.2. Some content 154
6.5. Conclusion 156
6.6. References 157
6.7. Appendices 160
    6.7.1. Appendix A: the program for the day (June 27, 2016) 160
    6.7.2. Appendix B: the 2017 program 161

Chapter 7. Transmitting Knowledge in the First Year of University: A Sociology of Work Perspective........ 163
Marie DAVID

    7.1. Introduction... 163
    7.2. Conventions in content and teaching methods 166
        7.2.1. Educational conventions......................... 166
        7.2.2. Conventions concerning the presentation of knowledge 170
        7.2.3. Conventions specific to teaching..................... 175
        7.2.4. The role of common evaluations..................... 177
    7.3. Knowledge markers.................................. 179
        7.3.1. The work of delimiting important knowledge 180
        7.3.2. Note-taking, a collective activity of teachers and students....... 183
    7.4. Conclusion 187
    7.5. References 188

Chapter 8. Postface: Synthesis and Perspectives............. 191
Emmanuelle ANNOOT

    8.1. University pedagogy: fields of research and fields of practice...... 194
    8.2. Research and expertise 195
    8.3. A disciplinary approach to university pedagogy 197
    8.4. The professional identity of lecturers and researchers and
their practices 201
    8.5. Conclusion 202
    8.6. References 203

List of Authors 207

Index 211

Introduction

University teaching practices have been the target of lively and varied interest since the beginning of the 2000s. As an institutional object, the teaching practices of academics are perceived as an object to be transformed, with this transformation aimed at the (seemingly inescapable) consideration of evolutions of the modes of knowledge appropriation by students and the modes of mediation (Albero 2015). Thus, for more than a decade, French higher education has been confronted with the need for "pedagogical innovations" supported, among other things, by the promotion of "digital technology". This is evidenced by the numerous calls for projects (IDEX, IDEFI, etc.) aimed at deploying specific digital training offers, developing and reinforcing the use of technological tools for teaching, or implementing innovative pedagogical devices (ICTE, e-learning, flipped classroom, etc.).

Considered as an object of research, the teaching practices of academics become an object to understand. In a collective work published in 2004, Emmanuelle Annoot and Marie-Françoise Fave-Bonnet presented the first summary of the questions associated with the study of teaching practices at the university. The aim was to shed new light on the daily practices of teachers and students, as well as on teachers' perceptions and the scope of their actions. The contributions structuring this synthesis paved the way for the development of further work; the exploration of the practices of lecturers and researchers was one of these avenues and aimed to question the idea of a common culture through the study of questions associated, for example, with the treatment of student heterogeneity (Altet 2004), with the gaps between

---

Introduction written by Stéphanie BRIDOUX, Nicolas GRENIER-BOLEY and Caroline LEININGER-FRÉZAL.

the planned course and the actual course (Trinquier and Terrisse 2004), or with the elements that constrain practices (Clanet 2004; Langevin 2008; Rege-Collet and Berthiaume 2009). On this point, and among the elements that constrain practices, while some are "institutional" in nature, others appear to be more related to the perceptions that lecturers and researchers have of teaching, learning and science.

Although a great deal of Francophone research in the wake of these pioneering works has since taken up the pedagogical practices of academics as its subject, few of them take on, or have taken on, the disciplinary dimension of these practices. In his survey of French articles published in the FRANCIS database on university pedagogy (1991–2005), Adangnifou (2008) indicates that the vast majority of articles published during this period focus on teaching and teacher training practices, information and communication technologies, student learning, as well as the evaluation of teachers and student learning, without intentionally targeting one or more disciplines. However, he points to five articles that specifically address issues of language and French learning and teaching but does not identify any articles that target a discipline in the fields of mathematics, the sciences or nature. It should be noted that the observation appears identical on a more international scale. Over the last 10 years, articles on disciplinary teaching practices at university have increased in number but are still relatively few in number.

However, some studies emphasize that the community of university teachers, particularly that of lecturers and researchers, is "shaped" by the academic discipline to which it belongs, and that it therefore shares "the same set of intellectual values, the same cognitive territory" (Becher 1994, p. 3). For Becher (1994), the sense of disciplinary belonging of lecturers and researchers is an essential (even primary) component of their identity and expertise as teachers; it includes a set of certainties about both what should be taught and how it should be taught. This leads him (and other researchers following him; Trede et al. 2012; Poteaux 2013) to advocate for the development of research on academic practices that take as their input the disciplinary specificity of actors and knowledge.

The objective of this book is to propose a panorama of the research carried out in didactics on the teaching and learning of sciences (mathematics, physics, chemistry, life sciences, earth sciences, geography) at university through the lens of university pedagogy. It will be structured in three parts. The different chapters will all be based on research on the teaching and learning of scientific disciplines at university. They will therefore be based on an explicit methodology and specific corpora.

The first part of this book questions the links between university pedagogy and didactics. In Chapter 1, Denis Berthiaume examines how and why English-language university pedagogy has come closer to French-language discipline didactics. He describes the nature and composition of disciplinary pedagogical knowledge and its role in higher education. This knowledge is at the intersection of the components of the pedagogical knowledge base, disciplinary specificity, and personal epistemology. In Chapter 2, Caroline Leininger-Frézal explores the place of this disciplinary pedagogical knowledge in higher education. This questioning is investigated on the basis of a participant observation carried out over 4 years at the University of Paris Diderot. In Chapter 3, Sacha Kiffer and Richard Wittorski approach the training of lecturers and researchers from the perspective of professionalization and its challenges.

The second part questions the teaching practices of university teachers with a disciplinary approach. In Chapter 4, Bridoux et al. present a piece of interdisciplinary research (chemistry, geography, mathematics and physics), which aims to study the impact of the research discipline of lecturers and researchers on their teaching practices. This question is approached by mobilizing the sociological concept of professional identity specified with regard to the relationship that lecturers and researchers have with the discipline from which they come (epistemological relationship), on the one hand, and with the way in which this discipline must be taught (pedagogical relationship), on the other hand. These two relationships are then characterized from interviews conducted with lecturers and researchers. The results show regularities between disciplines but also variabilities that may be linked to the disciplinary specificities of the lecturers and researchers interviewed. The question of the links between research activity and the practices of university teachers is also at the heart of the second chapter, written by Sabra Hussein (Chapter 5). It is approached here from the angle of the interactions between the resources mobilized by lecturers and researchers in their activity as researchers and in their activity as teachers. This question is studied by articulating concepts from the documentary approach to didactics and the anthropological theory of didactics. The results of interviews conducted with mathematics lecturers and researchers allow us to develop research avenues to shed light on the relationship between the two activities of research and teaching.

The third part offers a sociological perspective of the practices of lecturers and researchers. In Chapter 6, Stéphanie Tralongo analyzes the discourse on "higher education pedagogy" constructed by them in a set of various kinds of texts (regulatory texts, articles, scientific works, calls for projects, etc.). This analysis highlights a common discursive background on "higher education pedagogy" that the author then sets out to deconstruct. Stéphanie Tralongo shows that these discourses have a naturalizing dimension based in particular on the imperative need for change. Chapter 7 sheds light on higher education from another angle. Through an analysis of in situ teaching practices in several disciplines (physics, sociology, chemistry), Marie David shows that, beyond the discourses, teaching practices are based on teaching conventions that are partly disciplinary and concern the ways of teaching and presenting knowledge. These conventions are distinct from those used in research.

References

Adangnifou, N. (2008). Peut-on parler de recherche en pédagogie universitaire, aujourd'hui, en France ? *Revue des sciences de l'éducation*, 34(3), 601–621.

Altet, M. (2004). Enseigner en premier cycle universitaire : des formes émergentes d'adaptation ou de la "métis" enseignante. In *Pratiques pédagogiques dans l'enseignement supérieur : enseigner, apprendre, évaluer*, Annoot, E., Fave-Bonnet, M.-F. (eds). L'Harmattan, Paris.

Annoot, E. and Fave-Bonnet M.-F. (eds) (2004). *Pratiques pédagogiques dans l'enseignement supérieur : enseigner, apprendre, évaluer*. L'Harmattan, Paris.

Becher, T. (1994). The significance of disciplinary differences. *Studies in Higher Education*, 19(2), 151–161.

Clanet, J. (2004). "Que se passe-t-il en cours ?" Éléments de description des pratiques enseignantes à l'université. In *Pratiques pédagogiques dans l'enseignement supérieur : enseigner, apprendre, évaluer*, Annoot, E., Fave-Bonnet, M.-F. (eds). L'Harmattan, Paris.

Poteaux, N. (2013). Pédagogie de l'enseignement supérieur en France : État de la question. *Distances et Médiations des Savoirs*, 4 [Online]. Available at: http://dms.revues.org/362 [Accessed 27 June 2016].

Rege Colet, N. and Berthiaume, D. (2009). Savoir ou être ? Savoirs et identités professionnels chez les enseignants universitaires. In *Savoirs en (trans)formation : au coeur des professions de l'enseignement et de la formation*, Hofstetter, R., Schneuwly, B. (eds). De Boeck, Brussels.

Trede, F., Macklin, R., Bridges, D. (2012). Professional identity development: A review of the higher education literature. *Studies in Higher Education*, 37(3), 365–384.

Trinquier, M.P. and Terrisse, A. (2004). Entre prévisions et réalité du cours : regards croisés sur les pratiques et les représentations des enseignants de DEUG. In *Les pratiques dans l'enseignement supérieur*, Annoot, E., Fave-Bonnet, M.-F. (eds). L'Harmattan, Paris.

About the Authors

Emmanuelle Annoot is a professor of education and training sciences. She is a member of the Cirnef laboratory (Université de Rouen Normandie France). She is currently vice-president of the academic council of the Université de Rouen in charge of the field "Humanities, Culture, Societies". Her research focuses on university pedagogy, coaching practices and the professional development of university lecturers and researchers (especially those just starting out).

Denis Berthiaume is a university professor in educational psychology. His research and intervention work focuses on university pedagogy, quality approaches in higher education, strategic planning and educational leadership. He is currently Vice-Rector, Academic and Research, at the Université de l'Ontario français, Canada, a new higher education institution focused on transdisciplinarity and research intervention in the broad field of humanities and social sciences.

Stéphanie Bridoux is a lecturer in mathematics at the Université de Mons (Belgium). She is a member of the Laboratoire de Didactique André Revuz (EA 4434) where she is co-leader (with Nicolas Grenier-Boley) of the working group "teachers in higher education". Her current research is in the field of mathematics didactics and focuses on the study of teachers' discourse during moments in the course (moments of demonstrating knowledge) by focusing on how the notion of limit is taught.

Marie David is a lecturer in sociology and a social science associate. She is a member of the Centre nantais de sociologie (UMR 6025) and teaches at the Institut national supérieur du professorat et de l'éducation in Nantes,

France. Her current research interests are the sociology of work, the sociology of knowledge and the sociology of school, and focus on the production of knowledge in secondary and higher education. Her latest publication is: David M. (2020). "Travailler à l'université. La définition étudiante du niveau et de la direction des efforts à fournir", *Revue française de pédagogie*, no. 209.

Martine De Vleeschouwer is a lecturer in mathematics at the Université de Namur (Belgium). She is a member of the Institut de Recherche en Didactiques et Éducation of the Université de Namur (IRDENa). Her research interests are in the field of mathematics didactics, and more particularly in the area of the transition from secondary school to university.

Nicolas Grenier Boley is a professor in mathematics didactics and mathematics at the Université de Rouen Normandie. He is a member of the Laboratoire de Didactique André Revuz (EA 4434) where he is co-leader (with Stéphanie Bridoux) of the working group "teachers in higher education". His current research is in the field of mathematics didactics. On the one hand, he studies moments of the course and the in situ practices of mathematics teachers in secondary and higher education. On the other hand, he is interested in the transition between university academic mathematics and mathematics taught in secondary schools for future teachers or new teachers.

Cécile de Hosson is a university professor at the Université de Paris and a researcher in didactics of physics at the Laboratoire de didactique André Revuz, a research unit she directed from 2013 to 2018. Her research themes are structured around one objective: to identify the way in which physics knowledge circulates and is transformed when it moves from a "scholarly" space of enunciation to a space of reception. Since 2012, this objective has been embodied in the study of the discourse of physics lecturers and researchers, on the one hand, and in the analysis of popular science comics, on the other hand.

Rita Khanfour-Armalé is a lecturer in chemistry at CYU cergy Paris université and a researcher in chemistry didactics at the Laboratoire de Didactique André Revuz (LDAR). She is a science teacher at the Inspé de l'académie de Versailles for primary and secondary schools. Her main research interests are as follows: the professional identity of lecturers and researchers in chemistry, the practices of secondary school teachers in chemistry (conversational and didactic analysis) and within an interdisciplinary science project, and recently the practices of primary school teachers (scientific challenges and the investigative approach).

Sacha Kiffer is a pedagogical advisor at HEC Montréal (Canada). He holds a PhD in Education and Training Sciences and is a research associate at CREAD (Centre de recherches sur l'éducation, les apprentissages et la didactique) at Rennes 2 University (France). His research focuses on the professional development of university teachers and, in particular, the construction of their pedagogical skills.

Nathalie Lebrun has been a lecturer in physics at the Université de Lille since 1996 and has been on research assignment since 2013 at the Université de Paris at the André Revuz didactics laboratory (EA4434) following the completion of a master's degree in the didactics of experimental sciences in 2013 at the Université de Paris Diderot. She focuses on two research axes in the exploration of the practices of lecturers and researchers in physics: the comparative approach and mobilization of an approach using professional identity and the integration of the results of the research in physics teaching (taking into account the conceptions of students) in the teaching practices.

Caroline Leininger-Frézal is a senior lecturer in geography didactics at the University of Paris, attached to the Laboratoire de Didactique André Revuz (LDAR). Her research interests include the teaching of geography in higher education, particularly the curriculum, the use of cases and examples, the professionalization of students and the professional identity of higher education teachers. Her accreditation to supervise research is on the teaching of geography through experience from primary school to university.

Zoé Mesnil is a lecturer in didactics of mathematics at the Université de Paris, within the Laboratoire de Didactique André Revuz (LDAR). The theme of her thesis, the teaching of logic in high school, led her to focus on the transition from high school to higher education, in which a conceptual leap requires knowledge of logic that is not always built in high school or taken on in higher education. She is notably co-leader of the Logic and Reasoning group of the GDR DEMIPS (Didactics and Epistemology of Mathematics, links with Computer Science and Physics, in Higher Education).

Céline Nihoul has been a doctor in the Didactics of Mathematics at the Université de Mons (Belgium) since January 2021. Her thesis focuses on the teaching of equations of lines and planes in Belgian secondary education. She is a member of the Laboratoire de Didactique André Revuz (EA4434) and has been part of the "higher education" group since 2013.

Hussein Sabra is an associate professor in mathematics education at the Université de Reims Champagne-Ardenne. His work focuses on the documentational work of mathematics teachers. He develops methodological tools to address the issue of teachers' interactions with resources. His research considers the individual and collective processes of designing resources for teaching. His research is currently focused on two themes: the relationship between the research activities and teaching practice of mathematics lecturers and researchers, and resources for teaching mathematics in engineering education.

Stéphanie Tralongo is a senior lecturer in sociology in the Modes, Spaces and Processes of Socialization (MEPS) team at the Centre Max Weber in Lyon. From an approach of socialization, and particularly of the notion of appropriation, her work is deployed in the fields of sociology of culture, education, work and sciences. The effects of public policies on higher education training programs, teaching and research practices, and the knowledge produced, are at the heart of her most recent work.

Richard Wittorski is a professor at the Université de Rouen Normandie and director of the CIRNEF (centre interdisciplinaire de recherche normand en éducation et formation). His work focuses on work-training relationships and professionalization in the field of adult education and in various sectors (industry, labor inspection, educational work, adult education, etc.). He has produced more than 150 publications on these issues.

PART 1

The Links Between University Pedagogy and Didactics

1

Why and How has Anglophone University Pedagogy Moved Closer to Francophone Subject Didactics?

1.1. Introduction

Anyone working at the crossroads of different intellectual traditions has become aware of the "cultural specificity" of certain scientific knowledge. In the field of educational sciences, this is the case with the relationship between teaching and learning. If one examines it by looking at the Anglophone literature on the subject, one discovers an object of study that focuses mainly on the relationship between the teacher and the learner and on the psychological dimensions of this relationship (Shuell 1993; Andrews et al. 1996; Palincsar 1998; D'Andrea and Gosling 2005). If we examine the latter from the French-speaking literature, we discover a subject of study that focuses mainly on knowledge taught and knowledge learned (Chevallard 1991; Jonnaert and Lenoir 1993; Jonnaert and Laurin 2001; Terrisse 2001). On the Anglophone side, we opt for "pedagogy", whereas on the Francophone side, we opt for "didactics". However, the difference between pedagogy and didactics is not always very clear (Tochon 1991; Bertrand and Houssaye 1999).

In higher education, one would think that the didactic approach would dominate because of the prominence of taught knowledge – university teachers are first and foremost specialists in a discipline or profession which they have been assigned to teach (Menges and Austin 2001; Kreber 2009).

Chapter written by Denis BERTHIAUME.

Their own training rarely focuses on pedagogy or didactics, but rather on the discipline or profession they have been assigned to teach. Yet, in the French-speaking world of higher education, the notion of "university didactics" is very rarely mentioned as it is in German-speaking countries (*Hochschuledidaktik*). This can be explained in two ways. On the one hand, as Develay (1992, 1997) points out, the notion of "general didactics", that is, detached from a particular discipline, does not exist, unlike pedagogy, which is rather generic. On the other hand, the field was quickly occupied by English-speaking concepts from university teaching and learning (Beard and Hartley 1987; Cranton 1998; Lazerson et al. 2000; Fry et al. 2008). In fact, university pedagogy or higher education pedagogy is now used to describe anything that deals with teaching and learning at the tertiary level (Langevin and Bruneau 2000; Langevin 2007; Berthiaume and Rege Colet 2013; Rege Colet and Berthiaume 2015). The transposition of the concept took place in part in Quebec, a French-speaking island in the middle of an English-speaking ocean, since English-language university pedagogy developed in North America in the 1960s and in the United Kingdom in the 1970s. It appeared roughly in the French-speaking universities of Quebec in the 1970s and was imported into Belgium in the 1980s, Switzerland in the 1990s and France in the 2000s.

Over the years, researchers and practitioners in the field of higher education pedagogy have realized that the generic concepts of Anglophone pedagogy required some adaptation to the cultural and/or disciplinary context in which they were used (Alexander and Dochy 1995; Ghosh 1996; Gardiner et al. 1998). On the Francophone side, the object of study of "knowledge taught and learned" focused mainly on the primary and secondary levels of education, sometimes on the professionalizing tertiary sector (Chevallard 1991; Jonnaert and Laurin 2001; Terrisse 2001). The two intellectual traditions began to come together in the 1990s when English-speaking university pedagogy began to focus on "disciplinary specificity" (Becher 1994; Hativa and Marincovich 1995) and, at the same time, the French-speaking world of higher education began to question "university pedagogy", that is, the conditions of study and the future of university graduates (Dupont and Ossandon 1994).

In this chapter, we will explain how the two intellectual traditions came together, giving rise to the concept of "discipline-specific pedagogical knowledge". We will describe this form of knowledge, which is essential for all higher education teachers, whether they work in academic or professional higher education. We will highlight the different components of this knowledge and how they interact with each other to form what is known as "discipline-specific pedagogical knowledge".

1.2. Some contextual elements: pedagogy versus didactics

As a French-speaking Canadian (Quebecer), I have had the opportunity to pursue my university studies in both French and English higher education institutions. Montreal lends itself well to this as there are two French-speaking universities (Université de Montréal and Université du Québec à Montréal) and two English-speaking universities (McGill University and Concordia University). For a number of years, students registered at one of these universities have been able to take courses at any of the four universities, which I did during my graduate studies. I had the opportunity to study the same phenomena from the field of education from both the Anglophone and Francophone literature.

As early as my graduate studies in education, I became interested in the question of teaching and learning specific to each disciplinary or professional field taught at university. Drawing from both English and French sources, I discovered two parallel universes that seemed to have little contact with each other. This situation is paradoxical: on the one hand, one becomes aware of the potential richness of pooling the knowledge generated by these two intellectual traditions; on the other hand, one is surprised that this has not been done to date. My work has therefore addressed this situation and I have begun to examine the scientific literature from both intellectual traditions. To explain the difference between the two traditions, I will take a two-step approach. First, I will discuss the constituent disciplines of educational science according to each tradition, and then I will discuss the angle of observation favored by each tradition.

The field of educational sciences is constituted differently according to one or the other approach. In the Anglophone literature, psychology seems to dominate the disciplinary configuration. It is impossible to study the teaching-learning relationship without studying the underlying psychological processes (e.g. cognitive structures of the teacher or the learner, group dynamics, developmental stages of the actors). The subject matter (what is being taught) seems to be relegated to the background. Disciplinary specialization around blocks of disciplines such as social studies or natural sciences comes after having assimilated a set of generic concepts stemming mainly from educational psychology. In the Francophone literature, discipline didactics seems to dominate the disciplinary configuration. It is impossible to study the teaching–learning relationship without looking at the knowledge to be taught and to be learned (e.g. scholarly knowledge versus academic knowledge, didactic transposition, disciplinary structure, conceptual complexity). Psychological processes are present but seem secondary to the understanding of the observed phenomena.

To describe the difference in perspectives between the Anglophone and Francophone traditions, I will use Houssaye's (2014) pedagogical triangle (reproduced in Figure 1.1). Houssaye describes the relationship between teacher, learner (student), and knowledge using this triangle. The teacher's mission is ultimately to help the student learn the knowledge presented. However, the way to achieve this seems to differ according to each intellectual tradition. On the Francophone side, it is clear that the teacher seeks to "organize" the knowledge in such a way as to help the learner acquire it and then transform it into skills. For example, this is done through the establishment of a sequence of teaching concepts and the more or less present accompaniment of the teacher according to the level of complexity of the subject being taught. On the English side, the teacher's main objective is to support the learner's psychological processes so that the learner acquires the knowledge and develops the skills related to it. For example, the teacher seeks to support the learner's motivation, collaboration with other learners or participation in a discussion on the subject presented.

This is obviously not a dichotomous situation: one approach does not prevent the other. Focusing primarily on the organization of knowledge (what Houssaye calls the "teaching" process) does not mean avoiding consideration of the learner's development (what Houssaye calls the "training" process). The difference between the two intellectual traditions seems to lie rather in the angle of observation of the teaching–learning relationship, in the door that is used to enter this relationship. In the English-language literature, one enters through the door that corresponds to the "training" process, whereas in the French-language literature, one enters through the door that corresponds to the "teaching" process.

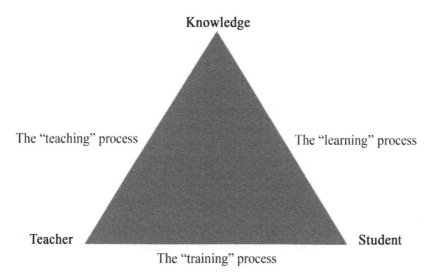

Figure 1.1. *Houssaye's (2014) educational triangle. For a color version of this figure, see www.iste.co.uk/bridoux/research.zip*

Studying the teaching–learning relationship from both intellectual traditions simultaneously thus allows for a much richer and more promising look at the notion of disciplinary specificity in this relationship. This is what I sought to do and what led me to develop a conceptualization, which I later empirically tested, of the disciplinary pedagogical knowledge of university teachers. If we take up Houssaye's triangle (see Figure 1.1), disciplinary pedagogical knowledge allows the teacher to help the learner by focusing on both the knowledge taught and the psychological processes underlying their relationship. Thus, we find ourselves drawing from both elements of didactics and elements of pedagogy.

1.3. English-speaking university pedagogy

University-based centers for teaching and learning began to emerge in North America (Canada and the United States) in the 1960s at the request of teachers who wanted to develop their knowledge and skills in teaching. The majority of them had a doctorate in a disciplinary and/or professional field but felt powerless to "teach" the elements of their discipline and/or profession to students. For example, the Centre for University Teaching and Learning at McGill University in Canada was established in 1969 with the mission, among others, of organizing training workshops for newly hired teachers (McAlpine and Cowan 2000). Such centers, although working in the field of teaching and learning, were generally located outside of faculties of education to avoid their activities being perceived as equivalent to pre-service training for primary and secondary teachers. Indeed, the audience for new university teachers is quite different from the audience for elementary and secondary teachers (Dunkin and Precians 1992; Menges and Austin 2001; Martin et al. 2002). Thus, newly hired university teachers do not necessarily see themselves as teachers but rather as:

– specialists in a discipline and/or profession that is broader and often more important to them than the institution by which they were recruited;

– highly qualified professionals with research, teaching and service responsibilities, with a strong emphasis on research;

– intellectuals who have the freedom to choose what they teach, ideally in connection with their research activities.

Thus, the training activities organized by the English-language university pedagogy centers focused very little in the early years of their existence on issues of disciplinary specificity. Training activities were based primarily on three conceptual areas:

– teacher education (e.g. learning theories, teaching expertise, pedagogical knowledge base, reflective practice);

– adult education (e.g. the needs of adult learners, professional development, experiential learning, conceptual change);

– instructional design (e.g. clarification of content and learning objectives, choice of teaching strategies and assessment methods, sequencing).

The choice and contribution of these rather generic conceptual domains was obvious, since they included specialists from all disciplines and/or professions taught at the university. The participants in the training activities shared a common need:

– to develop as a teacher of a discipline or profession, related to their research responsibilities;

– use conceptual tools to build training activities for students based on their own disciplinary and/or professional knowledge and skills;

– to integrate these new inputs into their previous and future professional experiences.

For example, early professional development activities for university teachers focused on learning, teaching strategies, assessment methods and the use of information and communication technologies for education (ICTE). These activities were considered "generic" as they applied to all disciplinary and/or professional areas. Teachers developing their knowledge and skills through these resources were then expected to work on adapting them to their disciplinary reality once the training was completed. For example, once the generic learnings about discussion as a form of teaching were completed, each teacher had to think about how to implement discussion as a teaching strategy in their own field (e.g. law, medicine, engineering, art history).

In the 1980s, researchers in English-speaking countries became interested in the link between pedagogical knowledge and the nature of the content taught. In the context of research on the pedagogical knowledge base of teachers, they began to question pedagogical content knowledge, that is, pedagogical knowledge related to the subject taught (Gudmundsdottir and Shulman 1987; Shulman 1986, 1987; Grossman et al. 1989). In this area of research, a set of essential knowledge for teaching (e.g. pedagogical knowledge, knowledge about learning, subject-specific knowledge) was identified. It was at this point that it was realized that knowledge at the intersection of pedagogical knowledge and content knowledge was central to the professional development of the teacher. In teacher education programs for elementary and secondary schools, there were generic elements that were the same for all students (e.g. elements of psychology, philosophy, sociology of education) and subject-specific elements (e.g. mathematics, social studies, natural sciences, language and culture). Shulman's work in particular highlighted the difficulty novice teachers had in linking these two categories of knowledge. Interest in pedagogical content knowledge was born.

During the 1990s, two developments paved the way for the emergence of disciplinary pedagogical knowledge. On the one hand, research on pedagogical content knowledge was increasing (Grossman and Yerian 1992; Baxter and Lederman 1999; Gess-Newsome and Lederman 1999; Magnusson et al. 1999). How it was formed, how it was used in various disciplinary fields (e.g. mathematics, natural sciences, social sciences, physical education and sports) and how it could be evaluated was studied. The aim was to study what was sometimes called the "psychologization of subject matter", a form of "applied epistemology" very close to the didactics of disciplines. On the other hand, researchers were beginning to take an interest in the notion of disciplinary specificity in higher education. Various works on the epistemological nature of disciplines and the similarities and differences between them emerged (Smeby 1996; Neumann 2001; Donald 2002; Neumann and Becher 2002; Lueddeke 2003). This work has reminded researchers – and university teachers – that it is not possible to ignore the specificities of each discipline when implementing new pedagogical strategies. One example is problem-based learning in medicine (Bligh 1995). This approach is very appropriate in medicine because it is based on the notion of the clinical case. But how can it be imported into disciplines that are close to it, such as biology, or further away from it, such as ethics?

There was a growing awareness among various stakeholders in higher education of the importance of considering discipline-specific pedagogical knowledge in the professional development of higher education teachers. However, it was not until 1995 that the concept of discipline-specific pedagogical knowledge emerged (Lenze 1995, 1996). At that time, Lenze used it to refer to pedagogical content knowledge but applied it to higher education. The transfer of the concept from the primary and secondary levels to the tertiary level had taken place. However, the situation was very particular since Lenze used the field of language teaching to transform pedagogical content knowledge into discipline-specific pedagogical knowledge. Yet, learning to use English at the primary, secondary or tertiary level does not seem quite equivalent to learning social studies at the primary level, history and geography at the secondary level and ancient history at the tertiary level. In fact, Lenze has simply transposed the concept of pedagogical content knowledge developed by Shulman for the primary and secondary levels to higher education. However, with the reality of tertiary education being more complex, the work on the disciplinary specificity of each field taught in higher education showed that the concept needed to be further explored in order to make it operational and representative of the reality. This is where the notion of disciplinary pedagogical knowledge specific to higher education emerged (Berthiaume 2007).

1.4. An approach to the disciplinary pedagogical knowledge of university teachers

It is in this context that I chose to focus on the operationalization of disciplinary pedagogical knowledge among university teachers. Since disciplinary specificity was becoming an inescapable part of thinking about university pedagogy, and since the notion of disciplinary pedagogical knowledge as conceptualized by Lenze was not entirely representative of the complexity of the knowledge taught in higher education, it was necessary to start again from scratch and to examine various areas of research in the educational sciences – mainly Anglophone, but also Francophone – in order to better define the outline of disciplinary pedagogical knowledge. According to Shulman's (and Lenze's) work, the starting point was simple: disciplinary pedagogical knowledge corresponds to a set of pedagogical resources (e.g. knowledge, beliefs, intentions) available to a teacher that allow him or her to better understand how to teach and "make known" the various concepts of his or her discipline (Berthiaume 2007). On the one hand, the university teacher draws on his or her knowledge base for teaching and, on the other hand, adjusts this pedagogical knowledge to the disciplinary specificity. It was therefore necessary to re-examine these notions and see how the two could be related to each other.

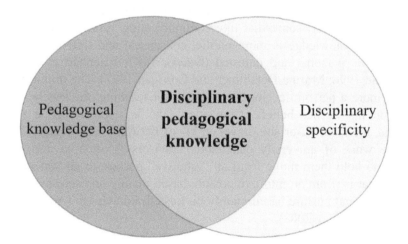

Figure 1.2. *Disciplinary pedagogical knowledge at the intersection between the pedagogical knowledge base and disciplinary specificity (Berthiaume 2007). For a color version of this figure, see www.iste.co.uk/bridoux/research.zip*

1.4.1. *The pedagogical knowledge base of university teachers*

Research on the pedagogical knowledge base of teachers has identified three main components (Donmoyer 1986; Reynolds 1989; Pajares 1992; Pratt 1992; Turner-Bisset 1999; Hiebert et al. 2002):

– Aims: elements that guide the teacher's action or implementation of decisions (e.g. wanting to engage students during instruction or seeking to develop autonomy).

– Teacher knowledge structures: elements that inform the teacher's action or the implementation of decisions (e.g. his or her understanding of a pedagogical principle or method, his or her understanding of a theoretical notion to be introduced in his or her teaching).

– Teacher beliefs: elements that also inform teacher action or decision making; however, unlike knowledge, beliefs are generally very non-consensual and rarely proven (e.g. the view that handwritten notetaking is absolutely essential to learning or that students must memorize definitions of certain concepts before learning anything else).

The pedagogical knowledge base is thus the terrain of a set of interactions between these three elements. Knowledge and beliefs set the "tone" while goals or intentions transform them into actions. Knowledge and beliefs are very complementary, somewhat like communicating vessels that feed each other. While knowledge is more public, consensual and tested, beliefs are more private, personal and untested (Nespor 1987; Eisenhart et al. 1988; Calderhead 1996; Morine-Dershimer and Corrigan 1997). The implication is that the more a person develops knowledge for teaching, the less he or she draws on his or her beliefs. Conversely, the less knowledge a person develops, the more he or she draws on his or her (untested) beliefs. This is why the work of university educational advisors is often to accompany teachers to help them move from an "intuitive" posture to an "intentional" posture, that is, from an intuitive posture based mainly on (untested) beliefs to an intentional posture based mainly on (tested) knowledge (Angelo 1994; Saroyan and Frenay 2008).

1.4.2. *Disciplinary specificity in higher education*

The reflection on the specificity of disciplines and/or professions taught at the university was launched in the English-speaking literature by the work of Biglan (1973a, 1973b). The latter sought to categorize university disciplines. It is to him that we owe the well-known typology of "hard" versus "soft" disciplines or "pure" versus "applied" disciplines. A third dimension mentioned by Biglan but less often used is that of disciplines studying "life" or studying "non-life". Various authors have used Biglan's typology to study the teaching-learning relationship in a comparative manner, from the perspective of the specificity of each disciplinary and/or professional field (Braxton and Hargens 1996; Neumann 2001; Neumann and Becher 2002). Although the categorization offered by Biglan has since been challenged, research on disciplinary specificity of an epistemological nature was born. At the same time, some have looked at disciplines but more from a sociocultural perspective (Becher 1987a, 1987b, 1989, 1990, 1994). Still using Biglan's typology, the specificities of each academic discipline were studied from the point of view of the norms, practices or representations shared by the members of that discipline.

All this research has made it possible to discover, on the one hand, that the nature of each discipline, its "epistemological structure", is different. For example, mathematics would be a cumulative discipline since in order to understand notion C, one must first understand notions A and B. On the contrary, a discipline such as philosophy is more comparative because there is not necessarily a predefined sequence in the learning of various thinkers: it is possible to start with Socrates as well as with Rousseau, the important thing being to compare one with the other. Moreover, some disciplines are more paradigmatically cohesive than others. For example, physicists generally agree on the notion of Earth's gravity, while economists agree less on the notion of the well-being of a population. Thus, physicists are more paradigmatically cohesive about gravity than economists are about well-being; this will of course influence teaching and learning practices.

On the other hand, it was discovered that teachers have common representations of how to teach or learn. Taking the example of mathematics, many teachers in this discipline agree on the importance of using a color code when presenting concepts on the blackboard (what is known in English as boardmanship). However, these representations may differ from one cultural context to another without the members of the discipline being aware of it. We then speak of sociocultural representations (Jodelet 1993; McNamara 1994; Billman 1999; Moscovici 2000). Research on disciplinary specificity was henceforth presented in two dimensions:

– the epistemological structure of the discipline;

– sociocultural representations specific to the discipline.

Since both areas of research – on the pedagogical knowledge base and on disciplinary specificity – are broken down into subspecializations, it is possible to refine the concept of disciplinary pedagogical knowledge by digging deeper. Thus, as Figure 1.3 shows, disciplinary pedagogical knowledge results not only from the linking of the pedagogical knowledge base with the specificity of a discipline, but also from the linking of the components presented above. Thus, goals, knowledge and beliefs are confronted with the epistemological structure and sociocultural representations specific to each discipline. It is therefore only through a process of translation or transposition that the teacher manages to adapt the generic elements of his or her pedagogical knowledge base (goals, knowledge or beliefs) to the particularities of the discipline being taught (its epistemological structure and associated sociocultural representations).

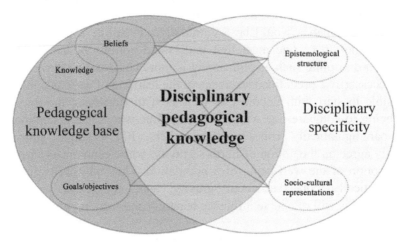

Figure 1.3. *Disciplinary pedagogical knowledge at the intersection of the components of the pedagogical knowledge base and the components of disciplinary specificity (Berthiaume 2007). For a color version of this figure, see www.iste. co.uk/bridoux/research.zip*

Disciplinary pedagogical knowledge is therefore multifaceted. Here are two examples from my practice as an educational consultant. When a university-level mathematics teacher explains that the student must "take the chalk", that is, come to the blackboard to solve a problem in order to understand the material, he or she is appealing to a belief (taking the chalk) that is linked to a sociocultural representation (coming to the blackboard to understand). This is a belief because it is not really proven; the teacher is not entirely wrong since the exercise of analyzing and solving a problem live helps the student to learn the targeted concepts, but this is not exclusive to the use of chalk and blackboard (e.g. solving a problem in a group using pencil and paper).

Another example would be that of a philosophy teacher who seeks to develop critical thinking in her students. On the one hand, she knows from pedagogical literature that guided discussion allows students to develop their critical thinking skills and leads them to the field of synthesis and evaluation according to Bloom's taxonomy (Anderson et al. 2001). On the other hand, since philosophy is a comparative discipline (not really a sequence in learning unlike mathematics where one has to understand A and B to study C), the teacher seeks to introduce various thinkers to the students by comparing them to each other and asking the students to explain how a particular thinker would react to what is being said. Her interventions in the discussion guide the students in developing their critical thinking skills. The teacher uses knowledge (teaching through guided discussion) and adapts it to the epistemological structure of her discipline (comparative rather than cumulative) as part of her instructional scenario.

The work of operationalizing disciplinary pedagogical knowledge has led to the identification of numerous dimensions for each component of the pedagogical knowledge base (e.g. short-term goals, long-term goals, disciplinary knowledge, pedagogical knowledge, beliefs about learning) as well as for the components of disciplinary specificity (e.g. teaching in the discipline, practicing in the discipline, subdivisions of the discipline). The operationalization work also clarified the potential relationships between these dimensions, as demonstrated in the previous two examples (Berthiaume 2008, 2007).

1.4.3. *The personal epistemology of university teachers*

A major difference between higher education and primary or secondary education is the famous issue of academic freedom or independence (Altbach 2000; Vrielink et al. 2010). While at the primary and secondary levels, the teacher is responsible for teaching the elements of a regional, national or international curriculum, this is not the case at the university level, despite recent reforms aiming to further harmonize the competences developed by students in higher education (e.g. the Bologna reform in the European Higher Education and Research Area; Barkholt 2005). Thus, each teacher in higher education is recruited on the basis of his or her scientific knowledge and skills, in a disciplinary and/or professional field. Moreover, since teaching is only one dimension of their work as a lecturer and researcher, they generally teach on subjects related to their own research activities. The higher education teacher is therefore not like other teachers. Their personal posture, that is, their way of seeing and understanding things, has a much greater impact on the teaching–learning relationship than may be the case at the primary and secondary levels of the education system.

This reality has led me to question the relevance of the model of disciplinary pedagogical knowledge located exclusively at the intersection between the teacher's pedagogical knowledge base and the disciplinary specificity of his or her teaching field. Indeed, since the university teacher's approach to his or her profession plays an important role in higher education, I tried to see what research on this could shed light on it. Thus, I turned to the notion of personal epistemology, which is the set of beliefs about knowledge held by an individual (not necessarily a teacher). According to this line of research, each of us holds beliefs about knowledge, about how knowledge develops, about the value of various forms of knowledge (Hofer and Pintrich 2002; Hofer 2004). These personal beliefs lead us to judge the validity of elements that are generally accepted by others. According to this line of research, each person has his or her own perception of a piece of knowledge, based on his or her identity and previous experiences. The notion of personal epistemology is similar to the notion of relationship to knowledge from the Francophone literature (Caillot and Maury 2002) but differs from the latter in that it is personal, rarely shared, often implicit, and even unknown to the individual.

Thus, I hypothesized and confirmed in the operationalization of the conceptual model that the personal epistemology of the university teacher mediates between his or her pedagogical knowledge base and the specificity of the discipline he or she teaches. This is because it is about beliefs about knowledge, and knowledge is both elements of the pedagogical knowledge base and elements of disciplinary specificity. An example of a personal epistemology can be found in the following situation: I need to change a window in my house but I don't know anything about it. How will I go about developing my knowledge and skills so that I can change this window? On the one hand, I could get a home improvement book and learn how to change a window. On the other hand, I can turn to my neighbor, who I saw change some windows in his house last summer. Some people will prefer to consult the book, others the neighbor. Others will even do both. Their respective evaluations of the sources of knowledge (book versus testimonial) differ. If we apply this logic to higher education, it is possible to find teachers who feel bound by norms, rules, or practices that they perceive as immutable (e.g. the primacy of lectures over other pedagogical methods), while other teachers will not hesitate to challenge them (e.g. wanting to build in moments of discussion with students so as to obtain evidence of their understanding of concepts presented through a lecture). For example, a literature teacher in a department where the usual pedagogical practice is to read a text to students may feel empowered to use a new method such as discussion after attending a workshop on this method. A colleague who has taken the same workshop may not feel empowered to do things differently than the rest of her colleagues. These two teachers have different personal epistemologies: one is more of a conformist and the other is more of a free spirit. Their respective personal epistemologies will influence their willingness, ability and even manner of adapting generic elements from their pedagogical knowledge base to the specifics of their disciplinary or professional field.

The role played by the teacher's personal epistemology in the production of disciplinary pedagogical knowledge thus undermines the idea, held by some researchers interested in disciplinary specificity, that all historians teach the same way, that all biologists think about learning the same way, or that all nursing teachers proceed in the same way to teach an aspect of the common curriculum (Becher 1994; Neumann 2001). Therefore, disciplinary pedagogical knowledge cannot, in reality, correspond to the graphic in Figure 1.3 due to the importance of the personal epistemology of the academic teacher. Figure 1.4 provides a more accurate representation of the components and relationships that make up the disciplinary pedagogical knowledge of a university teacher. Moreover, the exercise of operationalizing disciplinary pedagogical knowledge identified certain components and relationships between components that were present in all participants in the exercise, thus giving an indication of a common core across disciplines or professions. This is particularly important when considering how to support the development of disciplinary pedagogical knowledge for all university teachers, regardless of their disciplinary and/or professional area (Berthiaume et al. 2008).

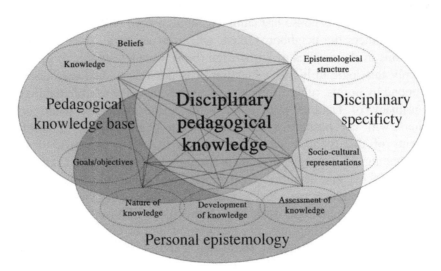

Figure 1.4. *Disciplinary pedagogical knowledge at the intersection of the components of the pedagogical knowledge base, disciplinary specificity and personal epistemology (Berthiaume 2007). For a color version of this figure, see www.iste.co.uk/bridoux/research.zip*

1.5. Conclusion

In this chapter, we have explained how a rapprochement between the Anglophone and Francophone intellectual traditions has taken place, giving rise to the concept of "discipline-specific pedagogical knowledge". We then described this form of knowledge, which is essential for all higher education teachers, whether they work in academic or professional higher education, and we highlighted the different components of this knowledge and how they interact with each other to form the whole that constitutes "discipline-specific pedagogical knowledge".

Because of its importance to the teacher, the development of "disciplinary pedagogical knowledge" should be a goal of all professional development activities organized by university pedagogy structures. Of course, activities aimed at the development of generic pedagogical knowledge and skills are still relevant. However, they can – and should – be accompanied by activities aimed at the development of discipline-specific or professional pedagogical knowledge and skills (Jenkins 1996).

University teachers' professional development involves various types of activities ranging from training workshops to individual counseling to teaching evaluation to applied research on one's teaching practices (Rege Colet and Berthiaume 2015). And each individual's development will depend on his or her prior experiences, aspirations and preferences. Fortunately, the concept of "disciplinary pedagogical knowledge" is highly adaptable to various forms of development, whether one is working alone (e.g. through reflective practice using a logbook or skills portfolio), in pairs (e.g. through a mentoring program or collaborative teaching observation with a colleague) or in groups (e.g. through a community of practice or applied research group about one's pedagogical practices). Regardless of the form of development chosen, the important thing is to ensure that personal reflections, dialogues or group discussions focus on the various components of "disciplinary pedagogical knowledge" and the relationships among them (Berthiaume and Weston 2015).

1.6. References

Alexander, P.A. and Dochy, F. (1995). Conceptions of knowledge and beliefs: A comparison across varying cultural and educational communities. *American Educational Research Journal*, 32, 413–442.

Altbach, P.G. (2000). Academic freedom: International realities and challenges. In *The Changing Academic Workplace: Comparative Perspectives*, Altbach, P.G. (ed.). Boston College Center for International Higher Education, Chestnut Hill, MA.

Anderson, L.W., Krathwohl, D.R., Airaisian, P.W., Cruikshank, K.A., Mayer, R.E., Pintrich, P.R., Raths, J., Wittrock, M.C. (2001). *A Taxonomy for Learning, Teaching, and Assessing: A Revision of Bloom's Taxonomy of Educational Objectives*. Longman, New York.

Andrews, J., Garrison, R., Magnusson, K. (1996). The teaching and learning transaction in higher education: A study of excellent professors and their students. *Teaching in Higher Education*, 1, 81–103.

Angelo, T.A. (1994). From faculty development to academic development. *American Association for Higher Education Bulletin*, 45(8), 2–7.

Barkholt, K. (2005). The Bologna process and integration theory: Convergence and autonomy. *Higher Education in Europe*, 30, 23–29.

Baxter, J.A. and Lederman, N.G. (1999). Assessment and measurement of pedagogical content knowledge. In *Examining Pedagogical Content Knowledge*, Gess-Newsome, J., Lederman, N.G. (eds). Kluwer, Dordrecht, The Netherlands.

Beard, R. and Hartley, J. (1987). *Teaching and Learning in Higher Education*. Paul Chapman, London, United Kingdom.

Becher, T. (1987a). Disciplinary discourse. *Studies in Higher Education*, 12, 261–274.

Becher, T. (1987b). The disciplinary shaping of the professorate. In *The Academic Profession: National, Disciplinary and Institutional Settings*, Clark, B. (ed.). University of California Press, Berkeley, CA.

Becher, T. (1989). *Academic Tribes and Territories*. Open University Press, Buckingham, United Kingdom.

Becher, T. (1990). The counter-culture of specialisations. *European Journal of Education*, 75, 333–346.

Becher, T. (1994). The significance of disciplinary differences. *Studies in Higher Education*, 19, 151–161.

Berthiaume, D. (2007). What is the nature of university professors' discipline-specific pedagogical knowledge? A descriptive multicase study. Unpublished PhD Thesis, McGill University, Department of Educational and Counselling Psychology, Montreal, Canada.

Berthiaume, D. (2008). Teaching in the disciplines. In *A Handbook for Teaching and Learning in Higher Education*, 3rd edition, Fry, H., Ketteridge, S., Marshall, S. (eds). Routledge, London, United Kingdom.

Berthiaume, D. and Rege Colet, N. (eds) (2013). *La pédagogie de l'enseignement supérieur : repères théoriques et applications pratiques, Tome 1. Enseigner au supérieur*. Peter Lang, Bern, Switzerland.

Berthiaume, D. and Weston, C. (2015). Développer son savoir pédagogique disciplinaire. In *La pédagogie de l'enseignement supérieur : repères théoriques et applications pratiques, Tome 2. Se développer au titre d'enseignant du supérieur*, Rege Colet, N., Berthiaume, D. (eds). Peter Lang, Bern, Switzerland.

Berthiaume, D., Horisberger, M., Chevalier, P.-A. (2008). Strategies for helping university teachers develop discipline-specific pedagogical knowledge. Communication effectuée dans le cadre de la rencontre annuelle du International Consortium for Educational Development (ICED), June, Salt Lake City, UT.

Bertran, Y. and Houssaye, J. (1999). Pédagogie et didactique: An incestuous relationship. *Instructional Science*, 27, 33–51.

Biglan, A. (1973a). The characteristics of subject matter in different academic areas. *Journal of Applied Psychology*, 57, 195–203.

Biglan, A. (1973b). Relationships between subject matter characteristics and the structure and output of university departments. *Journal of Applied Psychology*, 57, 204–213.

Billman, D. (1999). Representations. In *A Companion to Cognitive Science*, Bechtel, W., Graham, G. (eds). Blackwell, Oxford, United Kingdom.

Bligh, J. (1995). Problem-based learning in medicine: An introduction. *Postgraduate Medical Journal*, 71, 323–326.

Braxton, J.M. and Hargens, L.L. (1996). Variation among academic disciplines: Analytic frameworks and research. In *Higher Education: Handbook of Theory and Research*, Smart, J. (ed.). Agathon Press, New York.

Caillot, M. and Maury, S. (eds) (2002). Didactiques et rapports aux savoirs. Laboratoire Éducation et Apprentissages, Université René-Descartes (Paris V-Sorbonne), Paris, France.

Calderhead, J. (1996). Teachers: Beliefs and knowledge. In *Handbook of Educational Psychology*, Berliner, D.C. and Calfee, R. (eds). Macmillan, New York.

Chevallard, Y. (1991). *La transposition didactique : du savoir savant au savoir enseigné*. La pensée sauvage, Paris, France.

Cranton, P. (1998). *No One Way: Teaching and Learning in Higher Education*. Wall & Emerson, Toronto, Canada.

D'Andrea, V. and Gosling, D. (2005). *Improving Teaching and Learning in Higher Education: A Whole Institution Approach*. SRHE/Open University Press, Buckingham, United Kingdom.

Develay, M. (1992). *De l'apprentissage à l'enseignement*. ESF Éditeur, Paris, France.

Develay, M. (1997). Origines, malentendus et spécificités de la didactique. *Revue Française de Pédagogie*, 120, 59–66.

Donald, J.G. (2002). *Learning to Think: Disciplinary Perspectives*. Jossey Bass, San Francisco, CA.

Donmoyer, R. (1986). The concept of a knowledge base. In *The Teacher Educator's Handbook: Building a Knowledge Base for the Preparation of Teachers*, Murray, F.B. (ed.). Jossey-Bass, San Francisco, CA.

Dunkin, M.J. and Precians, R. (1992). Award winning university teachers' concepts of teaching. *Higher Education*, 24, 483–502.

Dupont, P. and Ossandon, M. (1994). *La pédagogie universitaire*. Presses Universitaires de France, Paris, France.

Eisenhart, M.A., Shrum, J.L., Harding, J.R., Cuthbert, A.M. (1988). Teacher beliefs: Definitions, findings, and directions. *Educational Policy*, 2, 29–50.

Fry, H., Ketteridge, S., Marshall, S. (eds) (2008). *A Handbook for Teaching and Learning in Higher Education: Enhancing Academic Practice*. Routledge, London, United Kingdom.

Gardiner, H.W., Mutter, J.D., Kosmitzki, C. (1998). *Lives Across Cultures: Cross-cultural Human Development*. Allyn and Bacon, Boston, MA.

Gess-Newsome, J. and Lederman, N.G. (1999). *Examining Pedagogical Content Knowledge: The Construct and Its Implications for Science Education*. Kluwer, Dordrecht, The Netherlands.

Ghosh, R. (1996). *Redefining Multicultural Education*. Hartcourt Brace, Toronto, Canada.

Grossman, P. and Yerian, S.Y. (1992). Pedagogical content knowledge: The research agenda. Communication made within the framework of the annual meeting of the American Educational Research Association (AERA), April. San Francisco, CA.

Grossman, P., Wilson, S.M., Shulman, L.S. (1989). Teachers of substance: Subject matter knowledge for teaching. In *Knowledge Base for the Beginning Teacher*, Reynolds, M.C. (ed.). Pergamon Press, New York.

Gudmundsdottir, S. and Shulman, L. (1987). Pedagogical content knowledge in social studies. *Scandinavian Journal of Educational Research*, 31, 59–70.

Hativa, N. and Marincovich, M. (eds) (1995). *Disciplinary Differences in Teaching and Learning: Implications for Practice*. Jossey-Bass, San Francisco, CA.

Hiebert, J., Gallimore, R., Stigler, J.W. (2002). A knowledge base for the teaching profession: What would it look like and how can we get one? *Educational Researcher*, 31, 3–15.

Hofer, B.K. (2004). Exploring the dimensions of personal epistemology in differing classroom contexts: Student interpretation during the first years of college. *Contemporary Educational Psychology*, 29, 129–163.

Hofer, B.K. and Pintrinch, P.R. (2002). *Personal Epistemology: The Psychology of Beliefs about Knowledge and Knowing*. Lawrence Earlbaum Associates, Mahwah, NJ.

Houssaye, J. (2014). *Le triangle pédagogique. Les différentes facettes de la pédagogie.* ESF Editeur, Paris, France.

Jenkins, A. (1996). Discipline-based educational development. *The International Journal for Academic Development*, 1, 50–62.

Jodelet, D. (1993). *Les représentations sociales.* Presses universitaires de France, Paris, France.

Jonnaert, P. and Laurin, S. (eds) (2001). *Les didactiques des disciplines : un débat contemporain.* Presses de l'Université du Québec, Canada.

Jonnaert, P. and Lenoir, Y. (eds) (1993). *Sens des didactiques et didactique du sens.* Éditions du Centre de Ressources Pédagogiques, Sherbrooke, Canada.

Kreber, C. (ed.) (2009). *The University and Its Disciplines: Teaching and Learning Within and Beyond Disciplinary Boundaries.* Routledge, New York.

Langevin, L. (ed.) (2007). *Formation et soutien à l'enseignement universitaire.* Presses de l'Université du Québec, Canada.

Langevin, L. and Bruneau, M. (2000). *Enseignement supérieur : vers un nouveau scénario.* ESF Éditeur, Issy-les-Moulineaux, France.

Lazerson, M., Wagener, U., Shumanis, N. (2000). Teaching and learning in higher education, 1980–2000. *Change*, 32(3), 12–19.

Lenze, L.F. (1995). Discipline-specific pedagogical knowledge in linguistics and Spanish. In *Disciplinary Differences in Teaching and Learning: Implications for Practice*, Hativa, N., Marincovich, M. (eds). Jossey-Bass, San Francisco, CA.

Lenze, L.F. (1996). Discipline-specific faculty development. *NEA Update*, 2, 1–4.

Lueddeke, G.R. (2003). Professionalising teaching practice in higher education: A study of disciplinary variation and "teaching-scholarship". *Studies in Higher Education*, 28, 211–228.

Magnusson, S., Krajcik, J., Borko, H. (1999). Nature, sources, and development of pedagogical content knowledge for science teaching. In *Examining Pedagogical Content Knowledge*, Gess-Newsome, J. and Lederman, N.G. (eds). Kluwer, Dordrecht, The Netherlands.

Martin, E., Prosser, M., Trigwell, K., Ramsden, P., Benjamin, J. (2002). What university teachers teach and how they teach it. In *Teacher Thinking, Beliefs, and Knowledge in Higher Education*, Hativa, N. and Goodyear, P. (eds). Kluwer, Dordrecht, The Netherlands.

McAlpine, L. and Cowan, S. (eds) (2000). *Reflections on Teaching and Learning: 30 Years at McGill.* Centre for University Teaching and Learning, McGill University, Montreal, Canada.

McNamara, T.P. (1994). Knowledge representation. In *Thinking and Problem Solving*, Sternberg, R.J. (ed.). Academic Press, San Diego, CA.

Menges, R.J. and Austin, A.E. (2001). Teaching in higher education. In *Handbook of Research on Teaching*, 4th edition, Richardson, V. (ed.). American Educational Research Association, Washington.

Morine-Dershimer, G. and Corrigan, S. (1997). Teacher beliefs. In *Psychology and Educational Practice*, Walberg, H.J. and Haertle, G.D. (eds). McCutchan, Berkeley, CA.

Moscovici, S. (2000). *Social Representations: Explorations in Social Psychology*. Polity Press, Oxford, United Kingdom.

Nespor, J. (1987). The role of beliefs in the practice of teaching. *Journal of Curriculum Studies*, 19, 317–328.

Neumann, R. (2001). Disciplinary differences and university teaching. *Studies in Higher Education*, 26, 135–146.

Neumann, R. and Becher, T. (2002). Teaching and learning in their disciplinary contexts: A conceptual analysis. *Studies in Higher Education*, 27, 405–417.

Pajares, M.F. (1992). Teachers' beliefs and educational research: Cleaning up a messy construct. *Review of Educational Research*, 62, 307–322.

Palincsar, A.S. (1998). Social constructivist perspectives on teaching and learning. *Annual Review of Psychology*, 49, 345–375.

Pratt, D.D. (1992). Conceptions of teaching. *Adult Education Quarterly*, 42, 203–220.

Rege Colet, N. and Berthiaume, D. (eds) (2015). *La pédagogie de l'enseignement supérieur : repères théoriques et applications pratiques, Tome 2. Se développer au titre d'enseignant du supérieur*. Peter Lang, Bern, Switzerland.

Reynolds, M.C. (ed.) (1989). *Knowledge Base for the Beginning Teacher*. Pergamon Press, New York.

Saroyan, A. and Frenay, M. (eds) (2008). *Building Teaching Capacities in Universities: From Faculty Development to Educational Development*. Stylus Publishing, Sterling, United Kingdom.

Shuell, T.J. (1993). Toward an integrated theory of teaching and learning. *Educational Psychologist*, 28, 291–311.

Shulman, L. (1986). Those who understand: Knowledge growth in teaching. *Educational Researcher*, 15, 4–14.

Shulman, L. (1987). Knowledge and teaching: Foundations of the new reform. *Harvard Educational Review*, 57, 1–22.

Smeby, J. (1996). Disciplinary differences in university teaching. *Studies in Higher Education*, 21, 69–79.

Terrisse, A. (2001). *Didactique des disciplines : les références au savoir*. DeBoeck Université, Brussels, Belgium.

Tochon, F.V. (1991). Entre didactique et pédagogie : épistémologie de l'espace/ temps stratégique. *The Journal of Educational Thought*, 25, 120–133.

Turner-Bisset, R. (1999). The knowledge bases of the expert teacher. *British Educational Research Journal*, 25, 39–55.

Vrielink, J., Lemmens, P., Parmentier, S. (2010). Academic freedom as a fundamental right. Paper, League of European Research Universities.

2

Teacher Training at University through the Prism of Disciplines

2.1. Introduction

New pedagogical expectations have been placed on higher education institutions since the 1990s and 2000s. These demands for change are based on the assumption that teaching practices at university are not very effective and are out of step with society's expectations and more specifically with those of students and their parents who hope for a quick return on investment, namely a job, after graduation. These demands are gathered under the banner of innovation and excellence, the watchwords of educational policies in higher education. Innovation is part of a profoundly renewed imagination of change (Martuccelli 2016, p. 41). "[...] Innovation [is] the bearer of an ordinary and permanent imaginary of change, instead of a vision of rupture and the extraordinary, which reflects its seduction at the level of organizations" (Crozier 1995; Alter 2000). Teaching practices are assessed, read and evaluated according to this imagination and these demands for change (Lemaître 2018). The social and political demand for the renewal of teaching practices in higher education has contributed to the development of training in higher education. The demand for training has recently been increased by legislative measures. Indeed, article 2 of the decree of May 25, 2016 on doctoral training stipulates that the employing university shall offer training to contractual doctoral students for all of the duties carried out, including pedagogy. While doctoral schools are in charge of research training, employing institutions are obliged to offer training on

Chapter written by Caroline LEININGER-FRÉZAL.

teaching. In the same vein, the decree of February 8, 2018 imposes mandatory pedagogical training for the teaching skills of trainee lecturers (40 h of mandatory training – Decree no. 2017-854 of May 9, 2017).

How can we develop a pedagogical training offer for beginner and/or experienced higher education teachers? This was the first question I asked myself when I was appointed director of the *Centre d'Accompagnement des Pratiques Enseignantes* (CAPE) at the Université Paris Diderot from 2014 to 2018. This service, now closed, was responsible for the initial and continuing education of teachers from primary to higher education. As part of this, the service was responsible for developing a pedagogical training program for higher education teachers, in collaboration with the *Service d'Accompagnement aux Pédagogies Innovantes et à l'Enseignement Numérique de l'Alliance Sorbonne Paris Cité* (SAPIENS). From the outset, this undertaking raised several questions: What are the needs and desires of higher education teachers for training? What forms can this training take with regard to the means at our disposal? What is the distribution of roles between the university services (CAPE) and the inter-university service (SAPIENS)?

These questions called for practical, strategic and political choices to be made in order to set up the training. They have also generated a research approach and questioning. As a researcher in geography education working on the teaching practices of geography lecturers and researchers, I decided to adopt an approach based on participant observation:

> Participatory observation [PO] implies that the researcher is totally immersed in his or her field, in order to try to grasp all its subtleties, at the risk of lacking perspective and losing objectivity. However, the advantage is clear in terms of data production: this method allows the researcher to experience the reality of the subjects observed and to understand certain mechanisms that are difficult to decipher for anyone who remains in a situation of exteriority. By participating in the same way as the actors, the researcher has privileged access to information that is inaccessible through other empirical methods. (Bastien, 2007, p. 128)

This text will be limited to the French context and to the analysis of a particular case study – that of the Université Paris Diderot. This participant observation is based on a logbook I kept during the course of my work as a lecturer and researcher from 2016 to 2019. This logbook allowed me to analyze the discourses held by lecturers and researchers in informal (discussion between colleagues, emails, training sessions, etc.) and formal (departmental meetings, pedagogical council, pedagogical seminar, etc.) moments of exchange. An analysis of this logbook shows that including the discipline in the proposed training courses was a point of tension between the various stakeholders in the training of higher education teachers. This is what we will develop in section 2.2. We will then discuss the resources available for developing training in higher education with a disciplinary approach (see section 2.3), and in section 2.4 we will look at the conditions necessary to develop training in higher education.

2.2. Difficulties of taking into account disciplines in the training of higher education teachers

Disciplinary entry into higher education teacher education first emerged as an informal request from teachers in questionnaires completed at the end of training.

> Logbook entry – March 2015
>
> Initially (2014–2015), CAPE implemented workshops on the topic of evaluation by involving researchers and trainers specializing in the issue: evaluation of training by students, essay evaluation, development of a multiple-choice questionnaire, internship evaluation, and the evaluation of student theses. The essay training was chosen by teachers of humanities and social sciences (history, sociology, law, language, literature). Two recurring remarks in the evaluation questionnaires referred to disciplines. Some of the teachers appreciated the fact that this workshop led them to think about a mode of evaluation specific to their discipline, and they appreciated the exchange of practices, particularly its interdisciplinary aspect. On the other hand, another group of teachers regretted that the disciplinary dimension had not been developed further, arguing that an essay in one discipline does not have quite the same methodology as in another.

Box 2.1. *The role of disciplines in training evaluation*

This request for subject-specific training came up regularly in the questionnaires. It was also expressed in a more formalized way by groups of teachers who asked CAPE to provide logistical and financial support towards the organization of training sessions on the teaching of their discipline.

> Logbook entry – March 2015
>
> In early 2015, a physics lecturer and researcher came to us to ask for our financial and logistical support to organize a training session dedicated to the teaching of her discipline within the framework of an emerging network (Teaching Physics at University day – journée Enseigner la Physique à l'Université). This day was part of an informal network of physics teachers that was being formed. This network is now structured and organizes training sessions twice a year. CAPE supported this initiative.
>
> Logbook entry – January 2016
>
> A sociology teacher contacted CAPE for advice and logistical support to organize a training day on teaching her discipline locally.
>
> Logbook entry – date not noted
>
> I facilitated a workshop on experiential learning (Kolb 1984) based on the example of a course conducted in a Licence 3 Professorat des écoles (3-year degree course in school teaching). This workshop generated interest and raised many questions. A physics lecturer and researcher questioned the meaning of experience in physics. On which experiment should a physics course be based? Are the tutorials that are experiments not part of experiential learning? Does not the work in physics education also fall within the scope of experiential learning? Despite my expertise in geography education, I was unable to explore this questioning. I lacked knowledge of epistemology and didactics of physics to enter into a dialogue with this teacher. I did try to discuss the differences between experience and experimentation, but in experiential learning, Kolb (1984) puts the two on the same level.

Box 2.2. *Expression of a disciplinary need*

Participant observation does not allow us to quantify this demand for training rooted in disciplines but simply to appreciate its recurrence alongside other areas of training such as digital and interactive approaches. The requests for disciplinary pedagogical training were justified by two types of intrinsically linked arguments. The first is that the content of the training should take into account the epistemological specificities of the discipline being taught. The second is utilitarian: given the limited time available to a lecturer and researcher, the training must be immediately rolled out by the teachers in their courses.

The following year, we[1] proposed developing disciplinary training days in view of recurrent requests and emerging initiatives in some disciplines such as geography and literature. By disciplinary, we mean training that took into account the disciplinary specificity of the knowledge and approaches to be transmitted. It was not a question of developing the disciplinary culture of lecturers and researchers who were already specialized. This reflection raised two questions:

– Is it legitimate to run training on disciplinary teaching in higher education?

– If it is, who is able to provide this training? Who can design and implement didactic training for teachers in higher education?

This last question highlighted several obstacles to the development of didactic training. In order to develop such training, it would have been necessary to involve people from outside the university – the instructional designers did not feel legitimate and neither did the CAPE team – which would have considerably increased the cost of the proposed training and consequently limited its number drastically. At the CAPE level, the budget was limited.

We considered introducing didactic training into the training offer for beginning higher education teachers. In a note that resulted from collaboration between CAPE and the human resources department of the University of Paris Diderot, we proposed recognizing and taking into account co-training in the compulsory training of new lecturers. This proposal is the result of discussions with the directors of the faculty and the heads of the pedagogical council. It was not retained by the human resources department. Several reasons were given.

The first is the difficulty of controlling the content and quality of these training sessions. The process of creating and implementing co-training is "bottom-up" and not "top-down". It is not the human resources department that identifies a training need, writes the specifications and chooses the speaker. This is done in groups of varying size that act autonomously at the

---

1 "We" here refers to the CAPE team. There were several of us working on these issues.

level of a department, a faculty or even at the level of a discipline or a specialism. Indeed, there are sessions dedicated to teaching in some conferences. These sessions can be related to research or reflective practice. There are also dedicated pedagogical seminars such as Teaching Physics at University (see above) or the seminar on teaching practices in geography at university initiated by University of Tours. These exchange times do not follow the same organizational logic as those governed by the human resources department. There are not necessarily well-defined training objectives, just an underlying desire to exchange and reflect on teaching practices on a specific subject or discipline.

The second difficulty stems from the fact that the human resources department thinks of continuing education in terms of profitability. The number of teachers per discipline is too small to guarantee a sufficient number of participants for training in a specific discipline. If we consider the new teachers recruited at the university, the target audience is very small (one to two at most per discipline). Since training is thought of at the university or university community level[2], it is difficult to envisage offering this type of training.

Thus, pedagogical training anchored in a discipline has developed in a modest and marginal way within the CAPE. Beyond the material, organizational or financial difficulties, considering developing training on teaching practices with a disciplinary entry point raised new questions:

– Do the resources necessary to organize this type of training exist and are they available in France? By resources, we mean research that can feed these training sessions and act as a basis for their content, but also competent people able to take part in training.

– How can this type of training be developed?

To explore this question, we have carried out a survey of articles published in French on higher education and taking a disciplinary approach. The choice to limit this inventory to France is explained by the question that guides us, namely, to find trainers able to come and provide training in higher education with a disciplinary approach. This state of the art has led us

---

2 A university community is a group of several universities united by common political actions of varying nature.

to note that the disciplinary dimension is rarely taken into account in research on higher education (in French).

2.3 Resources available for taking into account disciplines in higher education

The analysis of teaching and learning practices in higher education has been constituted as a field of research since the 1970s, in the Anglophone world under the term "teaching and learning". In his review of the issue, De Ketele (2010) emphasizes the abundance of journals dedicated to this subject. In French-speaking countries, higher education became the object of questioning in the mid-1990s and especially in the early 2000s. France was still behind other countries in the mid-2000s (2004). Rege Colet (2008) makes the same observation in her review of university pedagogical research in French-speaking Switzerland. The need to train competent professionals has probably encouraged a questioning of the quality of training (Poteaux 2014). Spaces for publication and exchange have developed. The French version of the Revue Internationale de l'Enseignement Supérieur (RIPES) was created in 2009. The International Association of University Pedagogy (IAUP) was revived in 2013. The perspective of research conducted on higher education in France is more sociological than pedagogical. "In France, work on the university (Duru-Bellat 1989; Coulon 1997; Musselin 2008) is mostly devoted to social issues, the evolution of the student public, the relationship to studies, living conditions, failure and success" (Poteaux 2015, p. 83).

Few studies take into account the discipline taught. This is what Adangnikou (2008) in his inventory of university pedagogy articles published in French in the Francis database (from 1991 to 2005). The vast majority of articles deal with teacher training practices, information and communication technologies, student learning, and teacher and student learning assessment, without intentionally targeting one or more disciplines. Five articles specifically address issues of language and French learning and teaching, but none of the articles relate to the teaching of geography, a discipline which we will turn to next. Two decades later, while university pedagogy has developed in France, does disciplinary research on higher education exist today? If not, why not?

Repeating this research with the methodology used by Adangnikou over the period 2006 to June 2018 (see box below), the results are significantly different.

> The survey was based on a search of the following keywords: teaching practice, pedagogical practice, pedagogical method, pedagogical innovation, learning, educational technology and evaluation. These keywords were cross-referenced with the terms university or higher education. Only articles in French and related to the French territory published between 2006 and June 2018 were retained.
>
> The criteria listed in the reference article leave some question as to how the search was conducted. The article does not indicate in which section of the advanced search the keywords were used. Second, I did not know if the French language and the fact that the article is about the French territory were entered as criteria in the "language" and "country of publication" sections or if they were selection criteria applied a posteriori by manual sorting. Finally, some of the queries generate a number of articles that are too large to be processed (more than 1,000) or indicate irrelevant articles. How did the author perform the sorting? Some articles do not have an abstract, so were the articles consulted?
>
> By default, articles without an abstract were not taken into account in the census if the title and keywords did not contain terms explicitly referring to higher education such as "student", "faculty", "university", "higher education", "IUT" (university institute of technology), etc. The title of the journal was also used as an index of the content as well as the discipline. Indeed, some journals are explicitly dedicated to higher education. In the same way, some disciplines such as psychology or medicine are only taught in higher education.
>
> To limit the number of results, I entered the keywords in the dedicated section, with quotation marks, and the language became a search criterion. Only articles in French were retained. On the other hand, I considered that taking France as a search territory was an a posteriori criterion. No heading corresponds exactly. The query crossing the keyword "learning" and "university" generated too many articles as such (986). I looked to see if there were any as-yet-unidentified articles listed on the first and last pages. Since this was not the case, we did not explore the entire 25 pages of results.

Box 2.3. *Methodology of the census of university pedagogy articles in the FRANCIS database, according to Adangnikou (2008)*

The volume of articles written on higher education is comparable between 2008 and 2018 to that published over the previous decade: 62 articles between 2008 and 2018 versus 66 between 1991 and 2005. In contrast, a larger proportion of articles have a disciplinary entry. Twenty-six of the 66 articles identified have a disciplinary entry or 42%. The discipline has become an entry point for research on pedagogical practices and learning in higher education. These results need to be put into perspective. The number of articles published in 10 years is low. We are talking about one to two articles per year.

The results are much the same for articles with a disciplinary entry in the RIPES journal. Since its inception, articles published have consistently addressed disciplinary teaching and learning issues. This is shown in Figure 2.1.

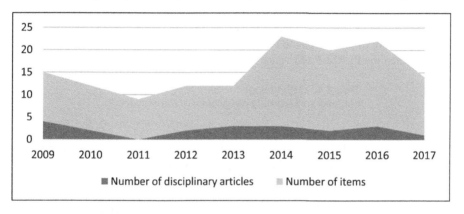

Figure 2.1. *Proportion of articles in the Revue Internationale de l'Enseignement Supérieur (RIPES) with a disciplinary entry compared to the total number of articles published each year. For a color version of this figure, see www.iste.co.uk/bridoux/ research.zip*

In order to establish this proportion, only articles mentioning an academic discipline or sub-discipline in their title were taken into account, which is an indicator of the disciplinary anchorage of the research. These articles represent between 10 and 30% on average of the articles published by the journal, with the exception of the year 2011.

Research has been developed on disciplinary teaching and learning practices, but it is very limited in volume. What about reflective practice? In order to go further in our review, we decided to focus on one discipline: geography. The choice of this discipline is strategic. On the one hand, geography is one of the disciplines that is absent from the overview of research carried out previously. On the other hand, in order to go further in the analysis, a good knowledge of the discipline was an asset since I am a researcher in geography education. French geographical journals were therefore analyzed. Unlike Anglo-Saxon research, very few French articles are dedicated to teaching or learning in higher education. The methodology of this census is presented in Box 2.4.

> To identify articles published in French on geography education, an "advanced search" was conducted on the FRANCIS, CAIRN and PERSEE databases. The keywords used are: "geography, higher education" and "geography, teaching, university".
>
> The search was restricted to the period 2008 to 2018 and to articles (as opposed to other types of publication) in French. The results obtained on PERSEE were too numerous to be fully searched (43,367 articles). I stopped the search when the PERSEE relevance indicator was equal to or lower than 50%.

Box 2.4. *Methodology for identifying articles on teaching and learning geography at the university*

This bibliographic search identified three articles that focus on the relationship of universities to their territory and student mobilities:

– Berroir, S., Cattan, N., Saint-Julien, T. (2009). Les masters en réseau : vers de nouvelles territorialités de l'enseignement supérieur en France. *L'Espace géographique*, 38(1), 43–58.

– Baron, M. and Perret C. (2008). Comportements migratoires des étudiants et des jeunes diplômés. *Géographie, économie, société*, 10(2), 223–242.

– Perret, C. (2008). Les régions françaises face aux migrations des diplômés de l'enseignement supérieur entrant sur le marché du travail. *Annales de géographie*, 662(4), 62–84.

– Baron, M., Barrera, C., Birck, F. (2014). Universités et territoires, du passé faisons table rase ? *Les Annales de la Recherche Urbaine*, 109, 18–27.

This work is largely in the field of spatial analysis and is mainly carried out by researchers from the PARIS team of the urban geography faculty (UMR geographie-cités). Two additional articles deal with the teaching and learning of geography at the university level, the first in relation to the preparation of students for the teaching exam:

– Candelier-Cabon, M. (2008). La France, mal aimée des concours ? *L'Information Géographique*, 72(3), 59–80.

The second is published by a historian in a journal of educational sciences. It deals with the teaching of "colonial sciences" under the Third and Fourth Republics, which includes geography but is not limited to it:

– Singaravélou, P. (2009). L'enseignement supérieur colonial. *"Un état des lieux", Histoire de l'éducation*, 2(122).

The research record is very meager. If the period considered were extended, the volume of articles listed would be much more substantial. The articles dedicated to the teaching of geography at the university are numerous at the end of the 19th century and in the first half of the 20th century (identifiable on PERSEE). This period corresponds to the creation of a certain number of institutions dedicated to geography: scientific journals, the Institut Géographie National, university chairs, a school discipline, etc. It is not surprising that articles propose a reflection on the teaching of the discipline at the time when it was being set up in schools and universities. What interests us here is the current state of research on the teaching of geography in higher education.

In addition to the systematic census carried out via the article databases, other publications were identified during bibliographic searches:

– Keerle, R. (2014). Acteurs, territorialisations et cartographie dans l'enseignement en IUT option animation. *Mappemonde*, 113.

– Leininger-Frézal, C., Douay, N., Cohen, M. (2016). L'étude de cas face à l'exemple : pratiques et enjeux dans l'enseignement de la géographie et de l'aménagement à l'université. *Recherche en éducation*, 27, 52–65.

– Zrinscak, G. (2010). Enseigner le terrain en géographie. *L'Information géographique*, 74(1), 40–54.

– In addition to these scattered articles, a dedicated issue of Carnets de Géographes from 2017 contains 13 texts of various natures in accordance with the editorial policy of the journal: an editorial, research articles (3), interviews (2) and feedback (7).

These articles fall under the umbrella of "Scholarship of Teaching and Learning" (SoTL) as defined by Boyer (1990). These articles are not just about teaching excellence or expertise. "SoTL involves sharing one's knowledge about teaching and learning in forms that can be evaluated by one's peers in the same way as other empirically tested knowledge" (Rege Colet and Berthiaume, 2009, p. 150). The articles by Régis Keerle and Georgette Zrinscak offer a distanced reading of teaching practices in IUTs for the former, and in the field for the latter, based on the collection and analysis of data. Similarly, the articles in the "Carnet de terrain" section of *Carnets de Géographes* are of the same order. These are lecturers and researchers, not specialists in didactics or educational sciences, who question their teaching practices. In the same vein, *Les feuilles de géographie*, a journal founded in the 1990s by doctoral students at the UMR Géographie-cités, "is an online space for the publication of materials and content for the teaching of geography at the University and more broadly in higher education" (journal website). This journal was relaunched in the mid-2010s after a decade of inactivity. These initiatives and texts are more numerous from the mid-2010s, which is consistent with the rise of university pedagogy. This reflects a need felt by the geography community to reflect on their teaching practices.

This inventory highlights the weakness of publications in geography on the teaching and learning of geography at the university level in French. This is not surprising given the small size of the geography teaching community in France (six lecturers and researchers able to supervise theses in 2021). There is a contrast with what is published in English. In scanning the *European Journal of Geography* (EJG) since 2011, when it was founded, and the *Journal of Geography in Higher Education* (JGHG), since 2008, 436 articles were identified as dealing with the teaching and learning of geography in higher education: 10 in EJG and 426 in JGHG. These two journals were chosen because they are peer-reviewed journals with an impact factor (0.567 for EJG and 1.213 for JGHG) whose editorial policy is favorable to articles in geography education. None of these articles were written by French authors. This observation shows that there are works in the field but no French specialists. In other disciplines, French researchers publish in English on disciplinary teaching at the university level, notably in mathematics and physics. In these disciplines, the communities of educationalists are often larger and more organized.

What can we infer from this inventory? Can we conclude that resources are limited? It would be presumptuous to draw a definitive and general conclusion. The first thing is that resources are not easy to identify. They are few in number in French but certainly much more numerous in English. It is likely that the number of potential trainers depends on the size of the community of researchers working on the teaching and learning of a discipline in higher education. There are certainly large disparities in the resources available across disciplines. We can hypothesize that the development of training in higher education may help to develop the SoTL literature in the coming years. "SoTL allows for the involvement of stakeholders, i.e., the teachers themselves, in the construction of the field" (Rege Colet and Berthiaume, 2009, p. 152).

2.4. How should we take into account disciplines in training in higher education?

Subject matter is central to describing, analyzing and understanding teaching practices in higher education. In her state of the question on pedagogy in higher education, Poteaux (2013, p.7) notes that "every lecturer and researcher who teaches has a certain perception of pedagogy through his or her empirical practice, which can, on the other hand, constitute an epistemological obstacle" (Bachelard, 1972). Disciplinary affiliation affects the teaching practices of lecturers and researchers, their discourse, their perceptions and their beliefs about teaching. It is the "disciplinary culture" that Becher (1994) defines as "a common set of intellectual values, a common cognitive territory". Disciplinary culture includes beliefs about what should be taught and how it should be taught. These beliefs are derived and result from the experience of teachers. It results from the way lecturers and researchers are socialized and trained, "training for research through research. There is no such thing as 'research pedagogy': training is done on the job, by imitation, randomly, depending on the laboratory and the team. In this context, the accompaniment by elders – companionship – operates in a person-to-person relationship of proximity and constant interaction" (Poteaux 2013). Training in pedagogy is also done in the form of companionship, even though there is a growing offer of training in university pedagogy, primarily for contractual doctoral students and for young lecturers and researchers.

While the discipline to which one belongs has an impact on the practices of lecturers and researchers, how can this disciplinary culture be taken into account in the pedagogical training of higher education teachers? Rege Colet and Berthiaume (2009) propose basing professional development on the empirical model of disciplinary pedagogical knowledge (DPK) (Berthiaume 2007). This model is presented in the previous chapter. We will therefore return to it only briefly. The model is a system that brings together three components of DPK:

– personal epistemology elements: beliefs about the nature of knowledge, learning from others, and the relative value of forms of knowledge;

– elements of basic pedagogical knowledge related to objectives (of the class, of the course), content, teaching, learning, assessment, content and pedagogical-disciplinary knowledge, and beliefs about teaching and learning;

– elements related to disciplinary specificity.

The strength of this model is that it is holistic and systemic, allowing for a complex approach to DPK. DPK is more than the sum of its parts but a whole resulting from their interactions. These elements of the system interact with each other, which generates, as in any system, positive feedback loops (which amplify the phenomenon) or negative feedback loops (which decrease the phenomenon). Berthiaume and Rege Colet use the empirical model of DPK to propose that the training and professional development of higher education teachers should be part of flexible arrangements that take into account the needs of teachers and their disciplinary constraints, which would involve the development of reflective practice or communities of practice. This proposal is similar to the one submitted to the University Paris Diderot. It is a call to stop thinking of training as a process where the majority of the offer is standardized and interdisciplinary, and to think of training in higher education in terms of disciplinary culture. What are the conditions that would enable this (r)evolution?

In light of the logbook, two conditions appear necessary.

The first condition is to make training in higher education an end and not a means. The purpose is to contribute to the professional development of the teacher and not to subject him or her to standards that are exogenous to the context in which he or she practices his or her discipline or profession.

The second condition is to change the environment on which higher education training is based. The latter has been based on university pedagogy and is constructed by researchers who claim to be in it as a field of research that "takes higher education and its teaching practices as its object of study. The question is [...] about the specificities of teaching and learning in a university setting (Biggs 1999; Hativa 2000, Langevin and Bruneau 2000)" (Rege Colet 2008, p. 627). De Ketele (2010) proposed a representation of university pedagogy and its objects.

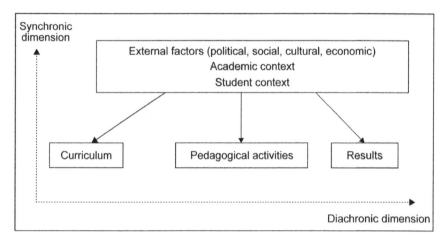

Figure 2.2. *"The field of university pedagogy: a system with multiple interactions", from De Ketele (2010)*

The field of academic pedagogy as defined here is not limited to teaching and learning practices. It also includes the curriculum, which involves what is prescribed, implemented and learned. Academic pedagogy is not strictly limited to teaching. The term academic pedagogy refers to both a field of research and the application of teaching and educational principles. This is an observation made by Nicole Rege Colet in her review of university pedagogy research in Switzerland: "university pedagogy is regularly relegated to the status of a practical application program in the form of teaching support" (Rege Colet, 2008, p. 628). Under the banner of university pedagogy, structures and actors with different purposes and discourses are thus found. On the one hand, there are researchers and laboratories that contribute to the construction of knowledge about higher education. On the other hand, university pedagogy services are in line with French and

European policies on higher education and aim to improve teaching practices, learning, student success, etc. These two forms of university pedagogy are complementary and feed off each other, as shown in Figure 2.3. University pedagogy services base their training on the results of research. They sometimes develop research projects. The research carried out is often action research aimed at improving the practices of higher education teachers. All of these actors form an ecosystem represented below.

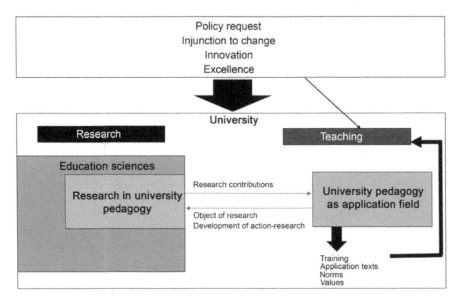

Figure 2.3. *Current environment for higher education training. For a color version of this figure, see www.iste.co.uk/bridoux/research.zip*

This ecosystem is not very conducive to the emergence of training on teaching that takes into account the disciplinary components of DPK. It is true that the role of disciplines in the professional development of lecturers and researchers is integrated into the theories developed by researchers in university pedagogy. However, in this environment, there is no real way to take into account the disciplinary culture of teachers. In order for this to be possible, it is necessary for lecturers and researchers who publish in SoTL to be able to integrate this milieu as facilitators, that they be able to develop support mechanisms, exchanges of practices, and training, and that these mechanisms be recognized. This will eventually lead to the emergence of networks of "smugglers" in the majority of disciplines taught in higher education. These "smugglers" are practitioners and researchers of the teaching of their discipline in higher education. They are not only didacticians who are interested in higher education. To be influential, these networks should be visible, known and recognized, which implies that they should be institutionalized with a structure and means. This is what Figure 2.4 attempts to represent.

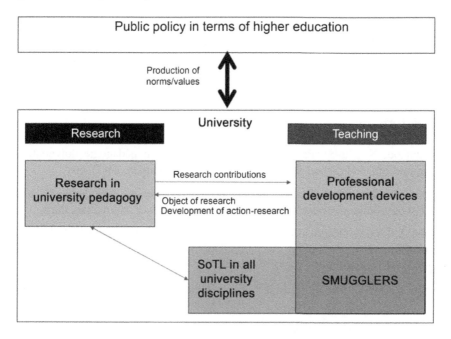

Figure 2.4. *Proposed evolution of the higher education training environment*

2.5. Conclusion

This text started with a practical question. How can we set up a training program on higher education for higher education teachers? What is the perceived and expressed need of teachers? It quickly became apparent that there was a need for training in higher education with a disciplinary approach. This tangible need was expressed several times on the margins of training courses organized by the Université Paris Diderot. Setting up this type of training is more complex than it first appears. The first difficulty was to identify competent people. Providing training in higher education from a disciplinary perspective is not completely part of the professional identity of instructional designers or lecturers and researchers. Publications on higher education with a disciplinary entry point in French are few and far between. In some disciplines, there are more in English. There are places and times for training, exchanges and co-training in higher education with a disciplinary approach, but they are not always recognized as such outside the circle of the community concerned. Developing this type of training thus comes up against sociological and organizational logics. The organization of training in higher education as it is implemented today is not compatible with the flexibility called for by Colet and Berthiaume (2009). Changing things means questioning the norms and processes that govern the organization of this training today.

2.6. References

Adangnikou, N. (2008). Peut-on parler de recherche en pédagogie universitaire, aujourd'hui, en France ? *Revue des sciences de l'éducation*, 34(3), 601.

Annoot, E. and Fave-Bonnet, M.-F. (2004). *Pratiques pédagogiques dans l'enseignement supérieur. Enseigner, apprendre, évaluer*. Harmattan, Paris.

Bastien, S. (2007). Observation participante ou participation observante ? Usages et justifications de la notion de participation observante en sciences sociales. *Recherches qualitatives*, 27(1), 127–140.

Becher, T. (1994). The significance of disciplinary differences. *Studies in Higher Education*, 19(2), 151–161.

Berthiaume, D. (2007). *What is the Nature of Professor's Discipline-Specific Pedagogical Knowledge? A Descriptibve Multicase Study*. MacGill, Canada.

Boyer, E.L. (1990). Scholarship Reconsidered: Priorities of the Professoriate. Special Report, Carnegie Foundation for the Advancement of Teaching. Jossey-Bass.

Colet, N.R. and Berthiaume, D. (2009). *Savoir ou être ? Savoirs et identités professionnels chez les enseignants universitaires*. De Boeck Supérieur, Paris.

De Ketele, J.-M. (2010). La pédagogie universitaire : un courant en plein développement. *Revue française de pédagogie. Recherches en éducation*, 172, 5–13.

Lemaître, D. (2018). L'innovation pédagogique en question : analyse des discours de praticiens. *Revue internationale de pédagogie de l'enseignement supérieur*, 34(34–1) [Online]. Available at: http://journals.openedition.org/ripes/1262.

Martuccelli, D. (2016). L'innovation, le nouvel imaginaire du changement. *Quaderni. Communication, technologies, pouvoir*, 91, 33–45.

Poteaux, N. (2013). Pédagogie de l'enseignement supérieur en France : État de la question. *Distances et médiations des savoirs. Distance and Mediation of Knowledge*, 1(4) [Online]. Available at: https://doi.org/10.4000/dms.403.

Poteaux, N. (2014). Accompagnement et pratiques pédagogiques dans l'enseignement supérieur. *Recherche et formation*, 77, 87–100.

Poteaux, N. (2015). De la recherche-action à la pédagogie universitaire : une démarche pour articuler enseignement et recherche. *Les dossiers des sciences de l'éducation*, 34, 75–90.

Rege Colet, N. (2008). D'une communauté de praticiens à un programme de recherche. Réflexions sur le développement de la pédagogie universitaire en Suisse romande. *Revue des sciences de l'éducation*, 34(3), 623–641.

3

Transforming Higher Education and Professional Learning for Academics

This chapter proposes to approach the issue of lecturer and researcher training from the perspective of the professionalization of higher education by drawing on the results of research on the construction of teaching skills by newly appointed academics. This research shows that the practices of constructing teaching competences, although eclectic and tendentially unstructured, describe very distinct patterns. This chapter also aims to show the interest of research in the pedagogical training of academics from the perspective of competence building (Kiffer 2016) with a view to professionalizing training (Wittorski 2007).

The academics' pedagogical development is often taken for granted, based on a common belief in universities that a good researcher is also a good teacher (Rege Colet and Berthiaume 2009). In addition, the scientific literature generally describes academics learning to occur "on the job" (Knight et al. 2006). These responses from the literature appear to be insufficient at a time when academics' pedagogical training is a statutory obligation in France. Since 2017, training novice academics in teaching has been a legal obligation[1]. It is now required that newly recruited academics should undergo teacher training during the first year of their employment.

Chapter written by Sacha KIFFER and Richard WITTORSKI.

1 Since the publication of Decree 2017-854, which set out the statutory provisions for academics and the Order of February 8, 2018, which set out a national framework for training aimed at deepening the pedagogical skills of trainee lecturers.

This compulsory 32-hour training course correspond to one sixth of their annual teaching service.

In addition to these regulatory changes, strong political and socio-demographic changes have gradually led to the diversification and growing complexity of academics' duties. These developments have led to the emergence of new professional learning issues.

This chapter has five sections. The first is devoted to describing recent developments in higher education with the aim of uncovering what can influence the practices of constructing the teaching skills of academics. Next, the problem of identifying the practices of academics will be formulated in terms of competences and the construction of competences in terms of professionalizing training (Wittorski 2007). Then, the theoretical framework of the research will be defined and the investigation methodology will be presented. Finally, the results will be presented and discussed in the light of the scientific literature.

3.1. Changes and increasing complexity within university education

Developments in university teaching over the last 30 years have led to a diversification of the activities of academics and, consequently, to the emergence of new professional learning issues for them.

Three major developments in higher education have marked the academic profession in recent years. First, the beginning of the 1990s was marked by the development of distance and hybrid training. Then, during the 2000s, European guidelines encouraged training institutions to formalize their training offers based on job descriptions. Finally, since the end of the 2000s, there has been a growing need for greater formalization and "traceability" of teaching activities and their products. Let us look at these three developments in detail.

– The first notable development is that universities and their teachers have been invited to develop a distance or hybrid training offer (combining face-to-face and distance learning) in response to the challenges of dealing with the democratization of higher education, which is putting new pressure on student numbers, and also to manage the costs associated with higher education as material and human resources become more streamlined. The development of these systems is not without raising a number of new questions for academics, for example:

- Beyond the attraction or fear that (new) educational technologies may arouse, how can we learn at a distance? And what do we learn? This last question is still relevant today.

- To what extent could the role (and perhaps the profession) of the teacher be transformed in these systems, less a transmitter of knowledge but more a "director of knowledge", architect, regulator, animator, facilitator, manager of communities on platforms, etc.

Second, the European guidelines of the late 1990s and early 2000s (notably the Bologna process), which were then progressively relayed (sometimes with a time lag of more than a decade) in the various countries of the European Union, have had the effect of inviting universities to base their training offers more on professional reference systems that allow for the registration of these courses in the French National Directory of Professional Certifications (*répertoire national des certifications professionnelles* [RNCP]).

Finally, a third evolution has been observed more recently, in connection with the development of evaluation, licensing and accreditation agencies (AERES[2] and then HCERES[3]): universities and their professionals have been invited to meet greater demand for formalizing their teaching (but also research) activities and their products, leading to evaluation meetings, first every 4 years and then every 5 years. These meetings then determine what is known as the budgetary dialogue between each university and its supervisory ministry. These evaluations are accompanied by a new reflection on the cost of training, which is new not for the university management teams but for the teaching teams.

The three developments mentioned above are part of clearly identified international and European challenges: to participate in greater economic competitiveness by raising the average level of qualification of the population and by facilitating geographic mobility. In our opinion, they

---

2 *Agence d'évaluation de la recherche et de l'enseignement supérieur* (French Research and Higher Education Evaluation Agency).
3 *Haut conseil de l'évaluation de la recherche et de l'enseignement supérieur* (French High Council for the Evaluation of Research and Higher Education).

reflect a desire to "professionalize" higher education in the sense that they seek to accompany the adaptation of its functioning in line with the issues mentioned (this is one of the meanings of the word professionalization). In this context, academics are in fact led to adapt their professional activity by diversifying it.

In addition to the activities that constitute the traditional core of the academic profession, there has been a significant diversification of the activities of academics over the past 30 years, resulting in new "invitations" to, for example:

– Ensure that the knowledge acquired in training is more closely linked to the fields of practice that correspond to it. In other words, thinking about how the knowledge being taught links to the occupations that the training is aimed at. This is of course linked to the emergence and generalization of bodies of knowledge.

– Develop relationships with other professional cultures, in particular with professional circles, trades, companies, training funders and even co-designers, both in the constitution of training reference systems in connection with trade reference systems and also in the organization of internship periods, which have become essential from bachelor's degree level onward and well beyond university work/study training courses.

– Develop a capacity to analyze the new stakes and purposes of training orders, particularly when the university is solicited by economic actors (companies, public administrations) to set up continuing education programs.

– Become architects of more complex and multi-actor systems insofar as university training offers are based, because of the developments mentioned, on terms that are often partnership-based and require thinking about the linkage between knowledge and skills (e.g. in connection with the latest orientations leading to thinking about training in terms of skill sets).

– Develop design and construction activities in connection with the 5-year evaluation of training offers and develop formalization activities about one's own activity in order to report on it (evaluation bodies).

The developments in higher education outlined above help to highlight the increasing complexity of teaching in the academic profession.

3.2. The heart of a problem: little recognition and training for teaching

Despite the complexity of the academic profession, teaching remains a less valued activity than research in an academic career. Indeed, promotion is based less on teaching activities than on the performance of research activities, measured by the number and quality of scientific publications. Investment in the pedagogical function of the profession is therefore, at least in part, to the detriment of career advancement (Déjean 2006).

Second, the relative absence of training structures in higher education is a founding element of the problem of the pedagogical development of academics in France. However, since the 1980s, teaching support initiatives have gradually emerged then have allowed academics to be trained or supported. This relative lack of recognition and training structures leads academics to adapt more or less alone to the situation (Altet 2004). Shulman (1993) even speaks of *pedagogical solitude* in the university.

However, the work expected by the institution is carried out and the results evaluated, which means that learning is built along the way. In this context, and taking into account the complexities of the academic environment, how do academics learn their trade as higher education teachers, especially when they are beginners, that is, when starting out in the academic career?

We hypothesize that this dynamic of professional learning and development in the deployment of the "new activities" mentioned earlier in this chapter is a "dominant logic of action" or learning by doing (Wittorski 1997, 2007). It is often a matter of learning by trial and error alone or with one's peers as the activity unfolds, without realizing it (when we act, we rarely ask ourselves how we are doing when the result is achieved or the activity is deemed successful. It is often when there is a perceived difficulty that the professional questions what they are doing).

The scientific literature seems to confirm this hypothesis. Some authors suggest that academics are self-taught teachers (Verrier 1999). The models of experiential learning (Kolb 1984) and the reflective practitioner (Schön 1983) are also regularly cited to describe learning the academic profession. Other research highlights learning the trade through experimentation (Ballantyne et al. 1999). More recently, Knight et al. (2006) have shown the predominance of "on-the-job learning". These researchers asked 2,401 part-time teachers to rate eight ways of learning according to their importance to learning the job by distributing 20 points. Respondents reported that they had learned the higher education teaching profession primarily "simply by teaching" (Table 3.1).

Ways of learning to teach	Points awarded (out of 20)
1. Simply by teaching in higher education	6.11
2. Experience as a student in higher education	3.31
3. Workshops and conferences	2.59
4. Discussions with colleagues in the same department	2.57
5. Formal education that has received an award	2.4
6. Conferences on teaching and learning	2.23
7. Assistance from a mentor	1.94
8. E-learning, on the Internet	0.81

Table 3.1. *Research findings from Knight et al. (2006)*

The findings of Knight et al. (2006) support the still overwhelming view in the university that learning to teach in higher education is natural (Rege Colet and Berthiaume 2009). In general, the work found in the literature is insufficiently precise to document the learning modalities used by novice academics to learn teaching. In light of this, it seems appropriate to deconstruct the term "on-the-job" learning in order to discover in greater detail the practices it covers.

3.3. Theoretical framework: competence building practices

In the field of education and training, there is no universally accepted definition of the concept of competence (Rey 2009). However, there seems to be agreement on a number of its dimensions (Prégent et al. 2009). The various authors who have conceptualized the notion (De Ketele 2000; Perrenoud 2000; Roegiers 2000; Scallon 2004; Tardif 2006; Jonnaert 2009; Le Boterf 2010) allow us to formulate the following definition: a *competence is the ability to mobilize a set of appropriate resources in a relevant way in order to successfully deal with problem situations.* In other words, the competent individual is the one who solves a problem situation. This definition has enabled us to break down competences into five skills, sequenced as follows: (1) identify the problems to be solved in problem situations, (2) identify the relevant resources to be applied, (3) select and combine these resources, (4) transfer them to the concrete situation and (5) ensure success in mastering the situation (Kiffer 2016).

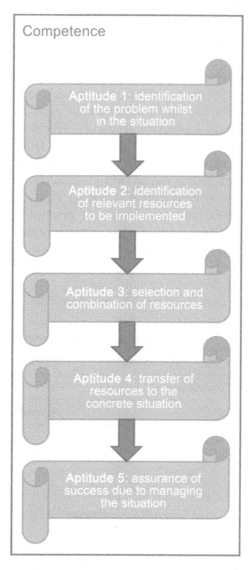

Figure 3.1. *A competence and its constituent skills. For a color version of this figure, see www.iste.co.uk/bridoux/research.zip*

The construction of competences is carried out through "learning practices" which we define as actions implemented by the learner – in this case, academics – in a more or less conscious manner in order to acquire competences. These actions are aimed at acquiring each of the five skills necessary to mobilize a set of appropriate resources in order to successfully deal with problem situations (Figure 3.1). The construction of competences is a part of the professionalization process (Kiffer 2016), more precisely of professionalizing training (Wittorski 2007).

From the avenues opened up in the literature, it was possible to identify *eight models* of practice that could answer the research question *how do academics who are just starting out learn their craft as higher education teachers*: observational-imitative learning (Bandura 1977, 2003), collaborative learning (Johnson and Johnson 1983; Dillenbourg 1999), the organized heteroformative setting (Bourgeois and Nizet 2005), tutoring (Houdé 1996; Baudrit 2007), formal and informal mentoring (Bernatchez et al. 2010); educational consultation (Clement et al. 2011); self-directed learning (Verrier 1999), and communities of practice (Lave and Wenger 1991; Wenger 2005). These eight models, which are defined in the rest of the text, are distinguished by their more or less structured training modalities, that is, they are either devices put in place with a view to training individuals to teach or devices – or more generally situations – which are not explicitly intended to train them, but which can have an effect in this sense.

Highly structured training practices	Weakly structured training practices
Training (organized heteroformative framework)	Self-directed learning
Educational consultation	Observation-imitation
Tutoring	Communities of practice
Formal mentoring	Informal mentoring

Table 3.2. *Learning practices*

3.3.1. *Highly structured learning practices*

The organized heterotraining framework refers to the more or less punctual training courses taken by beginner academics during which issues of pedagogy or university teaching are addressed. These trainings can address different topics such as the use of facilitation techniques, pedagogical methods, the use of specific tools. In this research, the specificity of the organized heteroformative setting is that the learner must have experienced, during the training, a socio-cognitive conflict in the sense of socio-constructivism (Darnon et al. 2008).

Academic consultation refers to the process by which a teacher seeks help from an academic advisor on any issue related to his or her teaching activity. Academic consultation is a free and voluntary process for the teacher (Morrison 1997). The advisor is a specialist in pedagogical and higher education issues but is not necessarily a teacher.

Mentoring is a partnership relationship between a mentor and a mentee. According to Eby et al. (2007), mentoring has four dimensions: a relationship between a mentor and a mentee (or protégé); a partnership based on learning; a relationship defined by two types of assistance, psychosocial and instrumental and a reciprocal but asymmetrical relationship. Mentoring can be formal or informal depending on whether it is defined by a training program that frames the mentoring relationship (Bernatchez et al. 2010).

Tutoring is characterized by a relationship between two individuals in which the tutor provides individualized assistance to the mentee. The nature of the help differs from that of mentoring in that it is exclusively instrumental, that is, it is based on technical and material aspects. It is not based on a relationship of affinity between the two partners and does not aim to create such a relationship. Tutoring does not have the psychosocial support dimension of mentoring (Houdé 1996). Like formal mentoring, the dyad is formed through a third party (a mentoring program, an institution, an organization, etc.). Finally, unlike mentoring, the duration of tutoring is usually limited and determined by a program (Barbier 1996).

3.3.2. *Weakly structured learning practices*

Observational learning – or vicarious learning – is based on the idea that individuals do not have to systematically have the disruptive experiences themselves that enable learning (Bandura 2003). In this conception of learning, individuals can learn by observing what others experience and then replicate it.

Self-directed learning describes voluntary self-learning that takes place outside of any organized heteroformative framework where the learner may have occasional recourse to one or more resource persons (Verrier 1999). In self-directed learning, self-learning refers as much to knowledge of a scholarly and cultural nature as to technical and practical knowledge, but also to know-how. Verrier (1999) specifies that self-directed learning is voluntary in order to emphasize the fact that it is an approach desired by the learner. The self-directed learner is autonomous in selecting the resources he or she deems necessary to achieve his or her learning goals. Nevertheless, it is not out of the question that the learner "may ask for help when needed" (Tremblay 1986, p. 28). Indeed, the definition of self-directed learning emphasizes that self-directed learners may need resource persons if they encounter "serious difficulty" (Verrier 1999, p. 89).

The theory of communities of practice is based on the idea that learning is a collective act (Lave and Wenger 1991; Wenger 2005). A community of practice is defined as a context in which opportunities are provided for community members to develop skills (Wenger 1998). For learning to occur within a community of practice, three conditions must be present simultaneously: a mutual commitment, a common enterprise and a shared repertoire. In Wenger's (1998) conception, mutual commitment corresponds to the set of "ordinary relationships that link the members of a community into a social entity" (Berry 2008, p. 29). The common enterprise refers to the set of common actions. They are determined on the one hand by what the institution requires in terms of objectives and activities, and on the other hand by the reality in the face of which these are accomplished, that is, what individuals actually do in their daily activities (Berry 2008). The shared repertoire includes "routines, words, tools, procedures, stories, gestures, symbols, styles, actions or concepts created by the community, adopted over the course of its existence, and made part of practice" (Wenger 2005, p. 91).

Collaborative learning refers to a situation in which a small group of individuals pursues a common goal, thereby maximizing the learning of each individual (Johnson and Johnson 1983). In other words, the collaborative learning situation is characterized by an interdependent relationship of the learning goals of the individuals. In the case of interdependence, a learner can only achieve his or her learning goals if other learners can also achieve their learning goals. Cooperative learning is the opposite of competitive learning and individualistic learning. In competitive learning, learners' goals are negatively correlated: one learner can only achieve his or her goals if the other cannot. In individualistic learning, learners' goals are independent of other learners. Collaborative learning is only possible if the people involved are at the same cognitive level, of equivalent status and able to work together to achieve the common goal (Dillenbourg 1999).

3.4. Methodology: the questionnaire survey

A survey was carried out to qualify the learning practices of novice academics in France based on the theoretical framework of the eight models of practice presented above. Each model was operationalized, that is, it was expressed in terms of empirically verifiable criteria. Specifically, for each model, a series of questions were incorporated into the questionnaire to determine whether the model was used – or not – by the respondents. For example, self-directed learning is a model made up of four dimensions, as defined by Verrier (1999): (1) self-learning, (2) voluntary, (3) outside an organized heteroformative framework and (4) possible and occasional recourse to resource persons. Each of these dimensions was operationalized by one or more questions. Details of the operationalization of the theoretical framework are available in Chapter 6 of the doctoral dissertation from which this chapter was derived (see Kiffer 2016).

To summarize, the questions asked in the questionnaire are designed to determine:

– the frequency of use of learning models in the sample;

– how to use each of the models;

– the distribution of models according to two main characteristics of the sample: gender and major discipline (age was excluded due to relative stability of these data in the sample);

– analysis of model combinations;

– analysis of the feeling of self-efficacy.

The questionnaire survey was administered in 2016 to 359 lecturers, with 1–4 years of experience in the academic profession. The sample is representative of the study population by three criteria: gender, age and major academic discipline (humanities; law; science and technology; medicine, pharmacy and dentistry).

The questionnaire survey was supplemented by four semi-structured interviews with experts in academic teaching training in France in order to discuss the trends that emerged. This part of the survey will not be discussed in this chapter. Readers interested in these additional details can refer to Kiffer (2016).

3.5. Presentation and discussion of the survey results

The results of the questionnaire show that the learning behaviors of novice academics are primarily autonomous. The responses also suggest that learning practices are not randomly chosen by academics, but rather correspond to specific learning needs. Second, the results show that academics act differently depending on their gender profile and discipline. Finally, the results show differences in effectiveness based on the learning practices implemented.

3.5.1. *Predominance of autonomous behavior*

Two rankings were established from the data collected (Table 3.3). The first ranking (individual treatment) corresponds to the addition of each model identified in the questionnaires. In other words, each time a respondent reported using a model, it was counted, then they were added together and eventually ranked according to their frequency of use. The second ranking (overall ranking) was derived from a question placed at the end of the questionnaire asking respondents to rank the eight models according to their importance in learning the trade. This ranking was obtained by sorting the frequency of use of each model in descending order. It should be noted that in order to answer these questions accurately, the respondents were able to read the definitions of the models posted throughout the questionnaire.

After counting the practices used, it appears that academics report using observational learning and collaborative learning most frequently. Another finding is that the least used models are educational consultation and tutoring (Table 3.3).

Learning practices	Ranking	
	Individual treatment	General ranking
Learning by observation-imitation	1	1
Self-directed learning	2	2
Collaborative learning	3	3
Community of practice	5	5
Mentoring	4	4
Heteroformative framework with socio-cognitive interactions and conflicts	7	8
Educational consultation	6	6
Tutoring	8	7

Table 3.3. *Ranking of learning practices by frequency of use*

Although teaching support structures are increasingly present in universities, the results of the survey suggest that these structures dedicated to training are not heavily used. The majority of academics who are just starting out prefer autonomy, which seems to be rooted in the university culture.

This being said, autonomy does not exclude the use of resource persons via informal discussions, which appeared as a recurrent modality in collaboration, learning by observation-imitation and self-training. In particular, self-directed learning is not a strictly autonomous practice, but a largely cooperative one, insofar as the respondents stated that they made extensive use of resource persons.

3.5.2. *Specific training needs*

Open-ended questions throughout the questionnaire allowed respondents to describe, for each learning practice they reported using, the specific "objects" of their learning. The objects can refer to a specific activity, a problematic situation, tools, etc. The data collected show that each learning practice can address specific learning needs, although some objects are represented in several practices (Table 3.4).

Learning practices	Description of the learning "objects"
Learning by observation-imitation	- Any type of teaching activity - Oral presentation techniques borrowed from fields other than teaching
Collaborative learning	- Co-facilitation of teaching - Co-organization - Joint pedagogical project
Training (organized heteroformative framework)	- Oral presentation techniques: use of voice, improvisation, public speaking, etc. - Methods to increase the interactivity of teaching (active pedagogies, problem-based learning, large group teaching, etc.) - Mastery of tools for teaching (ICTE) and for evaluation - Knowledge of the student (characteristics, expectations, conflict management, learning theories)
Tutoring	- Evaluation methods - Setting up examinations
Formal mentoring	- Teaching and evaluation strategy
Informal mentoring	- Managing problems with students - Use of teaching aids (documents, books, etc.)
Community of practice	- Management and administration of university courses - Innovation in education - Use of ICT - Educational outings (courses, trips, etc.) - Research (teaching of research methodology, dissemination and valorization of research)
Self-directed learning	- Identification of a problem in a situation - Identification of potential resources to solve it
Educational consultation	- Evaluation devices - Managing problems with students (conflicts, etc.) - Use of ICT - Innovation in education

Table 3.4. *Learning practices and pedagogical needs expressed by respondents*

Very few references in the scientific literature have addressed/documented the relationship between learning practices and the training needs of academics just starting out. Only the issue of training in an organized heteroformative setting is addressed. In this mode of training, Demougeot-Lebel and Perret (2011) noted that university teachers express training needs in teaching primarily for issues of interactivity, active pedagogical methods and the pedagogical use of software.

3.5.3. *Commonalities and differences in learning behaviors*

The method used here consists of dividing all the respondents to the questionnaire into several homogeneous categories from which comparisons can be made. Eight profiles of respondents were identified by crossing gender and major discipline. Then, for each profile, the three most frequently used learning practices were extracted from the responses to the "general ranking" question, which, as a reminder, asked respondents to rank the eight candidate practices according to their importance.

Profiles	Models ranked in first position	Models ranked in second position	Models ranked in third position
Female, humanities	Self-taught	Observation-imitation	Collaboration
Male, humanities	Self-taught	Observation-imitation	Collaboration
Female, science and technology	Self-taught	Observation-imitation	Collaboration
Male, science and technology	Observation-imitation	Self-taught	
Female, medicine, pharmacy and dentistry	Observation-imitation	- Mentoring - Self-taught - Educational consultation	
Male, medicine, pharmacy and dentistry	Observation-imitation		
Female, legal, political, economic and management sciences	Observation-imitation	- Self-taught - Mentoring	
Male, legal, political, economic and management sciences	Observation-imitation	Collaboration	Self-taught

Table 3.5. *Learning practices and lecturer and researcher profiles*

The results show that observation-imitation learning is a practice present among all novice academics, regardless of their profiles (Table 3.5). Other research on entering academia revealed the tendency of academics to imitate the teaching practices of their peers (Etienne and Annoot 2014).

The differences in learning behavior that can be seen in Table 3.5 can be explained by the epistemological and cultural specificities of academic disciplines. Endrizzi (2011) notes that training needs may vary depending on the discipline to which the academic belongs: in science and technology and medicine, training requests focus on the use of information and communication technologies (ICT), while in the humanities, requests are more focused on managing relationships with students. In their comparative study between History and Sociology, Boyer and Coridian (2002) show that the disciplinary universe of reference has consequences on the ways in which academics teach. More recently, Berthiaume (2007) has uncovered the existence of disciplinary pedagogical knowledge (DPK) that depends, among other things, on the culture of the discipline. If pedagogical knowledge is specific to each discipline, it is therefore possible to imagine that different learning paths may exist according to the profiles of academics. The data available to us here are not sufficient to conclude that such a relationship exists. This is an avenue of research that remains to be explored.

3.5.4. *Effectiveness of competence-building practices*

To measure the effectiveness of competence-building practices, a scale for measuring self-efficacy (Bandura 2006) was introduced in the questionnaire (Table 3.6). Specifically, respondents were asked to indicate, for each learning practice used, a score between 0 and 100, corresponding to their feeling of mastery of the five skills that constitute the competence (see section 3.3.).

0	10	20	30	40	50	60	70	80	90	100
Do not think I can do the task				Think I can probably do the task				Believe with certainty that I can perform the task		

Table 3.6. *Self-efficacy scale*

The results show that all self-efficacy scores increase, regardless of the skill-building practices used. Furthermore, it appears that the increase in the feeling of self-efficacy is significantly higher when observation-imitation community of practice–self-learning is combined. Finally, all the models appear to be equally effective in building teaching skills, except for self-directed learning and collaborative learning, whose effectiveness is more limited.

The question of the effectiveness of the competence-building practices of academics, whether beginners or experienced, is not addressed in the scientific literature. On the other hand, there is an abundance of work on the relationship between conceptions of teaching and learning and teaching and learning practices (Prosser and Trigwell 1999; Demougeot-lebel and Perret 2010). This research shows that academics' representations of their own teaching practices influence their teaching practices (Langevin 2007). However, a study of the links between teaching practices and competence-building practices is yet to be carried out.

3.6. Conclusion

Although the supply of pedagogical training for academics has been developing for many years in France, the results of this research reveal that novice academics declare that they are less inclined to turn to traditional heterodirected formal training than to informal learning practices. These learning practices, often "in situ", lead to the development of an experience that often becomes "embedded" (Leplat 1995) and therefore very attached to the activity and difficult to transfer to other situations and to communicate to other people.

From here, we can see the usefulness of complementing the "natural" development of this incorporated experience with devices aimed at "disincorporating" the learning produced, for example, through the development of a co-analysis of the activity (reflexivity) allowing one to "learn about oneself" but also to share with one's peers and to envisage "other possibilities". This is probably one of the major challenges of teaching training in university.

Institutional recognition of teaching activities in the academic career seems to be one of the levers for improving training for academics (Bertrand

2014; Cosnefroy 2015). By extension, we can envision that the recognition of informal learning practices, which are overwhelmingly what novice academics do according to this research, could contribute to the overall improvement of their pedagogical training in their early career. As such, we argue not only for the teaching activity to be recognized and valued by the institution, but also for informal activities that contribute to the construction of their pedagogical competences to be recognized and valued.

3.7. References

Altet, M. (2004). Enseigner en premier cycle universitaire : des formes émergentes d'adaptation ou de la "métis" enseignante. In *Pratiques pédagogiques dans l'enseignement supérieur : enseigner, apprendre, évaluer*, Annoot E., Fave-Bonnet, M.-F. (eds). L'Harmattan, Paris.

Barbier, J.-M. (1996). Tutorat et fonction tutorale : quelques entrées d'analyse. *Recherche et Formation*, 22, 7–19.

Ballantyne, R., Bain, J.D., Packer, J. (1999). Researching university teaching in Australia: Themes and issues in academics' reflections. *Stud. High. Educ.*, 2(24), 237–257.

Bandura, A. (1977). *Social Learning Theory*. Prentice-Hall, Englewood Cliffs.

Bandura, A. (2003). *Auto-efficacité. Le sentiment d'efficacité personnelle*. De Boeck Université, Paris.

Bandura, A. (2006). Guide for constructing self-efficacy scales. In *Self-efficacy Beliefs of Adolescents*, Pajares, F., Urdan, T. (eds). Information Age Publishing, Greenwish, CT.

Baudrit, A. (2007). *Le tutorat. Richesses d'une méthode pédagogique*. De Boeck Supérieur, Louvain-la-Neuve.

Bernatchez, P.-A., Cartier, S., Bélisle, M., Bélanger, C. (2010). Le mentorat en début de carrière : retombées sur la charge professorale et condition de mise en œuvre d'un programme en milieu universitaire. *Revue internationale de pédagogie de l'enseignement supérieur*, 26(1) [Online]. Available at: http://journals.openedition.org/ripes/374 [Accessed 28 September 2021].

Berry, V. (2008). Les communautés de pratiques : note de synthèse. *Pratiques de formation : analyses*, 54, 12–47.

Berthiaume, D. (2007). A description of discipline-specific pedagogical knowledge (DPK) encountered in the discourse of four university professors from four different disciplinary areas. PhD Thesis, McGill University, Montreal.

Bertrand, C. (2014). Soutenir la transformation pédagogique dans l'enseignement supérieur. Report, Ministère de l'éducation nationale, de l'enseignement supérieur et de la recherche, Paris.

Bourgeois, E. and Nizet, J. (2005). *Apprentissage et formation des adultes*. Presses universitaires de France, Paris.

Boyer, R. and Coridian, C. (2002). Transmission des savoirs disciplinaires dans l'enseignement universitaire, une comparaison histoire-sociologie. *Sociétés contemporaines*, 48, 4–61.

Clement, M., Di Napoli, R., Annelies Gilis, A., Buelens, H., Frenay, M. (2011). Educational consultation for reflective-dialogic partnerships: A possible model. *Recherche et Formation*, 67, 31–47.

Cosnefroy, L. (2015). État des lieux de l'accompagnement et de la formation des enseignants-chercheurs. Report, Institut Français de l'Éducation, Lyon.

Darnon, C., Butera, F., Mugny, G. (2008). *Des conflits pour apprendre*. Presses Universitaires de Grenoble.

De Ketele, J.-M. (2000). En guise de synthèse : convergences autour des compétences. In *Quel avenir pour les compétences ?* Bosman, C., Gérard, F.-M., Roegiers X. (eds). De Boeck Université, Brussels.

Dejean, J. (2006). Les réticences à l'évaluation de l'enseignement en France, signe de la culture professionnelle des enseignants-chercheurs ou trait de la culture française ? In *Les pratiques enseignantes en mutation à l'université*, Rege Colet, N., Romainville, M. (eds). De Boeck université, Brussels.

Demougeot-Lebel, J. and Perret, C. (2010). Les chargés de TD/TP ont-ils tous les mêmes inquiétudes avant leurs premières interventions face aux étudiants ? *Recherches en éducation*, 9, 99–113.

Demougeot-Lebel, J. and Perret, C. (2011). Qu'attendent les enseignants universitaires français en termes de formation et d'accompagnement pédagogiques ? *Revue internationale de pédagogie de l'enseignement supérieur*, 27(1) [Online]. Available at: http://journals.openedition.org/ripes/456 [Accessed 28 September 2021].

Dillenbourg, P. (1999). What do you mean by "collaborative learning"? In *Collaborative learning: Cognitive and Computational Approaches*, Dillenbourg, P. (ed.). Pergamon, Oxford.

Eby, L., Rhodes, J., Allen, T. (2007). Evolution and definition of mentoring. In *The Blackwell Handbook of Mentoring. A Multiple Perspectives Approach*, Allen, T., Eby, L. (eds). Blackwell Publishing Ltd., Malden.

Endrizzi, L. (2011). *Savoir enseigner dans le supérieur : un enjeu d'excellence pédagogique* [Online]. Available at: http://veille-et-analyses.ens-lyon.fr/DA-Veille/64-septembre-2011.pdf [Accessed 17 May 2021].

Étienne, R. and Annoot, E. (2014). L'entrée dans le métier d'enseignant-chercheur. In *28ème Congrès International de l'AIPU*, Mons.

Houdé, R. (1996). *Le mentor : transmettre un savoir-être*. Hommes et Perspectives, Théorie et Pratique, Revigny-sur-Ornain.

Johnson, R.T. and Johnson, D.W. (1983). Effects of cooperative, competitive, and individualistic learning experiences on social development. *Except. Child.*, 49(4), 323–329.

Jonnaert, P. (2009). *Compétences et socioconstructivime. Un cadre théorique.* De Boeck, Brussels.

Knight, P., Tait, J., Yorke, M. (2006). The professional learning of teachers in higher education. *Stud. High. Educ.*, 31(3), 319–339.

Kiffer, S. (2016). La construction des compétences d'enseignement des enseignants-chercheurs novices de l'université en France. PhD Thesis, Université de Strasbourg.

Kolb, D.A. (1984). *Experiential Learning: Experience as the Source of Learning and Development.* Prentice-Hall, Englewood Cliffs.

Langevin, L. (2007). *Formation et soutien à l'enseignement universitaire. Des constats et des exemples pour inspirer l'action.* Presses de l'université du Québec.

Lave, J. and Wenger, E. (1991). *Situated Learning: Legitimate Peripheral Participation.* Cambridge University Press.

Le Boterf, G. (2010). *Construire les compétences individuelles et collectives.* Eyrolles Éditions d'Organisation, Paris.

Leplat, J. (1995). A propos des compétences incorporées. *Education Permanente*, 123, 101–114.

Morrison, D.E. (1997). Overview of instructional consultation in North America. In *Practically Speaking: A Sourcebook for Instructional Consultants in Higher Education*, Brinko K.T., Menges, R.J. (eds). New forums, Stillwater.

Perrenoud, P. (2000). *Construire les compétences dès l'école.* ESF, Paris.

Prégent, R., Bernard, H., Kozanitis, A. (2009). *Enseigner à l'université dans une approche-programme. Un défi à relever.* Presses internationales polytechnique, Montreal.

Prosser, M. and Trigwell, K. (1999). *Understanding Learning and Teaching. The Experience in Higher Education*. Open University Press, Maidenhead.

Rege Colet, N. and Berthiaume, D. (2009). Être ou savoir ? Identité professionnelle et savoirs professionnels chez les enseignants universitaires. In *Savoirs en (trans)formation. Au cœur des professions de l'enseignement et de la formation*, Hofstetter R., Schneuwly, B. (eds). De Boeck université, Brussels.

Rey, B. (2009). Autour des mots. "Compétence" et "compétence professionnelle". *Recherche et Formation*, 60, 103–116.

Roegiers, X. (2000). *Une pédagogie de l'intégration : compétences et intégration des acquis dans l'enseignement*. De Boeck Université, Brussels.

Scallon, G. (2004). *L'évaluation des apprentissages dans une approche par compétences*. De Boeck, Brussels.

Schön, D. (1983). *The Reflective Practitioner: How Professionals Think in Action*. Basic Books, New York.

Shulman, L. (1993). Teaching as community property. *Change*, 25, 6–7.

Tardif, J. (2006). *L'évaluation des compétences. Documents le parcours de développement*. Les éditions de la Chenelières Inc., Montreal.

Tremblay, N. (1986). *Apprendre en situation d'autodidaxie : une étude des besoins des apprenants et des compétences des intervenants*. Presses Universitaires de Montréal.

Verrier, C. (1999). *Autodidaxie et autodidactes. L'infini des possibles*. Anthropos, Paris.

Wenger, E. (1998). *Communities of Practice: Learning, Meaning, and Identity*. University Press, Cambridge.

Wenger, E. (2005). *La théorie des communautés de pratique : apprentissage, sens et identité*. Presses de l'Université Laval, Quebec.

Wittorski, R. (1997). *Analyse du travail et production de compétences collectives*. L'Harmattan, Paris.

Wittorski, R. (2007). *Professionnalisation et développement professionnel*. L'Harmattan, Paris.

PART 2

The Teaching Practices of University Teachers with a Disciplinary Approach

4

Academic Territory and Professional Identity: Toward a Differentiation of Teaching Practices at University

4.1. Introduction

Over the past decade, many French universities have created professional development structures for university lecturers and researchers (LRs) with a view to "transforming pedagogy" in order to respond, in particular, to the questions posed by the diversity of students entering university and by the failure rate at the end of the first year of a bachelor's degree (Endrizzi 2011). Research has accompanied these changes, and as early as 2004, Annoot and Fave-Bonnet coordinated one of the first syntheses of issues associated with the study of pedagogical practices at the university. It should be noted that, until recently, research targeting higher education approached the study of teaching practices of LRs in a rather generic way, without taking into account the specific knowledge content of the disciplines taught, and more broadly, without taking into account the professional duality of "teaching and research" specific to the LR profession (Adangnikou 2008; Leininger-Frézal 2019). Paradoxically, and even if some research escapes this observation (Nixon 1996; Norton et al. 2005), it remains in the minority even though many researchers call for the development of research on teaching practices that include the discipline, that is, the subject that is being taught and forms the basis of the research activity of LRs (Trede et al. 2012;

Chapter written by Stéphanie BRIDOUX, Nicolas GRENIER-BOLEY, Cécile DE HOSSON, Rita KHANFOUR-ARMALÉ, Nathalie LEBRUN, Caroline LEININGER-FRÉZAL, Zoé MESNIL, Céline NIHOUL and Martine DE VLEESCHOUWER.

Poteaux 2013). Thus, according to Becher (1994), this inclusion is justified at three levels:

– at the macro level, to understand the university system, its environment and its relationship to the labor market;

– at the meso level, to analyze institutional management, evaluation methods and faculty development;

– at the micro level, to understand teaching practices and pedagogical activities.

University teachers, and more specifically lecturers and researchers, share a "disciplinary culture", "a common set of intellectual values, a common cognitive territory" (Becher 1994, p. 153). This shared culture also includes beliefs about what should be taught and how it should be taught. Each individual's beliefs also have a more personal dimension, as they stem from teachers' experiences, too. And of course, they influence practice, the study of which then becomes a means of accessing these beliefs and knowledge.

For some researchers (cf. in particular Calderhead 1996), teachers' knowledge and beliefs are in a way "encapsulated" in their professional experiences, to the point that they are inseparable from them. They are manifested through the acts of teaching, whether it be activity planning, interactions with students or assessment. They are expressed in the form of metaphors, actions or words. Their nature is as much a matter of mental images as of ideas or propositions, implicit or explicit, conscious or unconscious, inferred from what teachers say or do, which may be preceded by the phrase "I believe that...", in the case where they are declarative in nature. (Crahay et al. 2010, p. 87).

Yet, according to Becher, this disciplinary culture is not sufficiently taken into account in studies that are particularly concerned with the micro level: "It is difficult to see how faculty development can go beyond the most elementary level without a clear recognition that disciplinary cultures impose their own particular pattern in teaching as in other activities. Yet, neither practice nor the evaluation of practices commonly takes account of such variations" (Becher 1994, p. 158).

The notion of "disciplinary culture" refers to academic disciplines that have often been defined by their epistemological characteristics (Kuhn 2015), leading to their classification (Biglan 1973). Epistemologically, the boundaries between disciplines and subdisciplines are not strict, watertight lines but porous interfaces that can be debated. This is why we will retain an institutional understanding of the term discipline, understood as "the institutional division of a body of knowledge that delimits a domain in which the production of academic knowledge or the reproduction of the professional body of 'scholars' is carried out" (Lévy and Lussault 2003, p. 263). Neumann (2001) and Neumann et al. (2002) have shown that there are systematic pedagogical differences in epistemologically different disciplines. Knowledge of teaching (pedagogical knowledge) appears to be strongly related to the knowledge required to teach (disciplinary knowledge) (Rege Colet and Berthiaume 2009) and socially situated (Becher 1989; Neumann 2001). In other words, the pedagogical practices and values of lecturers and researchers (social dimension) are influenced by the structures of disciplinary knowledge that Becher (1989) calls academic territories.

Disciplinary didactics are characterized by taking into account the discipline in the study of teaching and learning phenomena; we sometimes speak of an "entry through the content". Thus, for several years now and in various disciplines, research in didactics in higher education has been conducted. In the didactics of mathematics, one of the oldest disciplinary didactics, it arrived almost from the beginning of the structuring of the field in the 1970s, and several international colloquia include working groups on higher education, which testifies to the still current importance of research at this level of education, even if it remains less important than for primary or secondary education. In the same way, research in the didactics of physics was deployed very early in higher education by examining the reasons for persistent errors made by general academic studies degree (DEUG) students, in particular in mechanics (Viennot 1979; Clement 1982; Halloun and Hestenes 1985). In other disciplines, for example in chemistry or geography, research on disciplinary content relevant to higher education is rarer, and if colloquia on the exchange of practices testify to the willingness of lecturers and researchers to reflect on their teaching, the contributions rarely fall within the field of research in didactics. However, it is not because didactic research exists at the university level that the LRs of the disciplines involved are aware of it (Lebrun and de Hosson, 2017).

As didactic researchers, we therefore support the hypothesis that the teaching and research discipline of lecturers and researchers is not neutral in the way they think about and conceive their pedagogical practices (Menges et al. 2001 cited in Rege Colet and Berthiaume 2009). We also argue that the dual dimensions of their profession, teaching and research, give them a different professional identity than pre-baccalaureate teachers (Rege Colet and Berthiaume 2009).

It is in this context that we conducted the research presented here based on four academic disciplines: chemistry, geography, mathematics and physics (Bridoux et al. 2019; Bridoux et al. 2020). This research formed part of a larger project with the goal of learning more about the LR audience. In the part of our research outlined in this chapter, we seek to understand, based on discourses of practice, how discipline membership influences the teaching practices of lecturers and researchers. Our questioning is based on the concept of professional identity, which we will present first. Based on the specificities of our disciplines, which we will then address, we will present in this chapter some results on the professional identity of the LR, showing regularities but also differences between the four disciplines studied.

4.2. Academic territory and professional identity: a theoretical environment to approach the pedagogical practices of lecturers and researchers

Various factors shape what researchers in the sociology of work refer to as "professional identity", which refers to a worker's sense of belonging to his or her professional group (Dubar 1996; Blin 1997). All these factors are likely to influence the "pedagogical action" (Leclercq 2000) of an LR. Our research is based on an assumption that is deliberately restrictive with regard to all of these factors: the way in which an LR describes his or her pedagogical practice, the way in which he or she "teaches", and what he or she expects of students are all driven by a set of beliefs about what should be known (and therefore taught) and how it should be done.

The scientific literature concerning the professional identity of university teachers is quite abundant (Tickle 2000; van Lankveld et al. 2017), yet it is (almost) as if the professional identity of LRs could be studied independently of the discipline that carries both their research and teaching activity. Insofar as the concept of professional identity has already been proven to shed light on the reasons why "teachers do what they do" (Kogan 2000; Tickle 2000), we have chosen to place our approach within this theoretical environment, but taking into account the "disciplinary culture" of LRs, that is, with regard to the relationship that LRs have with:

– the discipline from which they come (an "epistemological" relationship): what chemistry, geography, mathematics and physics are, for example, but also how knowledge in these disciplines is developed in research laboratories;

– the way in which this discipline (or the knowledge derived from it) should be taught (a "pedagogical" relationship), which is not independent of the needs they project onto their students.

This relationship will be all the easier to identify if the researchers in charge of exploring it know "what it is about", that is, if they have some familiarity with the knowledge of the discipline concerned. As mentioned in the introduction, research in disciplinary didactics appears to be relatively well equipped for this. Thus, considered in relation to a given academic territory, the concept of professional identity becomes an operative tool for entering teaching spaces through the door of knowledge and, in so doing, enriching knowledge on the professional identity of LRs (De Hosson et al. 2015a). More operationally, the professional identity of an LR specified according to his or her disciplinary culture can be inferred from the following (Cattonar 2001):

– Norms assigned to his or her profession and which he or she recognizes as such (this includes institutional norms related to his or her status, to the organization of teaching, to the way students are evaluated, or more tacit norms such as the types of knowledge that it is necessary to know at one level of teaching or another); more generally, this dimension refers to what the LR considers legitimate/illegitimate in the exercise of his or her profession.

– Qualities deemed necessary to carry out one's profession (these may be pedagogical qualities – being able to listen to students – or more disciplinary qualities – having a good command of the knowledge one teaches, doing research, etc.).

– Values (what one particularly appreciates in one's profession, which one would not be ready to delegate to others – a teaching topic, for example, and conversely, what one willingly delegates, which one considers not to be part of one's core profession).

In order to identify the norms, qualities and values attributed by a lecturer and researcher to his or her profession, we conducted individual semi-structured interviews.

4.3. The field survey

4.3.1. *Development of a survey tool*

The interview protocol was constructed from the one proposed by de Hosson et al. (2015b). We adapted it so that it would be operative for a given discipline on the one hand and would allow the implementation of a comparative approach on the other hand. Our objective was to trace the characteristics of the professional teaching identity (Cattonar 2001) from the declared and ideal teaching practices of the LRs. Given the inclusion of this research in the overall project, the interviews and their analysis take into account not only practices but also representations of the profession, students, etc. Different aspects of the profession were addressed, such as the ways in which teaching is organized and students are evaluated, the training of LRs in teaching, the difficulties encountered by students, the objectives of a course, etc. These aspects have allowed us to characterize the epistemological and pedagogical relationships that each LR has with the discipline he/she teaches. In Table 4.1, we give examples of questions from our interview protocol to the dimensions of professional identity to which they relate.

Dimensions of professional identity	Questions put to the LRs
Standards	What is the objective of a course? How do you ensure that it is achieved? What is the objective of an evaluation? What would be an ideal evaluation?
Qualities	What do you find difficult about being a teacher? Is teacher training for the LR desirable?
Values	What do you consider important in your teaching job? What would you be willing to delegate? What would you not be willing to delegate?
Discipline	What are the students' difficulties? How do you detect them? How do you address them? What makes a good course?

Table 4.1. *Interview guide*

Academic Territory and Professional Identity 77

We conducted 38 interviews (nine in chemistry, nine in geography, 12 in mathematics and eight in physics) with LRs who very often share the same training spaces, the first university year often cutting across several disciplines. The volunteer interviewees have varying degrees of university teaching experience and come from seven universities, two of which are located in Belgium.

In order to facilitate the characterization of pedagogical relationships, the interviews were conducted by researchers familiar with the knowledge of the discipline concerned. The identification of the epistemological relationships that the LRs have with their discipline was facilitated by the study of the epistemological specificities of the different disciplines concerned here. We present some of these specificities for each discipline.

4.3.2. *Epistemological specificities of the disciplines concerned by the survey*

The disciplines considered in this chapter are of different natures. Becher (1987) distinguishes four types of disciplines: pure sciences, pure humanities and social sciences, hard and applied technologies and applied social sciences. The nature of the knowledge at stake in these disciplinary groups and the disciplinary culture are different, as shown Table 4.2. By placing the four disciplines considered in the table, their diversity becomes apparent at first glance.

Disciplinary group	Nature of disciplinary knowledge	Disciplinary culture	Positioning of the disciplines considered in the chapter
Pure sciences	Cumulative; atomistic (crystalline/arborescent); is interested in the universal, quantities, simplification; leads to discovery/explanation	Competitive, gregarious; politically well organized; high publication rate; task-oriented	Mathematics Physical Sciences
Humanities and pure social sciences	Reiterative; holistic (organic/riparian); is interested in the particular, in qualities, complexity; leads to understanding/ interpretation	Individualistic, plural; not very structured; low publication rate; person-oriented	Geography

Hard and applied technologies	Finalized; pragmatic (know-how through concrete knowledge); concerns the mastery of the physical environment; results in products/techniques	Entrepreneurial, cosmopolitan; dominated by professional values; patents substitutes for publications; oriented toward a defined purpose	Chemistry
Applied social sciences	Functional; utilitarian (know-how via general knowledge); concerns the improvement of professional practice; leads to protocols/procedures	Forward-looking; status uncertain; dominated by intellectual fashions; reduced publication rates by expertise; power-oriented	

Table 4.2. *Positioning of the disciplines considered in this chapter with respect to Becher's (1987) typology (loose translation and adaptation)*

Chemistry is a natural science that studies matter and its transformations, and more precisely the chemical elements in their free state, atoms or ions. It also studies their associations by chemical bonds, transformations and reaction processes that change or modify the identity of particles or molecules. The analysis of all the substances that form the universe, the study of their properties and their transformations allow us to understand their evolution, but also to create new compounds, new materials, to invent new transformations. Kermen (2016) offers a synthesis of the epistemological and didactic specificities of chemistry. She states that chemistry is considered the science of transformations of matter, but at the same time it is an experimental science and an industry in society (Barlet 1999; Bensaude-Vincent 2004), which is a specificity compared to geography, mathematics and physics. "Chemistry is essentially a science of abstractions" (Gilbert and Justi 2006). And as a consequence, chemists seek to represent the phenomena they observe (at a macroscopic level) to explain ideas as events (at a microscopic level). According to Barlet (1999), chemistry has a specific culture marked by the incessant creation of new species and new materials, by a constant reference to the macroscopic and the microscopic, to the modeling of structures and phenomena. According to Le Maréchal (1999), the fact that theories and models in chemistry are based on a description of the structure and properties of microscopic entities (atoms, molecules, ions) which are not observable constitutes one of the specificities of chemistry. This specificity is a source of difficulty for students who must construct a microscopic representation of matter even though they only have access to macroscopic observations. For this, it is appropriate to distinguish objects, events and properties of the perceptible world separately from those of the non-perceptible world, consisting for example of objects, such as atoms and molecules, involved in events such as chemical reactions (Le Maréchal 1999; Pekdağ and Le Maréchal 2003). Theories are necessary in chemistry education, and essential to explain chemical concepts, experiments, or chemical properties (Tsaparlis 1997). The relationship to the experimental is strong and complex and is characterized by a back-and-forth between modeling and experimentation (Barlet 1999). To what extent and in what way do Chemistry LRs organize or not organize the links between experimentation, modeling and abstraction?

Geography is the science that studies space at the interface between societies and their environments. It takes into account the actors, the factors and their interactions to analyze the way in which people live, develop and practice a space. The discipline is marked by the predominant place of the "field", which designates both the place where geographers collect data (field surveys, samples, observations, interviews, etc.); the tool for apprehending the world: "doing fieldwork" designates a specific research methodology; and a research object: each researcher has "his" field, that is, the field of research on which he has built his expertise. Calbérac (2010) has shown that the field constitutes an "initiatory rite" in the training of geography students and researchers. This rite is based on the idea that practicing the field gives direct access to reality. This is the myth of the "real experience" that Karen Nairn (2005) deconstructed through an experimental device. This myth remains tenacious in pedagogical discourses, as evidenced by the responses made to Karen Nairn's article (Hope 2009; Owens et al. 2015). Yet, the epistemology of the discipline has largely been renewed in the field, now thought of as a construct (Calberac 2010; Volvey et al. 2012). This myth of real experience constitutes one of the elements of disciplinary culture in geography. How does this myth influence the pedagogical discourse and practices of LRs? Do LRs actually value what is based on spatial practices?

While the common view has long been to consider mathematics as a discipline that deals with objects such as numbers and magnitudes, this classical image that lasted until the 18th century was challenged in the 19th century when the reliance on geometric intuition gave way to a need to formalize mathematical notions in order to define them rigorously. This evolution continued in the 20th century when, as Bloch (2015) points out, tools that do not refer to any "sensible object" (e.g. general topology or measure theory) were developed by mathematicians, the efficiency of these theories being notably linked to their abstraction. Finally, the emergence of computers has led to the emergence of new fields, such as discrete mathematics, which continues to be explored in the 21st century. Thus, the activity of mathematicians varies greatly depending on factors such as periods, personalities or fields of research, and leads to a distinction between pure and applied mathematics. However, some common elements seem to us to be constitutive of the mathematical activity throughout its historical development and allow us to point out some specificities of the discipline. Thus, the cumulative character of mathematics leads mathematicians to have to organize a great deal of knowledge and to put them in relation. The construction of new definitions, the formulation of new results as well as the production of demonstrations are also central to mathematical activity, also testifying to the essential role of the formalization and abstraction processes that are associated with these activities (Rogalski 2012). As Robert (1998) points out, the mathematics taught at the beginning of university (and the phenomenon becomes more pronounced later in the course) resembles the mathematics of experts, both in terms of knowledge and expected practices. Schneider (2008) distinguishes two types of praxeologies, in the sense of Chevallard (1991), to characterize mathematical activity and to better understand what may be at stake in the transition between the two institutions of high school and university. In secondary education, notions often appear as objects installed by the monstration that designates them (Schneider 2008). Of course, these objects play an important role in learning and constitute mental objects in the sense of Freudenthal (1973). But the absence of a discourse that justifies the techniques involving these objects does not allow students to develop a deductive approach and leads them to procedural learning. This is what Schneider calls "type 1 praxeologies". In "type 2 praxeologies", formal definitions are more important. It is also a question of being able to deduce properties from previously demonstrated results. This type of praxeology makes it possible to develop a deductive structure but, as Schneider explains, too abrupt an entry into formalism can also lead to "hollow learning". Finally, students do not easily access important elements of mathematical activity familiar to mathematics LRs. How will mathematics LRs acculturate students to these processes of formalization and abstraction? What compromises will they have to make?

Physics is a science that seeks to understand, explain and model natural phenomena and their evolution. It is based on an approach composed of observations, experiments and formalism, as in mathematics. The hypothetico-deductive approach is the most widely used in both teaching and research. Like chemists, physicists develop models that allow them to explain and predict phenomena located in the world of objects (empirical field) (Coince et al. 2008). They can take the form of diagrams, concepts (e.g. the force model) or a law linking measurable physical quantities and have a field of validity depending on the phenomena studied. The work of physicists thus consists of simplifying, idealizing and modeling a phenomenon, thus making the link between the world of theories (theoretical field) and the world of objects (empirical field). The model is in fact an "operative" component of the theory and uses various symbolic representations. It is in this sense that physics enriches its models from the accumulation of situations, data and knowledge. The knowledge is in constant evolution but in the first years of university, teachers try to transmit knowledge developed over the course of time rather than new knowledge resulting from research, the latter being approached at the end of the undergraduate degree and during master's courses instead. The problems dealt with in physics are diverse (explanation and understanding of phenomena and objects, prediction of behavior, etc.). Yet, "globally, their solutions take the form of laws that are assumed to govern the how of inanimate nature, the how of its past and the how of its future" (de Hosson et al. 2015a). Do physics LRs value understanding and explaining natural phenomena? Do they value the experimental approach and do they go as far as the predictive nature of physics (models and laws)?

And in general, what trade-offs will LRs in different disciplines face in the tensions discussed?

4.4. Results

All the interviews confirm the influence of the research profession on the teaching profession. In this influence, some elements are independent of the discipline and are rather linked to some very general characteristics of the research activity: taste for the discipline, pleasure of the intellectual path to reach a goal which is not won in advance, etc. These results are in line with those of Fave-Bonnet (1994) where some physics LRs interviewed affirm that "research is thus necessary for what it brings to the teacher in terms of approach and method" and for others, the very definition of the university is at stake: "the maintenance of the research-teaching link is the only guarantee of a teaching that does not become sclerotic". Other elements more related to the teaching activity are also independent of the discipline, such as a certain distribution of responsibilities between teachers and students: the former are responsible for presenting the discipline and the latter for finding a personal work space that allows for an individualized encounter with the discipline. But other elements of this influence are marked by the epistemological characteristics of each discipline.

The results presented below are grouped into categories independently of the disciplines; within each category, we will highlight the disciplinary differences that appear. We have chosen to include numerous excerpts from interviews, some of which are quite long. Each extract is followed by the initial of the discipline (chemistry, geography, mathematics, physics) and a number identifying the interviewee. We do not seek here to quantify precisely how each excerpt is more or less representative of what was said in the interviews. We are trying to identify the problems that LRs encounter in teaching their discipline and how they try to solve them. This allows us to distinguish between what is widely shared and what is less common, and thus provides us with the overall picture.

4.4.1. *Showing the beauty of disciplines*

The LRs showcase and value certain aspects of their discipline in their courses. The first of these is what they consider to be the "beauty" of the discipline.

The LRs in the four disciplines were asked to characterize what they thought was a "good course in their discipline". This question showed that the LRs are keen to show what their discipline is and how much fun it can be. They want to inspire students to ask questions of their own, allowing them to learn more. We find there what we interpret as personal motivations of the LR for research: a taste for the discipline, pleasure of the intellectual path, etc.

To transmit this pleasure, this desire they have, LRs sometimes see themselves as storytellers, or as directors using different media (illustrations, examples, etc.). They consider themselves responsible for showing the beauty of their discipline, for proposing an interesting reflection. We find such positions regardless of the discipline:

> A good course is one that tells a story to the student and provides them with an intellectual pathway. I sometimes think I'm overdoing it but that's because when you like the discipline you want to convey certain key aspects of it. (C1)

> There's a theatrical aspect to it that takes you into something that makes you want to pursue physics. (P1)

> There is the beauty of math for its own sake. When I'm teaching it, I hope that the math student, will discover, appreciate and love math for what it brings them in itself in fact [...] There is the pleasure of doing math, and it's really this pleasure side that should be front and center in my opinion. Then there's the utilitarian side, which is about having the mathematical tools and making them love math. It's about succeeding in making them see and discover the beauty of the field. (M10)

We find in this extract a characteristic of mathematics, which is both "pure and applied". Here, the beauty of mathematics is presented as an intrinsic quality.

> For me, when my students are about to finish their studies, the most important thing is that I've taken them on a journey. (G3)

This formulation in terms of an invitation to travel is often used by geography LRs. Travel conveys the image of an Other and an Elsewhere that we can discover. The metaphor of travel is not without connection to the field. Both imply a displacement and a form of acculturation to be able to observe what there is to see. Travel and field are experiences that rely on spatial practices, whose importance in the epistemology of the discipline we have seen.

But for a course to be successful, it is not enough for students to be enthusiastic; they must also have been given the desire to pursue the reflection independently, and given the means to do so, as this second series of excerpts shows:

> A good course means that they want to listen, that they want to understand, that they want to look for information, because you can't say everything in two hours and if at the end of the course you haven't told them anything, they'll go look on Wikipedia. (C7)
>
> A [good] course makes students want to ask questions, to look in books in search of answers. (P1)
>
> Success is giving them a much more accurate intuition of objects and then a rigorous definition of them, which means that they are then able to reason for themselves about the objects. (M6)

Beyond the beauty of the discipline, LRs emphasize the usefulness and legitimacy of the content taught.

We note a variation in the way concepts are presented. Less theatrical staging is observed in the comments of the mathematics LRs interviewed compared to those in physics and chemistry. This can be explained by the emphasis on conceptual objects in mathematics, whereas in the other two disciplines it is the use of concrete examples from everyday life that is emphasized. We noted a unique feature in geography where the idea of travel prevails. This is probably due to the field activities in this discipline.

4.4.2. *Enhancing the usefulness and legitimacy of disciplines*

Regardless of their discipline, the LRs interviewed value what they believe is useful and legitimate to teach and learn, but what is designated as such varies from discipline to discipline.

The physics and chemistry LRs value that which has a link with reality, which can cover multiple realities:

> What I like is to show that physics has a link with reality, it is not a disembodied discipline, so that's why innovation tries to develop this approach to reality with either experimental or theoretical aspects. In this way, I also show them that knowledge advances and that they can also appreciate knowledge precisely because it advances during the program. (P4)

It is about understanding the natural phenomena that surround us, social debates, and applications in research:

> You have to incorporate researchers [into the first year of undergraduate degrees], because you have to show them the perspectives; when you talk to them about something you can show them a real application and a real problem behind it. The passion of a good researcher will be felt when they teach the class. (C7)

> It's about trying to understand things that we can't see with the naked eye. What is attractive about chemistry is the realization that everything is governed by the microscopic. We can apply different techniques to understand what is going on. Without chemistry there would be no life. (C12)

We find very explicitly the link with reality, which is a central element of the epistemology of these disciplines, experimental sciences as much manual as theoretical. In the extract from interview C12, the link between the microscopic and macroscopic aspects is mentioned, but this is the only interview where it appears.

In geography, the LRs value forms of teaching that are conceived through the prism of professional practices. In particular, they emphasize project workshops that are modeled on professional practices. The workshop corresponds to a response by students to a real or imaginary request from public or private sponsors. To respond to this request, the students collect data, analyze them and produce a report. These workshops often use the methodology of territorial diagnosis. These data are sometimes collected in the field, which is another form of professional practice, that of the researcher:

> I have always forced myself to involve some of my students in the professional world and it works because some of them have worked in companies today and they are very happy with it after a master's degree and even after a doctorate for two of them. (G5)

More generally, in geography, all active teaching practices are valued because they put students in a situation of action. Action seems to be inherent to the way knowledge is constructed in geography, namely the field:

> The geographer's field is at the same time the place where knowledge is acquired and the place for experimentation. It can also be seen as the test of what must be done and then what must be taken seriously. (G2)

These statements are also based on Dewey's (1938) underlying "learning by doing" model. This model is not cited as such, but it is implied. Geography LRs value putting students into action. This is probably an element inherited from the history of geography teaching. Indeed, when the discipline was institutionalized at the end of the 19th century, it was inspired by the theories of Rousseau (1762) and Pestalozzi (1882). Its teaching was conceived as lessons of things based on reflective observations of the world (Chevalier 1997). The teaching of geography at the university was based on a similar model, that of the field.

Mathematics LRs emphasize the usefulness and legitimacy of the concepts taught by presenting some applications:

> [We can for example not] start with very theoretical exercises, with lots of reading where surely they will drop out right away, but start with small things, practical applications; they are very interested in anything that can bring them to life and help them to earn a salary in the future. (M9)

The interest and motivation of the students are thus aroused by the application of the concepts taught in a context related to the chosen course of study:

> In math for chemists we give a book that is really the application of math in chemistry, so that gives them some motivation with math as well. (M2)

New notions are introduced in terms of the problems they can help solve, which are either related to mathematics itself or to another science:

> Sometimes a concept is introduced, but it's good if there's an added value; we can put it into a context, show a somewhat surprising application, and can see its usefulness in solving a problem. We were stuck and then suddenly ah well yes now with this new concept that was introduced in class, we can overcome the challenge. This is how science advances: there are problems and objects are introduced to solve problems. So, often when I teach my classes, I try to follow that approach. (M4)

Disciplinary affiliation shapes what LRs value in their discourse on their teaching practices. The imprint of the researcher's profession on the teacher's profession reaches its limits when it comes to teaching research products or training in undergraduate research.

As for the beauty of the discipline, geography is singled out by its emphasis on professional practices, with research activities close to those practiced in teaching. The LRs of the other disciplines place more emphasis on examples, but with some variation. In mathematics, the examples are closer to application exercises, while in physics and chemistry, examples from everyday life to understand nature prevail. We can therefore see that "learning by doing" is the common thread in all disciplines, but with more or less pronounced variations.

4.4.3. *Drawing on research, even if its results are not directly presentable*

Many LRs declare a link between the research part of their activity and the teaching part.

First of all, research is a reservoir of examples. In chemistry, mathematics and physics, the objects of research are often more distant from the content of the teaching at the beginning of the university. But this does not prevent some LRs from making links, even if the content is not directly accessible to students. It is no longer the discipline itself that is valued, but the research activity in this discipline, and its topicality. And once again, we find in several comments the dimension of pleasure, and the hope that this pleasure is visible, and transmitted, when the researcher teaches:

> I try to pass on my passion by making links between what I tell them and the examples I take from my research to show them, in general terms, which animates and interests them. As everything I do is also very applied in everything electronic today, this encourages the students, or at least interests them. (C7)

> I know that my research helps me a lot with my teaching, especially since I kind of have classes in my research, so I often tend to hide away in that a little bit, and then I explain it to them, I make all this stuff, make the connections, I give them glimpses of it in practice and everything, what it's for, and so on. I think they like that. (M12)

> In the master's program, as it is more often more specialized, it is more related to research. There I often make links with current events in research or daily news, but sometimes I also do it in the first year [of the bachelor's degree] to connect them to what we are explaining and to their daily lives, so I try to do these things in both types of courses. (P3)

> I find it interesting in terms of examples to show that physics is not a disembodied science and I think that the practice of research allows us in many ways to bring out this aspect (...) even in the teaching I did in the first year I also liked to show them that what we were teaching them was the state of knowledge at the time but that we could always be surprised by the evolution of knowledge. (P5)

We find in this last excerpt from a physics LR the idea that the evolution of knowledge and models is an important element of the epistemology of the discipline.

In geography, the knowledge issues are different. The LRs use the results of research to define the repository of knowledge to be taught and try to keep up with recent research results from the first year onward, in particular through regular bibliographic updates:

> All of my courses have a one-page handout with the syllabus, the objectives in 5-10 lines, and the essential bibliography. Usually it's one page, some courses it's two-sided but sometimes it's just one-sided. There's the course objective, the outline, and a basic bibliography. (G1)

For some other LRs, especially in mathematics, the content taught at the beginning of university is very far from what is studied in research. But it is part of a common background, especially in the first year of university, and one possible didactic choice is to recreate the research approach and the questioning that goes with it, and even to present notions that have already solved problems:

> When you do L1, L2, L3 [first, second, third year of a bachelor's degree], you are very, very far away from research. In fact, it's really very old math that has nothing to do with what you do in research. Which is not the case in other disciplines [...]. (M4)

> Compared to a lecturer and researcher, someone who is purely engaged in research is not in their comfort zone because they are looking for something, so inevitably they try to disrupt everything they know. As soon as there are things they don't understand, they try to understand them. They often find themselves facing difficulties. That's what we want to do in our classes. Present the structure and identify the points of equilibrium or the points of weakness in such and such a place. While this is sort of verging on what we know how to do, this is where it's interesting. (M4)

Indeed, beyond the content, the research process is often mentioned as being something that is ultimately expected of students who take the course.

Here, we note less variation between the four disciplines. While geography is more focused on teacher practices (use of research articles),

LRs in the other disciplines emphasize research methodology because the knowledge taught is far from the LRs' research field.

4.4.4. Staging the research process

We have already seen in sections 4.4.1 and 4.4.2 that the LRs consider that they have a responsibility to show the beauty of their discipline, and that the attitude they expect from students is not one of passive wonder, but rather of active participation in the intellectual process. Some LRs directly link this expected attitude with the research process; their objective is not to expose knowledge in a masterly way, even if this is done in a talented way, but to teach students to position themselves in front of knowledge as researchers:

> Because in research you also learn a number of things and certain attitudes towards problems so we can also instill that or get them to implement those attitudes directly into their daily practice. (P5)

> In teaching, I try to take a researcher's approach because a student who has to face a concept for the first time is probably finding it as hard as a researcher who is working on a problem whose solution is evading him (...). You have to go slowly and methodically, so it also gives them confidence in the fact that while they are a little confused, they can do it because they have experience in research too. (P8)

> There are practices using more digital tools, and practices using or getting closer to what is done in research labs so that students understand that there is in geographic research beyond undergraduate level – I'm talking about graduate and doctoral level –something else to imagine as a professional future, as opposed to just higher education and research. (G5)

This invitation to adopt a research attitude is sometimes translated into the implementation of specific teaching methods, such as the preparation of presentations, possibly accompanied by group work, or the reading of documents in geography:

> There is one thing that works well and is very successful, and that is the chemistry projects, as is done in physics, but we do this in the second year, not in the first year, and they have a subject that they come up with. It could be sunscreen, it could be photography, it could be wine, it could be anything, and they do a bibliographic work and set up experiments to demonstrate these topics, which is very tangible. (C2)

> [...] we have a small corpus of easy texts, 4, 5 well-chosen texts, and the students together, as we studied texts in philosophy in the last year of high school, have an approach, just an approach, and study Parisian geography by reading [...] by taking up Harvey's book on Paris translated by Giroux. It's super interesting. And why not approach it by asking how do we build an approach in geography? What is geography? [...] It's easy in M2 (the second year of a master's course) because we have the time to do it and we're here for that. It's impossible in L1, L2, L3 (at bachelor's degree level) because of the model, because of the 19 hour constraint, because of the end-of-semester evaluation, and because of the nightmare of catching up. (G6)

Finally, it is more at the master's level than at the bachelor's level that geography LRs seek to develop students' critical thinking skills. On the other hand, as early as the undergraduate level, taking students into the field is a priority for teachers, so much so that it is not conceivable to issue a geography license to students without them having done some fieldwork (Leininger-Frézal 2019).

The notion of critical thinking comes up in some comments as an important dimension of this research attitude:

> I give them the value and I ask them, "Does this make sense to you?" and I try to get them to understand that in chemistry there are concentrations that cannot be 10 to the minus 20 moles per liter and that the diameters of nanoparticles cannot be 10 to the 20 meters and they have to be told that it must come from the solar system and that they don't stop at that, so systematically, when there is an aberrant result, they have to be critical about that themselves. (C3)

Half of the chemistry LRs mention the difficulties students have in making sense of quantities, an important element of the experimental disciplines of chemistry and physics.

The excerpts mentioned so far in the first four categories of outcomes show the intentions of LRs. But these intentions sometimes clash with the reality of the student public, which does not always seem to recognize the beauty of the discipline, nor to adopt a research approach. This leads to tensions among LRs, particularly around evaluations.

All disciplines try to teach students the research process. The variation is in the teaching methods used to achieve this: reading of research documents is emphasized in geography, whereas group work and presentations are present in all disciplines. It should be noted that we did not find any sign of critical thinking in the interviews in mathematics and physics, whereas this aspect is apparent in the LRs of the other two disciplines, with ease in the master's degree for geography and in the bachelor's degree for chemistry.

4.4.5. *Adapting to current students*

The reasons that LRs give for the fact that their teaching does not necessarily go as they would like are multiple, and the responsibility is attributed either to the teachers (but in fact never to the teachers alone), or to the students (sometimes to the students alone, sometimes they share it with the teachers), or to the teaching at the high school, or to the discipline itself:

> Our expectations as teachers are out of step with the skills of our students, which is a criticism of either both or neither. We have to be able to match the two. What can we expect from the student in front of us? And the student, how will he/she respond to the teacher's expectations? Often the student expresses it like that. (C8)

> In the first year perhaps, I think that there is first of all a difficulty which is a difficulty of adaptation to our requirements. So, it's not necessarily related to the subject itself, but it's related to when we define a concept: what does it mean to understand a concept? (M1)

> In my opinion they come from high school with things that are not structured in their heads. They have a very disparate, non-hierarchical view of science. Moreover, the physics books go a long way in this direction. When you look at them, you get the impression that you have just a mail order catalog, if I caricature it a bit strongly. Things are not structured or poorly structured or not structured as a university education should be. (P1)

> Maybe it's a little generational difficulty. There are things that I can't stand that to them seem totally normal. Like texting during class, seeing two things on their screen. They are, I think, totally capable of that, listening and at the same time doing something else on their computer. I have to admit, I find that difficult. (G3)

We then find, in the difficulties mentioned, the epistemological specificities of each discipline:

> In chemistry there are abstract concepts. I'm thinking of quantum mechanics, and spectroscopy is very important in that regard. Spectroscopy follows on from quantum mechanics and it is essential. We can't do experiments in quantum mechanics; we can only do experiments in spectroscopy, which is the consequence, you see. For example, in quantum mechanics, so in atomic science, they find it difficult to do any kind of practical work. But with a Balmer lamp, it shows the spectrum of the hydrogen atom, so it's visual. They can see transitions; they can see the colors that are linked to electron transitions between one energy level and another energy level, but the physical chemistry behind it remains abstract for them, probably because they don't have the math, they don't understand it. All this mathematical baggage that we handle is important. The fact that it corresponds to chemical realities, I think it's a win-win situation if I can manage to get that across. (C7)

Chemistry LRs seek to develop in students in their teaching facets of chemistry such as abstract ability, manual skills and the connection between the two.

In physics and chemistry, disciplines for which, as we have seen, modeling occupies an important position, several LRs mention mathematical difficulties as being an important obstacle. Indeed, if they do not prevent students from accessing the experimental dimension, they do hinder the work in the model:

> The gaps in mathematical knowledge are really the problem. You'll write the integral and they'll be perplexed, you'll write a derivative and they'll be equally perplexed. So, they conclude that they don't have to spend time on that and that they aren't mathematicians, they're chemists, but it's really applied math. (C7)

> In the first year, some of the difficulties we have are related to the mathematization of the mathematical language used, which is a little more formalized than in high school. Having a poor grasp of high school mathematics when it has to be applied to university physics problems, that's a problem. Ultimately, they need to make the link between the mathematics seen in mathematics at school and apply the same mathematics to the physical realm, because we are in another context, a context of modeling. This means that we have to choose the right parameters, we have to manipulate them well. However, the notations are not necessarily the same as in mathematics, so some students are confused by the notations (...) They realize that a sine x or a sine represent variables and that this could be the same thing as x and t. (P5)

We see in this excerpt that in addition to the lack of mastery of simple mathematical tools, students also have difficulty transposing concepts seen in mathematics to a context related to another discipline.

Obviously, these mathematical difficulties mentioned for chemistry and physics students are also mentioned for mathematics students, and are linked by several LRs to the practice of mathematics in secondary education, which according to them favors formulas over an understanding of concepts, leading students to have a localized understanding of a course rather than a global vision:

> I think we have an awful lot of students who don't understand what it means to do math and have this sort of idea that they're going to try to learn things that are a little algorithmic, ready-made methods, that they're going to reproduce in a very similar context without any thought about the substance. (M8)

> I think that, at least unconsciously, we tell ourselves that students know what a demonstration is, when you can say that something is true or false, etc., but they may not have learned that in high school. It's a break between high school and university on the one hand, and it's also a break between the training that we, the teachers, had 10-15-20 years ago and the training that our students have had. (M5)

We find in this last excerpt one of the epistemological characteristics of mathematics, which is the important place of demonstration, a practice that for many LRs poses problems for students, as shown in this other excerpt:

> This happened to me personally in L1 (the first year of the bachelor's degree). I stated the theorem and then I began the demonstration and I was interrupted by someone asking me what I was doing. I said I was demonstrating the theorem, but they wanted to know whether it was true or false. They did not understand the concept of demonstration. (M4)

In geography, too, there is a disconnect between the knowledge taught in secondary school and that taught at university, but "the geography lecturers and researchers interviewed claim to be mostly unfamiliar with secondary school curricula, or even for some, seem to be disinterested in them," because "knowledge of what students have done previously does not appear to be a necessary prerequisite for what is taught at university for different reasons in history and geography" (Leininger-Frézal 2016, p. 4):

> I'm unable to tell you what they do in high school; I should do, I know that's silly... I rarely asked myself what they had covered before in high school. (G1)

Nevertheless, there seems to be a gap between the expectations of the teachers and the students' productions in terms of theoretical expectations. The LRs would like the students to be able to mobilize the terms seen in class and to position the content covered in the epistemology of the discipline.

> There's another element as well, which is related to this issue of understanding. The nuance is not fully understood between the vocabulary that I use versus the vocabulary that students use without fully understanding it. I can see my vocabulary cropping up in their own assignments, but it's being used in a different context or sense. So, I'm not conveying it properly. (G3)

> It's like when you go – and this is very pretentious of me – to the Collège de France to listen to someone, you go to hear about a subject and listen to a person speak about it. And if the student doesn't realize that he doesn't have a universal thought but that he only has the expression of Mr. what's-his-name on the subject, he misses the point because in fact he didn't understand that he was only getting the cognitive frameworks of one person on that subject. And that's what I have tried to convey in lectures, but it often hasn't been very successful. After a while I moved on to another topic and then came back to it. (G2)

This discrepancy pointed out by many LRs between what they want to do and what they do in class also results in a discrepancy between what they want to assess and what they actually assess. On the one hand, evaluation is used to see if the students have mastered the basic level, which consists of being able to reproduce techniques seen in class and in tutorials, and forces them to work:

> Objective number 1 is to make sure that a basic level of competency has been achieved; objective number 2 is to gauge whether what the teacher wanted to pass on has been conveyed. (C6)

> And so, the motivation aspect is not punitive per se but there is an element of forcing them to work. Continuous assessment can help with this. (C2)

On the other hand, for a large majority of LRs, the main objective of evaluation is to understand whether the students have gained a thorough understanding of the course. This is why many LRs want to assess this understanding, notably through problems in a context different from that of the tutorials, through the treatment of open questions. But they do not always succeed, either because of a lack of time or staff, or because it requires too much investment on their part to the detriment of research:

> I would like to assess them on their ability to investigate a little bit, and I would like to ask much more open-ended questions than what I actually ask in an exam to force them to investigate, think, etc. And we don't have time to do that. The exam is too short. (M5).

> We evaluate them with grades on specific exercises, but at the same time we don't evaluate whether they really understand the material. We would have to spend two hours with each student in order to ask them a lot of questions, to ask them to solve a small part of the problem. I think it's not ideal to do that for a large cohort of students but it's trying to think about whether there is any other way to do it (P6).

> No, I'm deeply dissatisfied with what I'm doing as an assessment. [...] I'd prefer a comprehensive continuous assessment where we could make sure that in some courses we would only do oral assessments, presentations, or individual assessments. (G6)

However, unlike the mathematics and physics LRs, we do not see a tension between understanding and student success in the geography LRs. Rather, there is a tension between the skills expected of students and their success.

Thus, whatever the discipline, the LRs have difficulty teaching as they would like to. One explanation shared by the LRs of chemistry, physics and mathematics concerns the lack of mastery of mathematics taught in high school, although there are variations that we have been able to link to the epistemology of the disciplines. In physics and chemistry, the students' difficulties are more related to disciplinary knowledge as mathematical tools at the service of physics and chemistry. In mathematics, on the other hand, difficulties are more rooted in high school practices, where operative techniques seem to be favored to the detriment of epistemological aspects such as demonstration or the links between concepts. We have also noted that these breaks between high school and university are much less present in geography, notably because the question of prerequisites seems less prevalent in this discipline. However, the difficulty of LRs to teach as they would like to leads to tensions at the level of evaluation, in each discipline.

This section reveals that there are many commonalities in the problems that arise within each discipline. However, we believe that what the LRs have said shows that the variations in how these problems are addressed are often a function of the epistemology of each discipline. With these results in mind, let us now return to the questions posed in section 4.3.2 for the different disciplines.

4.5. Returning to the questions of each discipline

We wanted to know to what extent and in what way chemistry LRs organize or do not organize the links between experimentation, modeling and abstraction. Through the interviews we conducted, we found that the chemistry LRs interviewed explain the course by telling the students a story and want this to spark an intellectual journey. They use applications in their courses to facilitate students' access to abstraction. These applications allow them to make chemistry visual despite the mathematical difficulties that prevent students from understanding the concepts, notions, and reactions behind them. Chemistry LRs make students think in small groups and encourage them to make presentations. Chemistry LRs report difficulty in doing chemistry with their students because of their difficulties. In addition to conceptual difficulties, the main difficulties mentioned were a lack of work and an insufficient mastery of mathematical tools. To help their students, the chemistry LRs interviewed regularly evaluate them to help them work and make the link between modeling and experimentation.

We hypothesized in geography that geography teachers' practices are influenced by LRs' emphasis on experience. The interviews we conducted show that the practices appear to be more complex. Geography LRs value pedagogical practices that are linked to social practices such as travel, professional practices such as planning projects or research practices such as fieldwork. Nevertheless, they also highlight in their discourse the difficulty of developing pedagogical approaches based on these practices in the bachelor's degree program. These types of practices seem to be favored in the master's program. The difficulties encountered at the undergraduate level are multiple: schedule, number of students, student difficulties, etc. On the other hand, whatever the level, active teaching is valued in various forms: presentations, analysis of documents, field projects, etc. This observation leads us to wonder if there has been a shift in the meaning of experience: since students cannot have spatial experiences in relation to spatial practices, the LR leads them to build courses where students will have a formative "experience" (socio-constructivist approach to learning). It would be worth conducting new interviews in line with this form of questioning.

We hypothesized that, given the specificities of mathematics, LRs would have to make compromises in order to show their discipline to students. The interviews we conducted confirm this hypothesis in several respects. First of all, the LRs interviewed are aware that there is in fact a significant gap between the mathematics taught in the first years at the university and mathematics research, which does not allow them to show certain aspects of it. They attribute this gap to various factors linked to both certain difficulties of the students (formalism, logic, demonstration practice, etc.) and to practices inherited from secondary education, which are issues that influence their teaching practices and which they take into account. Second, while LRs value an assessment practice based on a deep understanding of courses through problems in new contexts, or even open-ended questions, the interviews show that there is both a tension between what they would like to assess and what they actually assess, as well as between understanding and student success. From our point of view, this is a compromise linked on the one hand to the students' difficulties (see above) and on the other hand to time and availability. Finally, some LRs manage to show their discipline in a localized way, either by highlighting the legitimacy of the concepts, their usefulness through interesting applications (including in other disciplines) or by recreating (when the concept lends itself to it) the conditions that presided over its creation (questioning, research approach, etc.).

We hypothesized that physics LRs value explanation and understanding based on observations and experiments, and predict their evolution based on modeling. We found that the physics LRs interviewed use many examples related to everyday life in their courses. The explanation of natural phenomena observed in everyday life allows them to give meaning to their learning. The students are thus invited to advance their knowledge by questioning things themselves and by applying a methodology similar to that of a researcher (searching for answers in books, questioning concepts themselves, solving a problem based on their newly acquired knowledge). The use of topical subjects from research linked to everyday life allows the physics LRs interviewed to show that physics is not a disembodied science. Moreover, in order to face the difficulties of understanding physics concepts, they lead the students to solve problems in a progressive way and show them that, like the researchers, they can stumble when trying to resolve a problem, which should not be perceived as a failure. Thus, professional methods of knowledge production can be found in teaching practices. However, the mathematical tools are a block to go as far as the modeling stage and thus the prediction of observed phenomena. Moreover, we observed tensions between bringing them to solve problems not covered in the courses and the very strong time constraint, which means that there is not enough time to pose questions of students to see if they have understood correctly.

4.6. Conclusion and implications for university pedagogy

In this exploratory research, we sought to explore the imprint of discipline on LRs' teaching practices and pedagogical activities (micro scale introduced by Becher (1994)). We hypothesized that there are differences in pedagogical treatment across epistemologically different disciplines (Neumann 2001; Neumann et al. 2002) and that beliefs and knowledge drive pedagogical practices (Calderhead 1996). We decided to focus on their declarative pedagogical practices in order to identify possible tensions between what they want to do and what they do. To do this, we mobilized the concept of professional identity by identifying regularities and differences between the four disciplines studied (chemistry, geography, mathematics, physics) by exploring the values, qualities and norms in the statements of the LR interviewed (Cattonar 2001). Whatever the disciplinary affiliation of the LRs interviewed, we find certain identical values: to transmit a taste for the discipline while demonstrating their own passion to students. Thus, they share the same qualities: to make students autonomous by putting them in a position in which they can pursue the discovery of content on their own and make students experience a questioning and problem-solving process close to the activity of a researcher. However, certain tensions exist in the practice of the teaching profession between an ideal teaching model and the real teaching model that the LRs interviewed implement. Sometimes, these tensions are linked to the students' difficulties (lack of knowledge, know-how), and sometimes they are linked to institutional constraints (personnel, schedule, program to be finished). The imprint of the researcher in mathematics is more apparent in the teaching of the master's degree than in the bachelor's degree because it is not possible to do research, that is, to study mathematical objects that require rigor and abstraction, as early as the bachelor's degree. In physics, chemistry and geography, these tensions are less strong because it is possible to integrate from the first year of the degree a methodology that is close to that of research, especially in geography where, despite organizational constraints, the LRs undertake activities similar to those of research, such as field projects.

The results of this research corroborate shared intellectual values (Becher 1994), a grounding in professional experiences (Calderhead, 1996) and pedagogical practices designed around the disciplinary specificities of the LRs interviewed (Menges et al. 2001 cited in Rege Colet and Berthiaume 2009). However, our research has some limitations. The LRs interviewed are not necessarily representative of the university community. Therefore, there may be a bias in the selection of interviewees who may be more strongly inclined to pedagogical concerns than other LRs. It would be interesting to increase the number of interviews or to propose a questionnaire constructed from our findings to corroborate our results. In addition, we have limited ourselves to reported practices that may differ from actual practices. We are currently conducting field observations to corroborate the results of this exploratory research.

Currently, the training offered to new and experienced lecturers in university pedagogy centers is very much focused on general pedagogical concerns such as student motivation, group work. In the introduction, we stated that research in didactics in higher education was more or less developed depending on the discipline, but in any case, its results are little known by the research community and little used for training. However, our research shows that the professional identity of LRs is marked by their teaching and research discipline, and that their pedagogical practices are not neutral from this point of view. In other words, the LRs we interviewed share a set of norms, values and qualities, but some of them remain specific to their discipline (personal epistemology). Here, we agree with the work of Berthiaume (2006) who advocates taking into account the pedagogical knowledge, the specificity of the discipline and the personal epistemology of the LRs, which he calls disciplinary pedagogical knowledge (DPK). This

DPK model has, moreover, led to the emergence of pedagogical models for refining the "work of pedagogical coaching in the implementation of technology-supported university courses" (Bachy 2014). The results of our research advocate for the consideration of the discipline to which LRs belong in the content of this teaching training undertaken in university pedagogical services. Given the strong link between teaching practices and research practices observed in our study, it is important to consider the research dimension of the profession in order to accompany the transformation of LRs' teaching practices even if the content of the teaching is far from that of the TR's research field. The scholar of teaching and learning (SoTL) is a possibility to help LRs systematically reflect on their teaching practice (Biémar et al. 2015). Indeed, SoTL helps LRs translate their research approach into a teaching context. However, it should not be limited to having teachers reflect only on general pedagogy issues. It must also take into account the epistemology of disciplines and their didactics. In order for research to feed teaching practices, it seems necessary that knowledge remains an important component in university training, an essential basis for developing the critical spirit of young people and successful professional integration.

4.7. Acknowledgements

We thank the lecturers and researchers who granted us interviews at the following universities: Université de Cergy Pontoise, Université Rouen Normandie, Université Paris 1, Université Paris 4, Université Paris Diderot, Université Paris 13, Université Lille 1, UMONS and UNamur.

4.8. References

Adangnikou, N. (2008). Peut-on parler de recherche en pédagogie universitaire, aujourd'hui, en France ? *Revue des sciences de l'éducation*, 34(3), 601–621.

Annoot, E. and Fave-Bonnet, M.-F. (2004). *Pratiques pédagogiques dans l'enseignement supérieur : enseigner, apprendre, évaluer.* L'Harmattan, Paris.

Bachy, S. (2014). Un modèle-outil pour représenter le savoir technopédagogique disciplinaire des enseignants. *Revue internationale de pédagogie de l'enseignement supérieur*, 30(2) [Online]. Available at: https://journals.openedition.org/ripes/821#quotation [Accessed 28 September 2021].

Barlet, R. (1999). L'espace épistémologique et didactique de la chimie. *L'actualité chimique*, 4, 23–33.

Becher, T. (1987). The disciplinary shaping of the profession. In *The Academic Profession*, Clark, B.R. (ed.). University of California Press, Berkeley.

Becher, T. (1989). *Academic Tribes and Territories: Intellectual Enquiry and the Cultures of Disciplines.* SRHE and Open University Press, Milton Keynes.

Becher, T. (1994). The significance of disciplinary differences. *J. Stud. High. Educ.*, 19(2), 151–161.

Bensaude-Vincent, B. (2004). *Chimie et société : des relations tumultueuses. L'Actualité chimique*, (280–281), 22–24.

Berthiaume, D. (2006). A description of discipline-specific pedagogical knowledge (DPK) encountered in the discourse of four university professors from four different disciplinary areas. PhD Thesis, Université de McGill, Montreal.

Biémar, S., Daele, A., Malengrez, D., Oger, L. (2015). Le "Scholarship of Teaching and Learning" (SoTL). Proposition d'un cadre pour l'accompagnement des enseignants par les conseillers pédagogiques. *Revue internationale de pédagogie de l'enseignement supérieur*, 31(2) [Online]. Available at: http://journals.openedition.org/ripes/966 [Accessed 29 September 2021].

Biglan, A. (1973). The characteristics of subject matter in different academic areas. *J. Appl. Psychol.*, 57(3), 195–203.

Blin, J.-F. (1997). *Représentations, pratiques et identités professionnelles.* L'Harmattan, Paris.

Bloch, I. (2015). Concepts, objets, symboles, enseignement des mathématiques... Quelques réflexions sur l'épistémologie et la didactique. *Petit x*, 97, 71–79.

Bridoux, S., De Vleeschouwer, M., Grenier-Boley, N., Khanfour-Armalé, R., Lebrun, N., Mesnil, Z., Nihoul, C. (2019). L'identité professionnelle des enseignants-chercheurs en mathématiques, chimie et physique. In *Mathématiques en scène, des ponts entre les disciplines, Actes du Colloque EMF 2018*, Abboud-Blanchard, M. (ed.).

Bridoux, S., de Hosson, C., Nihoul, C. (2020). University teachers' in situ practices and comparison with students' experiences: A case study. In *Proceedings of the Third Conference of the International Network for Didactic Research in University Mathematics* (INDRUM 2020, 12–19 September 2020), Hausberger, T., Bosch, M., Chellougui, F. (eds). University of Carthage and INDRUM, Bizerte.

Calbérac, Y. (2010). Terrains de géographes, géographes de terrain. Communauté et imaginaire disciplinaires au miroir des pratiques de terrain des géographes français du XXe siècle. PhD Thesis, Université Lumière Lyon 2.

Calderhead, J. (1996). Teachers: Beliefs and knowledge. In *Handbook of Educational Psychology*, Berliner, D.C., Calfee, R.C. (eds). Macmillan, New York.

Cattonar, B. (2001). Les identités professionnelles enseignantes. Ébauche d'un cadre d'analyse. *Cahiers de recherche du GIRSEF*, 10, 2–35.

Chevalier, J.-P. (1997). La géographie scolaire : un des quatre pôles géographiques ? Cybergéo, 23 [Online]. Available at: http://journals.openedition.org/cybergeo/6498 [Accessed 28 September 2021].

Chevallard, Y. (1991). *La transposition didactique. Du savoir savant au savoir enseigné, 2ème édition augmentée.* La Pensée sauvage, Grenoble.

Clement, J. (1982). Students' preconceptions in introductory mechanics. *American Journal of Physics*, 50(1), 66–71.

Coince, D., Miguet, A.M., Perrey, S., Rondepierre, T., Tiberghien, A., Vince, J. (2008). Une introduction à la nature et au fonctionnement de la physique pour des élèves de seconde. *Bulletin de l'Union des Physiciens*, 102(900), 3–20.

Crahay, M., Wanlin, P., Issaieva, E., Laduron, I. (2010). Fonctions, structuration et évolution des croyances (et connaissances) des enseignants. *Revue française de pédagogie*, 172(3), 85–129.

Dewey, J. (1938). *Experience and Education.* Macmillan, New York.

Dubar, C. (1996). La socialisation : paradigmes, méthodes et implications théoriques. In *Formation et socialisation au travail*, Franck, B., Maroy, C. (eds). De Boeck Université, Brussels.

Endrizzi, L. (2011). Learning how to teach in higher education: A matter of excellence. *Dossier d'actualité Veille et Analyse*, 64.

Fave-Bonnet, M.-F. (1994). Le métier d'enseignant-chercheur : des missions contradictoires ? *Recherche & Formation*, 15, 11–34.

Freudenthal, H. (1973). *Mathematics as an Educational Task.* D. Reidel Publishing, Dordrecht.

Gilbert, J. and Justi, R. (2006). *Modelling-based Teaching in Science Education.* Springer International Publishing, Cham.

Halloun, I.A. and Hestenes, D. (1985). Common sense concepts about motion. *American Journal of Physics*, 53(11), 1056–1065.

Henkel, M. (2004). La relation enseignement-recherche. *Politiques et gestion de l'enseignement supérieur*, 16(2), 21–36.

Hope, M. (2009). The importance of direct experience: A philosophical defence of fieldwork in human geography. *Journal of Geography in Higher Education*, 33, 169–182.

de Hosson, C., Décamp, N., Browaeys, J. (2015a). Contribution à la rénovation des programmes de physique (lycée / collège) : la nécessaire place des mathématiques dans l'enseignement des mathématiques. *Bulletin de l'union des physiciens*, 972(109), 483–490.

de Hosson, C., Décamp, N., Morand, E., Robert, A. (2015b). Approcher l'identité professionnelle d'enseignants universitaires de physique : un levier pour initier des changements de pratiques pédagogiques. *Recherches en Didactique des Sciences et des Technologies*, 11, 161–190.

Kermen, I. (2016). Utilisation et rôles des exemples lors d'enseignements universitaires de chimie. *Recherches en éducation*, 27, 35–51.

Kuhn, T.S. (2015). *The Structure of Scientific Revolutions*, 4th edition. The University of Chicago Press, Chicago.

Kogan, M. (2000). Higher education communities and academic identity. *Higher Education Quarterly*, 54(32), 207–216.

van Lankveld, T., Schoonenboom, J., Volman, M., Croiset, G., Beishuizen, J. (2017). Developing a teacher identity in the university context: A systematic review of the literature. *Higher Education Research & Development*, 36(2), 325–342.

Le Maréchal, J.-F. (1999). Modelling student's cognitive activity during the resolution of problems based on experimental facts in Chemical Education. In *Practical Work in Science Education*, Leach, J., Paulsen, A.C. (eds). Kluwer, Dordrecht.

Lebrun, N., and Hosson, C.D. (2017). Repérer des conceptions d'étudiants : un pas vers l'enrichissement des connaissances professionnelles didactiques d'enseignants-chercheurs de physique. *Recherches en didactique des sciences et des technologies*, 15, 59–96.

Leclercq, G. (2000). Lire l'agir pédagogique : une lecture épistémologique. *Revue des sciences de l'éducation*, 26(2), 243–262.

Leininger-Frézal, C. (ed.) (2016). L'usage du cas et de l'exemple dans l'enseignement supérieur : pratiques, apprentissages et rapport aux savoirs. *Recherches en Éducation*, 27, 52–65.

Leininger-Frézal, C. (2019). Apprendre la géographie par l'expérience du primaire à l'université. HDR, Université de Normandie, Caen.

Lévy, J. and Lussault, M. (2003). *Dictionnaire de la géographie et de l'espace des sociétés*. Belin, Paris.

Nairn, K. (2005). The problems of utilizing "direct experience" in geography education. *Journal of Geography in Higher Education*, 29, 293–309.

Neumann, R. (2001). Disciplinary differences and university teaching. *Studies in Higher Education*, 26(2), 135–146.

Neumann, R., Parry, S., Becher, T. (2002). Teaching and learning in their disciplinary contexts: A conceptual analysis. *Studies in Higher Education*, 27(4), 405–417.

Norton, L., Richardson, T.E., Hartley, J., Newstead, S., Mayes, J. (2005). Teachers' beliefs and intentions concerning teaching in higher education. *Higher Education*, 50(4), 537–571.

Owens, C., Sotoudehnia, M., Ericksson-McGee, P. (2015). Reflections on teaching and learning for sustainability from the Cascadia Sustainability Field School. *Journal of Geography in Higher Education*, 39, 313–327.

Pekdağ, B. and Le Maréchal, J.-F. (2003). Hyperfilm : un outil de recherche en didactique de la chimie. In *Environnements Informatiques pour l'Apprentissage Humain, Actes de la conférence EIAH*, Desmoulins, C., Marquet, P., Bouhineau, D. (eds). INRP, Lyon.

Pestalozzi, J.H. (1882). *Comment Gertrude instruit ses enfants*. Delagrave, Paris.

Poteaux, N. (2013). Pédagogie de l'enseignement supérieur en France : état de la question. *Distances et médiations des savoirs*, 1(4) [Online]. Available at: http://journals.openedition.org/dms/403 [Accessed 28 September 2021].

Rege Colet, N. and Berthiaume, D. (2009). Savoir ou être ? Savoirs et identités professionnels chez les enseignants universitaires. *Savoirs en (trans)formation*, 137–162.

Robert, A. (1998). Outils d'analyse des contenus mathématiques à enseigner au lycée et à l'université. *Recherches en Didactique des Mathématiques*, 18(2), 139–190.

Rogalski, M. (2012). Approches épistémologique et didactique de l'activité de formalisation en mathématiques. In *Enseignement des mathématiques et contrat social : enjeux et défis pour le 21e siècle, Actes du colloque EMF 2012*, Dorier, J.-L., Coutat, S. (eds). University of Geneva.

Rousseau, J.-J. (1762). *Émile ou De L'Éducation*. Jean Néaulme, La Haye.

Schneider, M. (2008). Entre recherche et développement, quel choix de valeurs pour l'ingénierie curriculaire ? In *Ressources pour l'enseignement des mathématiques : conception, usage, partage, Actes des journées mathématiques*, Trgalova, J., Aldon, G., Gueudet, G., Matheron, Y. (eds). INRP, Lyon.

Tickle, L. (2000). *Teacher Induction: The Way Ahead*. Open University Press, Buckingham.

Trede, F., Macklin, R., Bridges, D. (2012). Professional identity development: A review of the higher education literature. *Studies in Higher Education*, 37(3), 365–384.

Tsaparlis, G. (1997). Atomic and molecular structure in chemical education. *Journal of Chemical Education*, 74, 922–925.

Viennot, L. (1979). Spontaneous reasoning in elementary dynamics. *European Journal of Science Education*, 1(2), 205–221.

Volvey, A., Calbérac, Y., Houssay-Holzschuch, M. (2012). Terrains de je. (Du) sujet (au) géographique. *Annales de Géographie*, 5–6, 441–461.

5

The Relationship Between Research Activity and the Design of Resources for Teaching – The Case of Mathematics at the University Level

5.1. General introduction

Research in Mathematics Education shows an increasing interest for research on teacher practices in higher education (Biza et al. 2016). In the latter study, one question was raised and mentioned as an avenue that requires exploration: that of the relationship between changing practices, changing resource offerings and the changing of teachers' professional knowledge. This chapter is a contribution to the research work around this question. We are particularly interested in the study of the impact of research activity in mathematics on teaching practices. We propose exploring this topic by looking at how mathematicians interact with resources for teaching and for research. We would like to mention that throughout this chapter, we designate "university professor" as the case of a mathematician that holds a teaching and research position in a university.

Our interest in this topic emerged from previous research (Sabra 2019); we identified, in some case studies of university professors, factors related to research activity that influence teaching practices. We found a need to characterize the relationship between research and teaching in mathematics

---

Chapter written by Hussein SABRA.

teachers' practices to better understand some of the choices made in a teaching context.

From an institutional perspective, the university professors training has been mandatory in France since the start of the 2018 academic year. We have also identified a need to support this institutional evolution by developing research results to characterize teaching practices in relation to research activity. This identified need is consistent with that highlighted in research with similar subjects to ours. As an example, Petropoulou et al. (2015) point out in their study of how mathematicians implement lectures that their practice and reasoning deserve to be studied because they can help other university professors; this help is particularly focused on how they – together with their students – construct the learning environment and foster learning in mathematics.

We therefore wish to contribute to this topic by providing elements that shed light on the understanding of mathematicians' teaching practices. In this chapter, we present a case study of three mathematicians through the prism of their interactions with resources. We focus particularly on how resources are mobilized in the context of the research activity. We then study they are used to design resources in and for teaching.

After this general introduction, which has allowed us to position the context of research, we shall continue with a literature review (section 5.2). This literature review deals with the way in which the theme of the relationship between teaching and research has been approached in research in the education sciences (section 5.2.1), as well as in research in the didactics of disciplines (section 5.2.2). This literature review will lead us to the formulation of a general question (section 5.2.3). In order to refine this question, we will present a theoretical framework, based on the Documentational Approach to Didactics (DAD) (section 5.3.1) and concepts from the Anthropological Theory of Didactics (section 5.3.2). This allows us to suggest new theoretical tools that we will put to the test in the framework of this study (section 5.3.3). We will continue by presenting our methodology based on interviews (section 5.4). Lastly, we shall present our analytical results (section 5.5) followed by a conclusion and perspectives for further study (section 5.6).

5.2. The relationship between teaching and research in higher education

The theme of the relationship between teaching and research in the practices of university professors is not a new one in the research landscape. Based on a literature review, we explore in this section the contributions of a resource-based approach to this theme.

5.2.1. *The relationship between teaching and research in educational science research*

Some research in the Education Sciences has attempted to characterize "positive" or "negative" relationships between research and teaching in general, that is, without specifically taking the content taught into account (Elton 1986; Neumann 1992). They have attempted to characterize the relationship that can occur between teaching activity and research activity (symbiosis, conflict, tension, etc.). In this subsection, we will consider the work of Elton (1986, 2001) and Neumann (1992), which are central research studies on this theme. They are cited in most research in the Educational Sciences. We have also used this work as a basis for our reflections in the following.

Neumann (1992) presents three types of connections (what she calls "nexus" in the article) that can characterize the "positive" relationship between teaching and research: the tangible nexus, the intangible nexus and the global nexus. We shall develop the definition of each type of connection as follows.

The tangible connection is generally related to a transfer of knowledge in terms of disciplinary content from research to teaching. In this regard, Neumann (1992) states that:

> The most obvious, or at least readily identifiable, association between the teaching and research activities, is the dissemination of the latest advanced knowledge. In some disciplines knowledge is advancing so rapidly that the text books cannot keep up and the first point of contact with new developments is in the lecture material presented to students. (Neumann 1992, p. 162)

This quote shows that according to Neumann, the tangible connection between teaching and research in a university professor's practices is not the result of a single teaching choice but is also dependent on the epistemological dynamics of the discipline at hand.

The intangible connection concerns the transfer of the researcher's actions into teaching practices and vice versa. Neumann (1992) characterizes it as a connection of a "qualitative" and subtle nature:

> These are qualitative links, relating to the approach and attitude towards knowledge that should be fostered in a university. Again, it was strongly argued that these subtle and diffuse links could only be conveyed by an active researcher. Thus, an active research involvement produces a qualitative difference in teaching, achieving an extra dimension that is not possible in other teaching institutions. (Neumann 1992, p. 163)

The intangible connection may reveal itself, according to Neumann (1992), in the way a university professor approaches the knowledge to be taught in order to encourage students to be critical of the knowledge involved. The intangible connection can also be manifested in the attitude of a university professor toward disciplinary knowledge. This attitude can take the form of a curiosity to explore new fields or a desire to discover new objects and learn new methods.

The global connection is on a broader scale that goes beyond the individual to consider a larger academic context:

> Not only is there a nexus between the research activity of the individual and their teaching activity, but there is also a nexus between the total research involvement of the department and the teaching activity of that department. Hence, it is not just the research of the individual academic that influences the teaching, but that of all the members of a department. This connection manifests itself in various ways. (Neumann 1992, p. 166)

Neumann (1992) distinguishes between "department's research activity" and "department's teaching activity" without explicitly defining these terms:

At the undergraduate level, a department's research activity furnishes the framework for the teaching. It was pointed out that disciplines today operate on such a large front that not all areas can be covered by one university. Hence, the research activity of the department determines the areas of broad concentration for that department's teaching and provides the direction for the undergraduate courses. (Neumann 1992, p. 166)

Global connection, then, is about connection at the scale of an academic device that goes beyond individuals, which Neumann calls "department".

In a more recent study, Elton (2001) examined the reasons for the presence or absence of a relationship between teaching and research in the practice of university professors. With a view to transforming the relationship between teaching and research, he proposes avenues for strengthening the "positive" articulations between the two types of activities. Elton (quoted by Henkel 2004) believes that "if there is a link between effective research and effective teaching, it may be because there is a third factor that can be said to generate both (Elton 2001)" (Henkel 2004, p. 27). This third factor, according to Elton, lies in models of teaching that focus on student activities rather than teacher activities. This allows Elton to view the relationship between teaching and research as a development of affinities between the students' education and the university professor research.

5.2.2. *The relationship between teaching and research in mathematics and science didactics research*

Numerous research studies in disciplinary didactics, not necessarily having as their main object of study the relationship between teaching and research, emphasize in the results of their studies that access to the research activity of mathematicians allows for the deepening of results related to the teaching practices of the latter (Mali et al. 2014; Petropoulou et al. 2015). Gueudet (2017) does not directly address the relationship between teaching and research. Instead, she highlights the fact that in the work of university professors in mathematics, the collective dimension is strongly present in the research activity, while it remains largely weaker in the teaching activity. She also underlines the interest of considering, in the context of a mathematician's teaching work, the role and place of resources resulting from research in the design of resources for teaching.

Madsen and Winsløw (2009), in a comparative study of the practices of university professors in physical geography and mathematics, highlight the fact that the forms of relationship that can take place between teaching and research depend strongly on disciplinary specificities (epistemological characteristics of the discipline). Using the Anthropological Theory of Didactics (Chevallard 1999), they highlight that the relation that can take place between the two missions of teaching and research depends closely on the perception that a university professor has of the specificities of his or her discipline. We will return to this study in more detail in section 5.3.

In the work conducted by de Hosson et al. (2015), the relationship between teaching and research is studied from the perspective of a university professor's professional identity. Following up on this research, Lebrun et al. (2018) conducted interviews with university professors in physics and mathematics. They point out that the professional identity of university professors in both disciplines appears to be a struggle between what should be done and what they do or think is achievable; interviewees in both disciplines highlight the importance of teaching according to methods derived from research activities (group work, problem solving, modeling, etc.). However, according to the university professors interviewed (see Chapter 5 in this book), these teaching choices are difficult to implement, particularly because of a lack of time and also because of a significant gap between academic expectations and what students are capable of mobilizing in terms of knowledge and also in terms of expected practices. A tension is thus observed between what the university professors want to evaluate in the students and what they actually evaluate. Differences are nevertheless pointed out according to the disciplines to which the interviewees belong.

In a similar manner to that of the previous work cited, Grenier-Boley (2019) addresses this question by taking as a starting point the practices of mathematicians in order to identify what is transposable to the classroom and what would be difficult to transpose. By questioning research practices in this way, he attempts to study what he calls the imprint of the research discipline on the teaching practices of lecturers and researchers. Some mathematics university professors report that there is a significant gap between the mathematics taught and the research, which does not allow them to show aspects of their research to students. Grenier-Boley (2019) refers to the characteristics of mathematics as a discipline to explain these statements; he notes that in mathematics, "since knowledge acquisition is characterized by a hierarchical progression and research results can generally only be 'shown' by their statement and proof, research is in fact very far from the mathematics taught at the beginning of university" (Grenier-Boley 2019, p. 122).

Buteau et al. (2014) conducted a survey of mathematicians on the use of programming software in their research and teaching. The results of this survey show that there is a *gap* (few mathematicians who use programming software in their research use it in their teaching). The participants in this survey mention different types of constraints explaining this gap: curricular, cultural and organizational (i.e. related to the institutional organization). This investigation motivated Broley's (2016) work on the place of "computer programming" in mathematics research practices. In her work, she investigates the relationship between teaching and research by considering the role and place of programming activity in both institutions (teaching and research). We note that in her work she is interested, among other things, in conducting a comparison between the activity of the student and the activity of mathematicians in the use of programming software.

The issue of the relationship between research activity and teaching practice is not new. It is studied from different perspectives in educational science research. Although it has been approached in an isolated way in research on the didactics of disciplines, it remains largely unexplored in Mathematics Education.

5.2.3. *Resources for understanding the relationship between research and teaching*

The work of Broley (2016) and Gueudet (2017) draws our attention to an avenue that could be promising for understanding certain aspects of the relationship between teaching and research in mathematics: the interaction with resources, particularly those derived from the research activity. The mobilization of these resources can take place at different moments of teaching practices: in the preparation of a class session, in the choice of content, in the implementation of resources in class and in the evaluation of learning.

A university professor conducts research in a field that has its own epistemology. There may be more or less proximity between the mathematical field he teaches and his research field (Grenier-Boley 2019).

His or her academic background and professional experience as a researcher may impact (or not) his or her teaching practices; they may manifest themselves in the choices of content to be taught, in the choice of their organization, in the modes of their dissemination, and in the forms of interaction with the students. In several research studies, the consideration of students as an object of study seems to be essential to better understand the relationship between teaching and research, in particular the impact of research on teaching practices (Elton 2001; Broley 2016).

For a particular teaching aim, the teacher designs resources that take into account all of the elements involved (the content and its organization, the forms of dissemination and interaction with students, etc.). Understanding teaching, in the case of lecturers and researchers, through the prism of resources (those mobilized and those produced) makes it possible to focus jointly on didactic choices, epistemological choices based on the potential of the available resources and the learning trajectory that one wishes to provide to students. Within this framework, understanding the factors that determine the place of research-based resources in the design of teaching resources will offer avenues for developing competencies in terms of "design capacities" (Brown 2009). Hence, our general question is as follows: how are resources from research re-appropriated and adapted by a mathematician in his or her teaching work?

5.3. The articulation of two approaches: the documentary work of a university professor in teaching and research institutions

In this section, we will provide a brief presentation of the DAD. The choice of this approach to study our research question is related to the possibility it offers to study the process of using research resources in teaching, from the selection of such a resource to its implementation (section 5.3.1). We will focus on some key concepts of this approach while discussing their adaptation to the case of university professors in mathematics. We will continue with a presentation of another framework: the Anthropological Theory of Didactics as adapted in the work of Madsen and Winsløw (2009). This will allow us to place the use of resources in their specific institutional context, that of teaching and research (section 5.3.2). We will conclude with a presentation of the nature of the articulation we make between these two approaches and the consideration of a particular type of critical resources to study the relationship between teaching and research.

5.3.1. *The documentational approach to didactics*

The DAD developed at a time when a framework was needed to conceptualize theoretically the emerging field of research around resources for teaching in order to study central issues related to this field (Trouche et al. 2019). It is conceived as an extension of the instrumental approach (Rabardel 1995), while taking into account not only a single technological tool that the teacher integrates into his or her work, but by considering a large set of resources with which a teacher interacts, sometimes simultaneously, for a well-defined teaching aim (Gueudet and Trouche 2009). In this section, we will present the main concepts of DAD (resource, scheme of use and document) and the processes that their articulation generates.

We shall use the concept of resources in the sense of Adler (2000), as both a noun and a verb, and therefore as an object and an action:

– An object that directs our attention to tangible material elements such as a manual, a book and a sheet produced with a colleague.

– Action that allows the activity to be "re-sourced" several times and not always in the same way; the concept of resource as an "action of resourcing" directs our attention to the different possible uses of the same resource in the context of mathematics teaching.

The concept of *scheme* (Vergnaud 1998) is central to DAD; we rely on the definition given by Vergnaud to define a *scheme of use*. Vergnaud (1998) suggests considering a scheme as a functional dynamic totality that has four interacting components:

– An identifiable *aim* that identifies the intent and purpose of the activity.

– *Rules of action* which are ways of acting generated by the scheme in order to reach the aim; they can include the taking of information and the controls which allow the conduct to be adapted to the particularities of each situation.

– *Operational invariants* that influence the rules of action. They can be concepts-in-action (which allow the available information to be selected and categorized for a given situation) or theorems-in-action (propositions held to be true by the subject, which allow him to process the available information in order to generate rules of action that suppose the achievement of the aim).

– The *possibilities of inference*, which offer the possibility of adapting to the variety of situations and play an essential role in the development of the scheme.

A scheme of use is also defined as an invariant organization of the activity for a *class of situations* (Vergnaud 1998), that is, a set of situations that correspond to the same teaching aim. By associating it with a class of situations having the same aim, a teacher mobilizes the same scheme that develops over the course of the experience.

DAD views the teacher's activity as a continuous process. It distinguishes between resources (plural) and document. The concept of document, developed by a teacher for a given teaching aim, is considered as a hybrid entity composed of a set of resources and a scheme of use. Following the resource/document dialectic, the construction of a document starts from a set of resources and goes through phases of selection, appropriation and transformation (combination and adaptation) by the teacher until the actual implementation in the classroom.

Vergnaud (1998) expresses a need to study the links between a teacher's teaching activity and his knowledge. According to him, the teacher's work consists of proposing situations and activities aimed at helping students to learn, clarifying the objectives to be achieved and accompanying the students to achieve the objectives. In this framework, he considers the teacher's role as a "mediator" (Vergnaud 1998, p. 238) who has to manage a complex process that can be influenced by many conditions, constraints and variables: (1) it [the teacher's role] begins outside the classroom, where the teacher organizes a complex implementation process taking into account variable parameters from one teaching situation to another; (2) it continues in the classroom through a large number of decisions and acts of mediation in a very limited time. Vergnaud (1998) proposes referring to the different components of the schemes to analyze these decisions and acts of mediation.

DAD considers the work of mathematics teachers as a whole and in its complexity. The work carried out according to this approach considers that a teacher's interactions with resources influence and are influenced by his or her training and teaching experience, his or her conceptions and/or *beliefs* about mathematics and its teaching (Rezat 2010); and the disciplinary content and its teaching context. Indeed, we want to discuss the potentialities of this approach in the case of a university professor's *documentation work*, with the consideration of a *resource system* that generates resources for teaching and resources for research. But before that, we wish to discuss the question of the relationship between teaching and research from the institutional point of view and from the perspective of Anthropological Theory of Didactics (Chevallard 1999).

5.3.2. *The complex relationship between teaching and research institutions*

A university professor develops professional experience by interacting simultaneously with a teaching institution and a research institution (Madsen and Winsløw 2009).

In a study focused on discipline specificities, Madsen and Winsløw (2009) explored the nature and conditions of a positive "link" between teaching and research in the case of physical geography and mathematics. Specifically, they examined the extent to which the relationship between teaching and research is discipline dependent. They proposed an analytical model for studying the relationship between research and teaching activities related to a discipline. We will not go into the theoretical details of this model based on the Anthropological Theory of Didactics (Chevallard 1999). We will present below a few aspects that will allow us to situate our theoretical choices (section 5.3.3) as well as our data collection and analysis choices (section 5.4).

Chevallard (2003) refers to Douglas (1999) when he talks about institutions. An institution is defined by Chevallard (1998) as being a "total" social device, which allows – and forces – its subjects, that is to say the people who come to occupy the different positions offered within this device, to put into play their own ways of doing and thinking. He emphasizes the cognitive dimension of institutions, which he places at the heart of his theoretical approach. He is interested in the relationship of a subject (teacher or student) to institutions and of objects (such as mathematical knowledge) to institutions, without taking into account the internal dynamics within these institutions. By moving from one institution to another – from the research institution to the teaching institution (or vice versa) in our case – we can consider in a different way the subjects of knowledge and the tools to produce this knowledge (mathematical or scientific, Chevallard 2003).

Madsen and Winsløw (2009) start from a basic principle in the Anthropological Theory of Didactics, which is that all human practice can be modeled in terms of praxeology, which we synthesize as follows: within the framework of an institution and for a given subject, the relationship to the objects of knowledge is shaped by the set of tasks that are accomplished according to well-defined techniques and are justified by knowledge that is called a theoretical block.

Madsen and Winsløw (2009) have developed a model based on the distinction between research praxeologies and teaching praxeologies, while embedding them in two distinct institutions: *research institution* and *teaching institution* (Madsen and Winsløw 2009). In their article, they distinguish between research organization (within a research institution) and didactic organization (within a teaching institution).

To study the relationship between teaching and research institutions, they identified the tasks of the research institution and those of the teaching institution. Then, they determined the knowledge and skills attached to each task. On the basis of the identified tasks, they conducted interviews in each of the disciplines considered.

The perception of the discipline in the research institution could be a parameter to be taken into account: a horizontal versus vertical metaphor of the discipline (Madsen and Winsløw 2009). They understand a vertical discipline as one in which many preconditions are necessary for contemporary knowledge, as theories are constructed in a cumulative manner. A horizontal discipline is one in which there is a juxtaposition of knowledge, sometimes interacting, but not relying on each other as strict preconditions. This ties in with Grenier-Boley's (2019) point about the impact of the discipline's epistemology (section 5.2.2).

Taking into account the institutional context will allow us to identify additional elements for understanding the interactions with resources, linked to the institutional conditions and constraints specific to each institution.

5.3.3. *The documentation work of a university professor, explored using pivotal resources*

In the case of a university professor, the definition given for a resource by Adler (2000) can be extended to cover both types of activity (teaching and research). We assume that in the case of lecturers and researchers, the resources mobilized and produced by research mainly feed the research activity. In this chapter, we are particularly interested in understanding how resources in/for research influence the design of resources for teaching, and thus the construction of a document.

To address our problem, we rely particularly on a model of documentation work based on the dialectic of scheme/class of situations. We also rely on the modeling proposed by Madsen and Winsløw (2009) to analyze the way a university professor develops a professional experience by interacting simultaneously with the teaching institution and the research institution (section 5.3.2). We consider that the interaction with the resources in each institution is linked on the one hand to the specific classes of situations (classes of research situations, classes of teaching situations) and on the other hand to the specificities of the discipline (Madsen and Winsløw 2009; Grenier-Boley 2019; section 5.3.2).

From the point of view of the interaction with resources, the relationship between research activity and teaching practices could take the form of a migration and adaptation of resources produced in the research institution to the teaching institution, or vice versa. This relationship can also take the form of resource use that reflects professional knowledge developed in the context of research activities (the "operational invariants" component of the resource's scheme of use, Gueudet and Trouche 2009).

We distinguish in fact:

– the *teaching document*, which corresponds to an aim related to a class of teaching situations in the sense of Gueudet (2017);

– the *research document*, which corresponds to an aim related to a class of research situations.

Each type of document is considered in its institution with the corresponding conditions and constraints.

Gueudet (2017) mentions that university teachers develop a resource system for research and a resource system for teaching. This is an assumption that we adopt as our working hypothesis. On the other hand, we would like to discuss it at the end of this exploratory study; insofar as our study takes into account certain aspects of the university professor profession, it seems appropriate to us to question these two resource systems: are they two interacting resource systems or rather a single resource system, the structure of which is determined by the two components of the profession?

The consideration of two resource systems requires new theoretical and methodological extensions to study their interrelation. We propose to explore the interaction process between the two systems by identifying what we will call *pivotal resources* in the research activities of a university professor.

The concept of *pivotal resources* has been characterized in previous studies using DAD (Trouche et al. 2019), but by being considered in the teaching context only. We propose to expand it to consider pivotal resources in the research institution. A pivotal resource is a resource that intervenes in multiple classes of situations (Gueudet 2017). We define a "pivotal resource" in the case of university professors as a resource that for a given teacher contributes to the construction of many research documents in a research institution. In other words, it is a resource that is mobilized by a university professor in several classes of research situations. Frequent use of a pivotal resource could influence some of the research activity.

For us, if there are relationships between research and teaching activities, they will be in terms of classes of situations where pivotal resources are mobilized. In this chapter, "pivotal resources" are considered in the literature review of classes of teaching situations. We assume that there is at least one pivotal resource in the research work of a given mathematician. This may be numerical computation software (Broley 2016), simulation software, a seminal work in his or her field of research, etc. Therefore, we shall rephrase our general question as follows: to what extent and how do pivotal resources from a research institution enrich the teacher's ability to design resources for teaching?

5.4. Methodology

A university professor in France has to teach a variety of content at different levels, ranging from the basic level in a discipline (at undergraduate degree and preparatory level) to very specialized courses related, if necessary, to their own research interests (at master's level). In this context and in order to explore our research question and to test the theoretical tools we are proposing (section 5.3), we conducted a study based on three interviews with mathematics university professors (see Table 5.1 for profiles). To preserve anonymity, we will call them M1, M2 and M3.

	Research experience	Research area	Teaching experience	Teaching level
M1	16 Years	Mathematical modeling of physical phenomena	16 Years	Undergraduate (mathematics and computer science) and master (applied mathematics)
M2	6 Years	Mathematical modeling of scientific phenomena	6 Years	Undergraduate (mathematics)
M3	17 Years	Number theory and combinatorics	17 Years	Undergraduate (mathematics) and master (pure mathematics)

Table 5.1. *Profile of the three university professors interviewed*

We developed an interview grid in two distinct parts: one part that focuses on research activity and one part that focuses on teaching practices. Although there are elements in common, the interview grid we developed differs from the one developed by Madsen and Winsløw (2009; section 5.3.2) in two respects: (1) we did not ask explicit questions about the relationship between research activity and teaching practice, but we chose to interpret this on the basis of the analyses; (2) the part that deals with research activity does not revolve around a precise task (or a precise example); we wished – in conformity with our research questions and theoretical choices (section 5.3.3) – to deal with a large number of classes of research situations. In addition, we did not ask direct questions about resources to ensure that the interviewees could express themselves freely about their research and teaching activities. This choice allowed us to identify resources freely cited by the interviewees and belonging to several classes of situations.

This will allow us to identify the pivotal resources (those cited spontaneously and belonging to several classes of research situations). With this choice, we do not, however, claim to identify all the pivotal resources.

The interviews lasted between one and one and a half hours; they were semi-structured; each interview took place in the university professor's office. All interviews were audio recorded. The transcripts of the interviews were coded in order to identify for each interviewee the teaching documents and the research documents (section 5.3.3), and the coding focused in particular on the different components of the resources' scheme of use.

For each interview, we created two types of tables: teaching document tables that correspond to classes of teaching situations, and research document tables that correspond to classes of research situations (see Table 5.2). The tables allowed us to identify the list of documents in each of the two institutions: research institution and teaching institution.

Research document tables			
Aim (of the research activity)	Resources	Rules of action	Operational invariants
Teaching document tables			
Aim (of the teaching activity)	Resources	Rules of action	Operational invariants

Table 5.2. *Presentation of the research document tables and the teaching document tables*

To construct the teaching document tables, we proceeded in the same manner as Gueudet (2017). We located in the transcript of the teaching part of each interview each response given as an aim of a teaching activity mentioned by the university professor. For each aim, we located the resources explicitly mentioned in the transcribed statement. Then, we identified stable elements in the way these resources were used (rules of action). For the regularity of these actions, we relied on the teacher's statements (e.g. "for..., we always start with..."). Finally, we noted the operational invariants; they correspond to statements of the type "I do so... because I think that...". We proceeded in the same way for the research part of the interview, in order to build the tables of research documents.

Once both tables were constructed, we first identified the pivotal resources in the research document table (see Table 5.3). Next, we checked whether or not the pivotal resource in the research document table (resource 1 in Table 5.3) was mentioned in the teaching document table. When this was the case, we took into account the teaching document where this resource appears (horizontal analysis of the table row corresponding to the document). If not, we tried to understand the reason for the lack of this resource in terms of operational invariants in the research institution and/or in terms of constraints in the teaching institution.

\multicolumn{4}{c}{Research documents table}			
Aims (A_i)	Resources	Rules of action (RA)	Operational invariants (OI)
A_1	Resource 1	RA_1	OI_1
A_2	Resource 2	RA_2	OI_2
A_3	Resource 3, Resource 1	RA_3	OI_3
...	...	...	...
A_n	Resource 4, Resource 1	RA_n	OI_n
\multicolumn{4}{c}{Teaching documents table}			
Aims (A_i)	Resources	Rules of action (RA)	Operational invariants (OI)
A_1	Resource 1	RA_1	OI_1
A_2	Resource 5	RA_2	OI_2
A_3	Resource 6, Resource 1	RA_3	OI_3
...	...	...	...
A_n	Resource 7, Resource 8	RA_n	OI_n

Table 5.3. *General form of the research document tables and teaching document tables, with Resource 1 as the hub resource*

This methodology allows us to question the process of mobilization of resources from the research institution to the teaching institution, considering a horizontal analysis of each document in each institution.

5.5. Forms of the relationship between research and teaching in terms of resources

Through our analysis, we have identified three forms of the relationship between research and teaching in terms of resources. We shall present each of these forms in the following three subsections.

5.5.1. *First form: the mobilization of a research resource in instantiation processes*

In the case of M1, we identified aims belonging to seven classes of situations in the research institution, in which [aims] software (Matlab, Maple, etc.) is fundamental in numerical modeling and simulation research (6 out of 7 identified aims). M1 uses this software to conjecture and validate (a conjecture or a modeling method). He says, "First of all, when I have to solve a problem, I start by looking at what happens on the computer and then I might be interested in the properties of my methods". The role of the software determines the thread of his research approach.

At the teaching institution, we have identified two teaching documents where the software is used. He uses the software with the master's degree students in order to make them aware of the characteristics of a modeling activity in mathematics (see Table 5.4 for an example of these documents). To do so, he chooses to provide a part of the software potential and a problem to model (rule of action). He describes this rule of action as follows: "I typically use Matlab. Matlab allows you to write small programs in a fairly simple way in order to numerically model a given problem". He adapts the problem to allow students to manipulate and deduce properties (rule of action):

> In reality, we adapt the problem because it's not a matter of bringing them a turnkey solution. We usually let them look for it and say what they think [...] What's interesting about the digital tool is that we have to run several executions of a program, look at it and try to deduce its properties.

He justifies these rules of action as follows (Operational Invariant): "It's really something exploratory, it's really experimental. I think that's the great thing about digital, I'm experimenting and trying to derive results".

	M1, teaching document
Aims	To make students aware of the characteristics of a modeling activity in mathematics.
Resources	Numerical calculation software. Resources from previous years around problem solving.
Rules of action	Choose a software used in the research. Choose and adapt a problem to solve that allows for manipulation, observation and experimentation.
Operating invariants	Modeling activity in mathematics is exploratory and experimental.

Table 5.4. *Presentation of a teaching document where the pivotal resource is used*

In this case (Table 5.4), we refer to the use of the pivotal resource in research at the teaching institution as *an action of instantiation*. Instantiation of the pivotal resource consists of mobilizing it from research institution to teaching institution in a particular way; as far as possible, this mobilization is done in a similar situation, with a similar role for the resource in both institutions, but with a more restricted domain of validity in the teaching institution. The teaching document (Table 5.4) illustrates two types of nexuses (section 5.2.1) which are tangible and intangible in the same class of situations: tangible in the sense that the document constructed is about an adaptation of the content from the research (from the modeling situations) and intangible in the sense that M1 develops an exploratory attitude toward the modeling activity.

5.5.2. *Second form: a research resource to scaffold learning of given content*

In the case of M2, we have identified six aims related to his research activities, in which software (Matlab, Maple, Scilab, etc.) is essential in numerical computation and graphical simulations (four aims out of six identified). His research activities using software include analyzing, modeling biological phenomena, validating experimental results, and communicating results to the biologists he works with.

In the teaching institution, the numerical simulation software appears in two teaching documents. In Table 5.5, we develop one of them, which corresponds to the aim "to design sessions of experimentation and discovery of mathematical properties with software". To achieve this aim, M2 selects a problem that is adaptable to the level of knowledge of his students (rule of action). He describes his approach as follows:

> I select my problem or subject, then I go on to select the mathematical tools. There are problems that you can illustrate, after some adaptations, with very basic tools. For example, we can study the population dynamics of urban pigeons from the stability phenomena of a dynamical system.

He then proceeds to develop, using the software, a support to show the stability phenomena from the representations (rule of action):

> [...] I use computational software that helps make graphical representations, so the student will have a model and an input. He [the student] says to himself I can vary this parameter, and he'll see how the data in his model reacts.

He justifies this rule of action as follows (Operational invariant):

> The fact that we have a tool that can give results in a visual way opens up avenues for analyzing a problem or discovering properties. For example, I show a phenomenon of stability of an equation or a solution of a differential equation on a graph to be able to discuss a notion or a property hidden behind it.

It continues (Operational invariant):

> The way we get people to discover a few things is essential. I think we ... we university teachers, we need to stimulate the spirit of imagination and inquiry in our students [...] they need to be asked to explain what they observe.

	M2, teaching document
Aims	Design teaching sessions to experiment and discover mathematical properties with software.
Resources	Numerical analysis software. Resources corresponding to the course in question.
Rules of action	Select a phenomenon of stability of differential equations. Show stability on a graphical representation. Offer the possibility to vary values and parameters to provoke a discussion on the properties.
Operational invariants	A software program is a tool that allows you to hide properties from students and display results in a visual way. We need to stimulate the imagination to make connections between mathematical properties and their representations.

Table 5.5. *Presentation of a teaching document related to the aim "Designing teaching sessions to experiment and discover mathematical properties with software"*

M2 attributes the same role to the software in the knowledge constructed in both institutions (research and teaching), while the operational invariants show that M2 uses the software in the teaching institution *to scaffold the content at stake*, in the design of the resource as well as in the implementation. Although this is a mobilization of software from research into teaching, we cannot say that it is a tangible connection in the sense of Neumann (section 5.2) because it does not concern disciplinary content. We can say that it is an intangible connection (a method is developed by relying on the software to approach knowledge), supported by a tangible resource from the research.

5.5.3. *Third form: the form of non-relation in terms of resources*

In M3's case, there is a pivotal resource in the research papers table; however, it is not mentioned in the teaching documents table. This finding is reinforced by M3's words in the interview, acknowledging that there is a gap between the research activity and the teaching activity in mathematics:

> There are obviously differences between the mathematics that is taught and the mathematics that is practiced by mathematicians, because when we do mathematics, well, we do rigorous assessments to gather evidence. From hypotheses and

properties, we show things. It's not the same things that we assume and that we use as properties and hypotheses and that we have to demonstrate with the students.

From his point of view, if there is a link, it will be in the "way of teaching" and in the problem-solving process because he thinks that "it is the same process" (Operational invariants). He describes the teaching of proof following the same process experienced in his research: he makes hypotheses and then determines the properties to be mobilized.

There are no common resources between the teaching and research institutions. There is a perceived "divorce" between the two institutions. He does not place his students in research situations. In his view, in order to do so, the entire class community does not need to be able to solve tasks. The connections that may exist are not tangible (section 5.2.1). They correspond, for example, to the relations to the way of teaching "to follow the same research process" in the treatment of evidence.

We can infer that there is a relationship between teaching and research that can be seen through the process of using the resource in the classroom and not just as a process of resource migration from a research institution to a teaching institution. This result is consistent with those identified by Tabchi (2018) in the case of university professors in graph theory. We characterize the interactions between research and teaching institutions as an action of disseminating the scientific attitude (research process) into teaching practices.

5.5.4. Results and discussions

It appears that the relationship between research and teaching is closely linked to the perception that university professors have of the specificity of both their research field and their research resources. We recall that our methodological choice requires the identification of the pivotal resources for the research activity. We then study, based on these pivotal resources, the relationship between research and teaching. The results of the analysis support our hypothesis that the pivotal resources influence an important part of the research activity and therefore if there are relationships between the research activity and teaching practices, they may occur in terms of classes of situations where these resources are mobilized.

The study of the relationship between teaching and research through the prism of resources appears to reveal new aspects of this relationship. The case studies of M1 and M2 show the limits of the typology of connections developed by Neumann (1992): in the same teaching situation, the connection can be tangible and intangible (case of M1). The DAD offers the possibility of characterizing tangible nexus based on the mobilization of material resources from research in teaching (the case of M2).

The analysis of the documents (resources and schemes of use) allowed us to identify intangible links (Neumann 1992), in particular the "operational invariants" component, which makes it possible to characterize the way in which the professional knowledge resulting from the research activity partly determines the teaching practices (M1, M2 and M3).

In terms of comparing the results against other work on the same issue (section 5.2), we can say that considering the resources of a university professor in general and those resulting from research in particular opens up avenues for better understanding the relationship between the two types of activity (teaching and research). Elton (2001, section 5.2) suggests that the way students are viewed in teaching models is a factor in understanding the relationship between teaching and research. This proposal is consistent with Broley's (2016) attempt to identify similarities between the activity of mathematicians and the activity of their students to characterize the impact of research on teaching. We suggest an additional factor: that of the teacher resource developer.

5.6. Conclusions and perspectives

This contribution does not have the simple objective of presenting a study of three mathematicians. We wanted to show the contributions of a resource-based approach to the theme of the relationship between teaching and research in the practices of mathematicians.

We have approached this theme by mobilizing mainly the DAD. We have proposed an extension of the use of this approach to cover the interactions with resources in the context of research situations, by considering concepts such as "research document" and "pivotal resources in research". We wish to continue exploring this issue by varying the case studies: the research field of mathematicians, which seems to be an important element to consider; the content taught and the teaching institutions (training of future mathematicians, training of future engineers, etc.).

From a methodological point of view, this case study reveals the need for a broader data collection methodology, based on a joint long-term monitoring of research and teaching activities. This type of monitoring, which includes several methodological tools (interviews, observation of in-class and out-of-class activity), makes it possible to infer in a fine-tuned way the schemes of resource use, particularly the "operational invariants" component of these schemes.

The three forms of relationship between teaching and research offer an avenue for their application in the training of teachers in higher education in order to develop capacities for the design and use of resources from research (choice of content, adaptation of content, the different ways in which these resources can be mobilized, etc.). This may be particularly important in a context where mathematicians believe that there is a gap between research in mathematics and the mathematics taught (case of M3 which confirms the result of Grenier-Boley (2019), section 5.2.2).

The study of the relationship between research activity and teaching practices through the prism of interaction with resources also opens up avenues for new research. Taking into account the resource/document dialectic has allowed us to identify the limitations of the typology proposed by Neumann to characterize the types of nexus between teaching and research. Although this typology remains valid in the case of research that does not take into account resources as a mediation tool, we believe that a refinement of the typology is still possible in order to broaden it to take into account resources. All this offers new avenues for future research and collaboration.

5.7. References

Adler, J. (2000). Conceptualizing resources as a theme for teacher education. *J. Math. Teach. Educ.*, 3, 205–224.

Biza, I., Giraldo, V., Hochmuth, R., Khakbaz, A., Rasmussen, C. (2016). *Research on Teaching and Learning Mathematics. ICME-13 Tropical Surveys*. Springer, Hamburg.

Broley, L. (2016). The place of computer programming in (undergraduate) mathematical practices. In *Proceedings of INDRUM 2016 First Conference of the International Network for the Didactic Research in University Mathematics*, Nardi, E., Winsløw, C., Hausberger, T. (eds). University of Montpellier and INDRUM, Montpellier.

Brown, M.W. (2009). The teacher-tool relationship: Theorizing the design and use of curriculum materials. In *Mathematics Teachers at Work: Connecting Curriculum Materials and Classroom Instruction*, Remillard, J.T., Herbel-Eisenmann, B.A., Lloyd, G.M. (eds). Routledge, New York.

Buteau, C., Jarvis, D., Lavicza, Z. (2014). On the integration of computer algebra systems (CAS) by Canadian mathematicians: Results of a national survey. *Can. J. Sci. Math. Technol. Educ.*, 14(1), 1–23.

Chevallard, Y. (1998). Analyse des pratiques enseignantes et didactique des mathématiques : l'approche anthropologique. In *Analyse des pratiques enseignantes et didactique des mathématiques – Actes de l'université d'été*, IREM de Clermont-Ferrand (ed). La Rochelle.

Chevallard, Y. (1999). L'analyse des pratiques enseignantes en théorie anthropologique du didactique. *Recherches en Didactique des Mathématiques*, 19(2), 221–265.

Chevallard, Y. (2003). Approche anthropologique du rapport au savoir et didactique des mathématiques. In *Rapport au savoir et didactiques*, Maury, S., Caillot, M. (eds). Fabert, Paris.

Douglas, M. (1999). *Comment pensent les institutions*. La Découverte, Paris.

Elton, L. (1986). Research and teaching: Symbiosis or conflict? *High. Educ.*, 15, 299–304.

Elton, L. (2001). Research and teaching: Conditions for a positive link. *Teach. High. Educ.*, 6, 43–56.

Grenier-Boley, N. (2019). La recherche en mathématiques : une ressource pour les didacticiens ? HDR, Université de Paris Diderot (Paris 7) Sobonne Paris Cité, Paris.

Gueudet, G. (2017). University teachers' resources systems and documents. *Int. J. Res. Undergrad. Math. Educ.*, 3(1), 198–224.

Gueudet, G. and Trouche, L. (2009). Towards new documentation systems for mathematics teachers? *Educ. Stud. Math.*, 71(3), 199–218.

Henkel, M. (2004). La relation enseignement-recherche. *Politiques et gestion de l'enseignement supérieur*, 2(2), 21–36.

de Hosson, C., Décamp, D., Morand, E., Robert, A. (2015). Approcher l'identité professionnelle d'enseignants universitaires de physique : un levier pour initier des changements de pratiques pédagogiques. *Recherches en Didactique des Sciences et des Technologies*, 11, 161–190.

Lebrun, N., Bridoux, S., de Vleeschouwer, M., Grenier-Boley, N., Khanfour-Armalé, R., Mesnil, Z., Nihoul, C. (2018). L'identité professionnelle des enseignants-chercheurs de physique – Comparaison avec celle des mathématiciens. In *Ardist2018 : 10èmes rencontres scientifiques de l'ARDiST*, March 2018, Saint-Malo.

Madsen, L.M. and Winsløw, C. (2009). Relations between teaching and research in physical geography and mathematics at research-intensive universities. *Int. J. Sci. Math. Educ.*, 7, 741–763.

Mali, A., Biza, I., Jaworski, B. (2014). Characteristics of university mathematics teaching: Use of generic examples in tutoring. In *Proceedings of the Joint Meeting of PME38 and PME-NA36*, Vol. 4, Liljedahl, P., Nicol, C., Oesterle, S., Allan, D. (eds). PME, Vancouver.

Neumann, R. (1992). Perceptions of the teaching-research nexus: A framework for analysis. *High. Educ.*, 23, 159–171.

Petropoulou, G., Jaworski, B., Potari, D., Zachariades, T. (2015). How do research mathematicians teach Calculus? In *Proceedings of CERME9*, Krainer, K., Vondrová, N. (eds). Charles University in Prague, Faculty of Education and ERME, Prague.

Rabardel, P. (1995). *Les hommes et les technologies : approche cognitive des instruments contemporains*. Armand Colin, Paris.

Rezat, S. (2010). The utilization of mathematics textbooks as instruments for learning. In *Proceedings of the 6th Conference of European Research in Mathematics Education*, Durand-Guerrier, V., Soury-Lavergne, S., Arzarello, F. (eds). INRP, Lyon.

Sabra, H. (2019). The connectivity in resources for student-engineers: The case of resources for teaching sequences. In *Proceedings of the Eleventh Congress of the European Society for Research in Mathematics Education*, Jankvist, U.T., van den Heuvel-Panhuizen, M., Veldhuis, M. (eds). Freudenthal Group & Freudenthal Institute, Utrecht University and ERME, Utrecht.

Tabchi, T. (2018). University teachers-researchers' practices: The case of teaching discrete mathematics. In *Proceedings of the Second Conference of the International Network for Didactic Research in University Mathematics*, Durand-Guerrier, V., Hochmuth, R., Goodchild, S., Hogstad, N.M. (eds). University of Agder and INDRUM, Kristiansand, Norway.

Trouche, L., Gueudet, G., Pepin, B. (eds) (2019). *The "Resource" Approach to Mathematics Education*. Springer, Cham.

Vergnaud, G. (1998). Towards a cognitive theory of practice. In *Mathematics Education as a Research Domain: A Search for Identity*, Kilpatrick, J., Sierpinska, A. (eds). Kluwer Academic Publishers, Dordrecht.

PART 3

A Sociological Perspective of the Practices of Lecturers and Researchers

6

Beyond the Disciplinary Approach: Toward a Socio-historical and Critical Reflexivity of its Teaching Practices

6.1. Introduction

Between 2016 and 2019, three study days devoted to sociology teaching practices in higher education were organized, followed by the publication of a special issue in the journal *Socio-Logos*. The intention of these events was to create a space, and more precisely an opening, in order to present, analyze and compare teaching practices within higher education from a disciplinary point of view. While this space was intended above all as a place for the development of a collectively committed reflexivity, the announcement was nevertheless unequivocally a call for mobilization. The time was ripe for the pursuit of significant transformations in higher education and research that had been under way for the last 20 years. Increasingly numerous demands were specifically aimed at transforming teaching practices. It seemed urgent and essential to take stock of existing practices and to re-examine them from the point of view of the anticipated changes.

The purpose of this chapter is to revisit the reasons for this call. The intention is to reinscribe the calls to change teaching practices in the current political context. This context is generally passed over in silence and masked under a technical discourse. The challenge is then to show that the recent deployment of a discourse promoting a "university pedagogy" or "higher

---

Chapter written by Stéphanie TRALONGO.

education pedagogy"[1], together with devices and practices, circumscribes in a narrow socio-cognitive framework the space of the thinkable within which to consider its practices and transformations. We will call the set of propositions it contains a common discursive fund. This term is borrowed from Bernard Lahire's work on the construction of illiteracy as a public problem (Lahire 1999). It allows us to develop a discourse analysis by identifying the redundant commonplaces (or topics) that produce a finite series of propositions to define the social problem. This cognitive, rhetorical and lexical construction has effects on the categories of perception, the imagination and the practices of the actors by delimiting the space of the thinkable and the possible in terms of pedagogical creativity.

In the first part, entitled "The content of the common discursive fund on 'higher education pedagogy'", we will present the main proposals it puts forward. In the second part, entitled "Deconstruction, denaturalization: the political underneath the obvious", we propose to uncover the illusion of obviousness that surrounds a certain number of proposals formulated by this discourse. Finally, in a third part entitled "Teaching practices in sociology in reverse", we will illustrate some of the discrepancies between this common discursive background and the ordinary practices of teaching sociology, using examples presented during the study days and the special issue. In doing so, we will recall the scientific vigor of a set of disciplines, such as sociology, education sciences, political science, etc., whose specificity is the construction of an intelligibility of the social from elements of various natures. These disciplines thus provide resources for reaffirming that any pedagogical question, even the most technical or seemingly tiny one, for example the use of voting boxes in a lecture hall, can never be separated from the political and social issues within which it is embedded. Each questioning indeed refers to the types of men and women that societies aim to shape. And it encompasses the means, including of course economic and material means, that they use to achieve this. Repositioning the discourses in this ensemble, tying up threads where practices and injunctions may appear in discontinuous, technical, depoliticized, purely local, substantialist, or individual ways, then has an ambition: to contribute to introducing the

---

1 Although the term "university pedagogy" is much more widely used in the discourse, in this chapter we will opt for the term "higher education pedagogy", which makes it possible to refer to the space of higher education and research, and not only to universities. It is not by chance that the university is mentioned so often in the discussions, since it is the primary target of the transformations under way.

conditions of a plural, contradictory, and conflicting thought, informed by the disciplinary history of teaching and research practices.

METHODOLOGICAL NOTE.– This article is based on fieldwork conducted between 2013 and 2019, using a corpus composed of six regulatory texts and official reports; 11 books and 53 scientific articles; five regular calls for projects and 65 responses; a hundred texts of technical documentation on a University Pedagogy Center (UPC hereafter) including job descriptions, job offers, and training programs; six association websites; and participant observation of several activities (responses to calls for projects, participation in study days, invitations to conferences). The analysis grid combined the search for redundancies in the themes addressed in order to bring out the topics, with attention to the functions and social positions of the speakers and to the precise contexts of enunciation of the discourses. The analysis focused on the ways in which the speakers justified the theme of "higher education pedagogy"; on the content of the proposals for transforming teaching and on the ways in which they were achieved.

6.2. The content of the common discursive fund on "higher education pedagogy"

6.2.1. *Recent and growing discourse and practice*

The constitution of the corpus consisted of retaining all the discursive entities (oral and written) explicitly referring to "university pedagogy" or "higher education pedagogy". The documents were then classified according to their nature, the functions of their speaker and the places of enunciation. The enumeration of these different elements is instructive: it shows in what capacity, for what occasions, and from what institutional places actors write and speak on this topic. Thus, we find articles by researchers, mostly in the educational sciences, announcing an "emerging trend" (de Ketele 2010), special issues of journals, works developing certain associated topics (digital technology, evaluation of teaching, teacher training, pedagogical techniques for higher education), a journal (RIPES) and announcements of study days and conferences. This first set of documents indicates that this topic is part of the scientific field. A second set shows an activity rooted in the world of ministerial bureaucracy through the publication of regulatory texts, official reports and calls for projects published by bodies of the Ministry of Higher Education, Research and Professional Integration. A third space concerns the universities whose actors produce diversified discursive entities: announcement of study days, calls for and response to projects; job offers for pedagogical advisors or engineers; training programs to prepare for these functions of advisors/engineers; technical and organizational documentation of UPC, etc. A fourth set shows the development of associative networks aimed at the promotion and the defense of certain practices and activities in connection with "higher education pedagogy". These networks can be regional, such as PENSERA[2] and GRAPPE[3], or national, such as the Réseau SUP (UPC network). They are focused on one topic, for example the program approach or digital technology. These four forums thus show a configuration of activities that materialize in diversified practices the existence of this topic in the daily life of many actors in higher education. These actors are either lecturers and researchers, non-teaching university staff, ministry officials, or even elected politicians.

This abundance is not insignificant, especially for activities that are, after all, quite recent: discourses and practices on "higher education pedagogy" in France date back to the last 30 years. Two phases can be identified. The first appeared between 1990 and 2007. At that time, the topic of "pedagogy in higher education" was approached mainly through official reports and publications by certain researchers, who played the role of "experts" in the political world, as analyzed by Sandrine Garcia (Garcia 2008). The second phase is that of a more generalized implementation of UPCs, the creation of calls for projects, the multiplication of events (study days, colloquia), the publication of official reports and a decree on the training of new lecturers and researchers in 2018[4]. At first sporadic and very marginal in the first decade, activities and publications would continue to multiply thereafter.

Several questions can be raised. First of all, why this acceleration? It is not by chance, nor is it the result of a sudden generalized awareness of an unacceptable lack of training in teaching for lecturers and researchers that needs to be urgently addressed. This is the case even though one of the

---

2 *Pédagogie de l'Enseignement Supérieur en Rhône-Alpes.*
3 *"Groupe d'Appui à la Pédagogie"* of Midi-Pyrénées pedagogical advisors (https://grappeblog.wordpress.com/).
4 Order of February 8, 2018 establishing a national framework for training aimed at deepening the pedagogical skills of trainee lecturers JORF No. 0054 of March 6, 2018, text No. 23 NOR: ESRH1732884A ELI: https://www.legifrance.gouv.fr/eli/arrete/2018/2/8/ESRH1732884A/jo/texte.

arguments most often put forward concerns a lack of training and is based on numerous experiences, some of them painful, of lecturers and researchers who have suddenly gone from being doctoral students to teaching in higher education. Since the situation is not new, why did it suddenly become unacceptable in the 2000s? Why then, despite the very clear increase in the number of actors participating in the area of "higher education pedagogy", do we observe a homogenization of statements? The intention of this part of the chapter is to present the structuring lines of these discourses, whose homogeneity allows us to draw up the content of the common discursive fund. The next part will focus on the functions and relations between the speakers. The track followed is that of a link between the functions and relations of the speakers among themselves and in relation to higher education. This link is explanatory of the conditions of possibility for the actors to access the common discursive fund and to appropriate it in order to produce their own statements on "higher education pedagogy".

6.2.2. Circular and self-referential content

The discussion of "higher education pedagogy" evokes a series of topics that always seem to go together: it centers around change, why it is necessary, and how to implement it.

Thus, in 2014, Michel Beney and Jacques Dejou[5] presented to the Conference of University Presidents the "UPC network", an association for the promotion and defense of university pedagogical services:

> The context in which teachers, researchers and lecturers are now evolving generates a mutation of the profession that must be accompanied by the institution. Indeed, they are confronted with new requirements, both in terms of training, the public, the institutions and the tools (such as the use of Information and Communication Technology for Teaching). It is therefore important to support them to improve the pedagogical quality of the institutions. This is the role of the UPC.

---

5 Beney is a lecturer and researcher at the Université de Bretagne Occidentale and a researcher at the centre de Recherche sur l'Education, les Apprentissages et la Didactique (CREAD), while Dejou is dean of the Faculty of Dentistry at the University of Aix-Marseille.

In 2016, a MOOC (or online course) dedicated to teacher training in higher education was published by FUN Campus. In the first course of the four sessions, a PDF document signed by Patricia Arnault[6] was entitled "the Bologna Process, the internationalization of higher education". After two pages summarizing the "European context" as well as "the requirements of the Bologna Process", the author concludes that:

> At this stage, when we are aware of the major changes in the objectives of higher education, the diversity of students and their expectations, and the importance of the challenges of education for today's society, it has become imperative to train and support higher education teachers in the diversity of their missions, and to evaluate their activities in order to better recognize and value them. This is based on the reality of political leadership of pedagogical transformation by institutions or sites of higher education, and by the establishment or consolidation and development of support services for pedagogy.[7]

These exemplary speeches take up a certain number of topics that are widely found. First of all, they state that change is not only expected but unavoidable. They justify this need for change by referring to the "Bologna Process" and the "Lisbon Strategy", which have their own "requirements" that must be met.

The speeches also specify the targets on which the change must be focused: these are lecturers and researchers and educational institutions in higher education, which are, it should be remembered, also run by lecturers and researchers. This change is seen as desirable because it will allow for the "professional development" of lecturers and researchers, the "success of students" and the transformation of higher education institutions from training elites to training the masses (Rege-Collet and Romainville 2006); it will also allow society to be competitive and to intervene in the unemployment problem.

---

6 Expert of the MiPNES (Mission de la pédagogie et du numérique pour l'enseignement supérieur), DGESIP (Direction Générale de l'Enseignement Supérieur, et de l'insertion professionnelle), Ministry of National Education, Higher Education and Research, University of Poitiers.

7 Available at: https://www.fun-mooc.fr/courses/ENSCachan/20012/session01/about (accessed March 1, 2017).

From the point of view of its implementation, the speeches advocate that this change should be initiated thanks to various measures aimed at "supporting" lecturers and researchers. They are expected to be trained in pedagogy, which will lead them to transform their conceptions of teaching, their ways of teaching and their ways of evaluating students. In order to bring about these transformations, the discourses are based on theories (from psychology and education sciences on learning, students, etc.). They recommend the use of digital tools (Béjean and Monthubert 2015), a logic of "alignment" and a "reversal of approaches", in order to focus the approach "on learning" and students rather than on teaching, an approach by "competence" and "program", as well as certain "good practices" or "innovative practices", such as flipped classes, tutoring, courses in "fablab", "learning center", "flipped pedagogy", etc... (Bertrand Report 2014; Filâtre Report 2017; job offers; training programs; days on the future of higher education). For example, a job offer for an educational advisor/engineer published in 2016 begins as follows:

> Training Engineer/Pedagogical Advisor (cat. A); 1 year fixed-term contract, renewable
>
> This post is part of the X project [funded]. This cross-cutting project aims to promote success for all by strengthening support for students and promoting changes in teaching practices. One of the goals is to encourage teaching that focuses on student learning by supporting the professional development of university teachers in a change support approach.

Still on the subject of its implementation, the comments emphasize that this change will be facilitated by the creation of UPCs, which require financial, human and material resources. The financial resources will be provided in part by responses to calls for projects formulated by the State, which will make it possible to structure various forms of support for "higher education pedagogy" at the institutional level, such as local calls for projects, time off for "innovative" lecturers and researchers, etc. Human resources will consist of contractual or permanent recruitment of master's or doctorate graduates in the social sciences to fill the positions of educational advisors or engineers, who are in the process of being professionalized. The material means will include well-equipped digital support services, dedicated places, specific adequate furniture, etc.

It is also indicated that this change will meet with resistance from lecturers and researchers for various reasons: fear of change, backward-looking conceptions of teaching, a lack of initial and ongoing training and above all, a lack of career recognition of investments in teaching combined with an over-investment in research. The speakers advise imagining actions that take into account the gap that needs to be bridged, and among the avenues envisaged, some mention a link to disciplinary issues.

Finally, the speeches announce that this change can and must be evaluated through policy, strategies and performance measurement tools, in line with quality development.

6.2.3. *Some areas of traffic*

On the whole, this provides a tightly woven network within which lecturers and researchers, as the "governing bodies" of higher education institutions, have the double distinction of being the first recipients and some of the producers of the common discursive fund. Thus, depending on their status (doctoral student, postdoctoral student, young resident lecturer and researcher or former lecturer and researcher), there is no shortage of requests and demands to take part in various activities concerning the "pedagogy of higher education". The doctoral student, who tends to be just starting out in teaching, is strongly invited to refer to the UPC services, which offer training in teaching in higher education. These training courses can lead to certificates, which will be attached to the application file when recruiting for the position of maître de conférences (senior lecturer). In the application file, as in the oral exam, candidates may be asked to provide details, explanations and summaries of their teaching experience. Thus, being able to problematize this experience with regard to what the theme of "higher education pedagogy" consists of is not just anecdotal with regard to the expectations of a future lecturer and researcher. In the same vein, since 2018, a decree making the training of young senior lecturers mandatory has been promulgated. It stipulates that this training must be organized by the senior lecturer's host institution, that the participation of the latter will be the subject of an opinion counting for obtaining tenure and finally that the existence of this type of training will allow the institution to show its investment in the quality of its training.

Once the recruitment process has been completed, and the young lecturer and researcher has qualified as a lecturer and researcher, summons for teacher training invite him or her to get closer to the UPCs and/or to take part in actions proposed outside their university (by associations, by networks, etc.). These training invitations also concern academics in the middle of their career. The intention is to bring about a change in practices, justified by the idea that it is now necessary to "professionalize" this dimension of the activity of lecturers and researchers.

At the same time, the lecturer and researcher may be asked to participate in activities of an administrative nature aimed at creating, directing or participating in UPCs, vice-presidencies, or other functions relevant to the topic of "higher education". If he/she accepts, he/she will also be invited to get involved in associative networks or groups supported by the Ministry of Higher Education and Research. They will also be encouraged to produce scientific texts on "higher education pedagogy", to organize colloquiums or study days, to participate as a member of a panel on selection committees (awarding prizes, selecting projects, etc.). He or she may also set up a diploma or participate in the training of future pedagogical advisors. Finally, if the lecturer and researcher accumulates many years of experience in "higher education pedagogy", it will be possible for him/her to become an expert who will participate in panels for calls for projects, advise on the creation of UPCs or train future pedagogical advisors, whose functions are gradually becoming institutionalized and professionalized through training, job descriptions, and a listing in the interministerial directory of state professions[8].

This network thus relates to a series of calls to take part in the "pedagogy of higher education" which, as dedicated structures are deployed at the level of higher education institutions, are becoming increasingly present. And it is within the latter that lecturers and researchers are then called upon to demonstrate great creativity in rethinking their practices, transforming them, and getting their colleagues to do the same.

---

8 Available at: https://www.fonction-publique.gouv.fr/conseillereconseiller-pedagogique-de-lenseignement-superieur.

6.3. Deconstruction, denaturalization: the political under the obvious

One of the characteristics of talking about "higher education pedagogy" is its naturalizing dimension: with the world having changed, higher education, and more specifically the university, must adapt. However, it is worth taking a closer look at what are considered to be exogenous justifications, as well as at the rhetoric of the imperious necessity that they convey. There is nothing natural about all this, but a progressive construction, indicating recompositions in the relationship between politics and higher education.

The discourses refer to the "Bologna Process", the "Lisbon Strategy", and this socio-history will do the same. However, the intention is not to imply that this is a process and a strategy that "demands" or "dictates" the expected change from outside, but rather to reveal the ways in which the ideas of externality, necessity and imperiousness have been imposed.

6.3.1. *Denaturalizing the chronology*

A little more than 20 years after the Sorbonne declaration in 1998, research shows that it was indeed an impetus for the construction of a European Higher Education Area (EHEA). It is worth recalling that in May 1998 a conference was held at the Sorbonne, organized on the initiative of Claude Allègre, then Minister of Higher Education and Research, during which the "project of an EHEA structured around a common architecture of degrees at two main levels of study aimed at improving the mobility and employability of European students, and the attractiveness of the European higher education system" was formulated for the first time (Ravinet 2011). The project was launched with the signature of four ministers (German, French, Italian and British). The following year, a series of conferences began in Bologna as part of a "process" that would bear the name of the organizing city, and whose declaration, based on that of the Sorbonne, was signed by the ministers of 29 European countries in June 1999. This was followed by conferences in various cities, including Lisbon, which gave its name to a "strategy", aiming to "make the European Union the most competitive and dynamic knowledge-based economy in the world by 2010, capable of sustainable economic growth with more and better jobs and greater social cohesion". From 2010 onward, it was succeeded by the

"Europe 2020 strategy", following a renewed focus on economic growth and increased employment, using an "open method of coordination" (Monte and Rémi-Giraud 2013).

6.3.2. *Recomposing democratic functioning*

The construction of the European higher education area raises interesting questions concerning public policies, from their creation to their deployment and appropriation by citizens. We can thus ask ourselves "who" pilots "Bologna" (Croché 2006), "who" judges "university quality" (Garcia 2008), whether there was a clear initial intention, an initial rationality and consensus among the different stakeholders (Ravinet 2011), through what channels the norms aimed at the professionalization of university degree models are transmitted (Stavrou 2013), "who" benefits from "good practices" (Dakowska 2017) and, essentially, what recompositions in the exercise of democracy they signal (Cussó and Gobin 2008). These questions have been the subject of research that highlights the presence of a surprisingly stabilized semantic set, in other words, a common, homogeneous discursive fund that is constantly repeated from one actor to another.

Looking at the lexical stock circulating about higher education, Roser Cussó and Sandrine Gobin highlight a "tendency towards a deep homogenization of institutionalized political discourse", the result of an "intense lexical circulation of lexemes or technical-sounding words" among a wide range of actors (from politicians to bankers, from the media to "university professors", not to mention experts). Their analysis is that:

> Since the 1980s, we have been in a progressive but intensive context of transnationalization and concentration of political decision-making, through the weight that collegial power bodies (G8, European Union) and international economic organizations (World Bank, International Monetary Fund, World Trade Organization, etc.) have assumed. This displacement of the production of the central locus of the program and of the matrix discourse of reference, from the national sphere to technocratic spheres, which has rarely been subject to contradictory debate, seems to result in the production of a dominant internationalized collective imaginary

that is not presented as a politicized and partisan discourse, but as a neutral one. (Cussó and Gobin 2008)

The characteristics of this discourse are that it relies on experts, that it appears to be neutral and depoliticized, and that its argumentative structure is strongly marked: by avoiding conflict, it uses the rhetoric of the serious problem to be solved by technical solutions that are also provided, while mobilizing a representation of reality that tends to "paraphrase" it. "From then on, objectives and solutions have often been confused in a self-fulfilling and circular rhetoric", to the point that it has become impossible in the rhetoric on employment policy, for example, "to determine whether more growth is needed to promote job creation or to create jobs to boost growth (Gobin 2005)" (Cussó and Gobin 2008). We then witness a "form style" of "discourses produced in the reports of international organizations that seem to be built on a sequence of stereotyped and generalizing formulas generating an overall impression of emptiness of speech" (Cussó and Gobin 2008).

The influence of international organizations in the production and circulation of these discourses has been the subject of works in sociology and political science. Tracing the history of the influences, collisions and collusions of international organizations on higher education since the 1945s, Dorota Dakowska shows that a specific "multilateralism" has developed in stages, first "through Keynesian-inspired policies and the promotion of the right to education by UNESCO; then, via the OECD's activism in this field from the 1960s onwards, and finally, through neoliberal policies promoted by the World Bank and relayed, to varying degrees, by the OECD, the EU and the World Trade Organization" (Dakowska 2017). The production and dissemination of a common discursive fund then largely exceeds the national framework, in a global context marked by both Europeanization and transnationalism.

One of the particularities of this discourse is that it is not neutral. It is even ideologically marked: "monetarist thinking and the promotion of free trade" are its constitutive features (Cussó and Gobin 2008, section 19), within which globalization and competitiveness create a discourse "on the necessary adaptation of education to employment" by mobilizing the notion of the "knowledge society" (Cussó 2008). The reform of education systems, including higher education, and in particular universities, are the places where this ideology is applied. This ideology, defended by the European

Commission, is based on the theories of human capital and the knowledge economy (Garcia 2008). The solutions proposed, in other words the "good practices", are not proposed in themselves, but with regard to the transformation that constitutes the subordination of higher education to the needs of the market.

6.3.3. *Effects on the perceptions and practices of lecturers and researchers*

The notion of "academic freedom" is very present in higher education. Thus, to consider that there is an "official discourse of higher education" is not self-evident, writes Sophia Stavrou, "so much has the sacrosanct academic freedom always been a central issue" (Stavrou 2013). Her aim was to study the transformations at work in the program models between 2008 and 2012 within the University, using the example of the master's degree in the humanities and social sciences. She shows, however, the content and forms in which this "official discourse" is materialized and inscribed in the discourse, practices and categories of perception of a whole series of actors, initially in lecturers and researchers. Her work illustrates that this discourse aiming at transformation (via the professionalization of models) is above all political, that it "appropriates the theme of higher education and establishes legitimate orientations through a series of national and transnational communications, legislative and regulatory texts". The need to change the university toward a socio-economic rationalization is achieved through the transformation of the programs and the rise of a logic of quality.

A few years earlier, Sandrine Garcia conducted a study on the rise of the discourses of expertise and quality in higher education. Based on a field survey focused on the issue of teaching at the university, she showed how experts had been able to act as intermediaries from the 2000s onward in the economization of higher education, in other words the adoption of higher education as a means of supporting the needs of the market. The constitution of a discourse and practices centered on "university pedagogy" took a prominent place, allowing experts to pursue their careers, expertise to be used as "leverage to adapt the academic profession to economic issues", and international organizations to build scientific legitimacy through this expertise in order to intervene in fields in which they have no decision-making power and proceed by prescription (Garcia 2008).

All of this work shows that there is no natural tendency in the slope that the history of higher education has taken over the last 30 years and that the advent of a "pedagogy of higher education" involves issues, relationships and interests that are much broader than the sole success of students, which is itself reduced to the question of their subsequent professional integration. Everything that is "common sense", such as the idea that training is needed to learn to teach in higher education, does not arrive as it is in the minds of lecturers and researchers and other actors, but under the manufactured prism of a problem to be dealt with using solutions provided out of hand. The same is true for the call to be inventive, which is widely disseminated and expected both at the level of university "governance" (in their incentive practices) and at the level of the actors (in charge of stimulating practices or leading courses).

The common discursive fund on "higher education pedagogy" is thus a robust socio-cognitive framework, whether in its semantic aspect or in the practical declensions it provides from diversified devices. It has every chance of making sense to an increasing number of actors with training backgrounds and professional statuses that are also diversifying within higher education. For some of these actors, their raison d'être within this space is only due to the legitimacy of "higher education pedagogy". This socio-cognitive framing obviously questions the margins of maneuver of the different universes in relation to the political world. Essentially, it is the questions of autonomy and power that are being replayed here. The analyses presented tend to show that the adoption of the common discursive fund at all levels considerably weakens the idea of a "sacrosanct academic freedom". However, it is important to make a distinction between the discursive analysis, which shows this convergence, and the analysis of practices, which the survey protocol established here does not allow us to approach other than through discursive traces. Discourses are never reflections of practices, and between the two there are possibilities of more or less heterodox appropriations. An example of this is the organization of study days and the publication of a special issue on questions of teaching practices in sociology, for which part of the funding came from responses to calls for innovative projects in the field of "higher education pedagogy".

6.4. Teaching practices in sociology in reverse

6.4.1. *Creating a space to express one's practices*

Three study days and the publication of a special issue of the journal *Socio-Logos* were carried out between 2016 and 2019. The first day was organized in June 2016 in Lyon, jointly by the University Lyon 2, the Max Weber Center, the French Sociology Association (and more specifically the thematic networks "RT4. Education and training", and "RT46. Formation, certification, qualification"), as well as the Association des Sociologues de l'Enseignement Supérieur. It was entitled: "Social sciences, knowledge and practices for and in teaching" and was composed of 10 papers (see Appendix A).

The second meeting took place in November 2017, again in Lyon, under the aegis of the same partners, and the LLE (Laboratoire de l'Education, ENS Lyon), in which 13 papers were presented (see Appendix B). It is from these papers that a selection of eight articles would form the core of issue 14 of the journal *Socio-Logos*, which was entitled "*Enseigner la sociologie dans le supérieur*" (teaching sociology in higher education).

The intention of the general approach was spelled out in the text presenting the first day. Starting from the observation of the rise of discourses and devices aiming at the promotion of "higher education pedagogy", the text recalled that:

> In political terms, there is a strong case for not depriving higher education teachers and disciplines of all legitimacy and possibility of producing a discourse, analyses and reflexivity about their current pedagogical practices. [...] Moreover, since higher education teachers are regularly solicited during the revision of pedagogical models, it seems unavoidable that they be equipped theoretically and practically to position the components and disciplines as informed interlocutors in the face of universities caught up in a movement of economization between competition and impoverishment of means[9].

---

9 Text announcing the study day "*Les sciences sociales, des savoirs et pratiques à et pour enseigner*" (Social sciences, knowledge and practices to and for teaching) (2016).

The ambition of the study days and of the issue of *Socio-Logos*, a journal of the Association Française de Sociologie, was then "to question the practices of teaching social sciences in higher education from a disciplinary point of view" by calling for papers and articles dealing with "both the presentation of research and the presentation of teaching experiences". And this, with the perspective of producing a collective space for reflexivity around these themes by collecting a set of practices giving insight into what had been done, sometimes for several decades, rather than making up what should be done (Tralongo et al. 2019).

In total, some 30 doctoral students and current lecturers and researchers presented sociology teaching practices in higher education. Different types of courses (lectures, tutorials, field placements), but also levels (from the first year of the bachelor's degree to the master's degree), or fields and places (ranging from sociology to education sciences, to professional courses) were discussed.

6.4.2. *Some content*

The papers and articles will show that beyond these variations, which were strongly expected and encouraged in the interventions, several common points brought them together. These points constitute as many shifts with the common discursive fund on the "pedagogy of the higher education". More specifically, they will illustrate the relevance and some of the consequences of mobilizing sociology and, more broadly, the social sciences to analyze these practices. These disciplines, which are thus solicited both to invent courses and to anchor practices, provide avenues of escape from the common discursive fund, including in the ways of defining and implementing creativity and reflexivity. Thus, we observed quite stimulating, diversified and ingenious ways of teaching sociology, which took up the issue of academic failure. Failure was thus finely re-interrogated on the scale of a course, sometimes by mobilizing the notion of "rational pedagogy", of Bourdieu and Passeron (1964), without excluding from the accounts the doubts, the failures and the trials and errors.

We discovered that, far from the image of a bookish or off-the-grid discipline whose teaching should be transformed to make it more "professionalizing", teaching sociology today consists of teaching a practice (therefore gestures, tricks, postures, tinkering) as much as knowledge, and putting reflexivity at the heart of it. This is a complex task, which is nourished by scientific knowledge, by epistemological reflection on the conditions of production of this knowledge, by methodological know-how and by a back and forth between these different dimensions of sociological practice. Much of the difficulty for teachers lies in the need to articulate these different components while taking into account the material, temporal and institutional constraints specific to their institution, their component, their degree and their public. Nicolas Jounin's book, which outlines a field teaching practice of providing confrontational situations between students from working-class neighborhoods to the beautiful neighborhoods of Paris, is an exemplary illustration (Jounin 2014).

Among the papers and articles, several dealt with the teaching of survey methods, whose introduction into sociology degrees is the result of a long history. This has close links with the development of sociology in higher education (after the creation of a bachelor's degree in 1958), and with the pluralization of methodologies in the framework of research. The dialogue between teaching and research, which did not wait for the injunctions of the last 20 years to be established, was underlined (Beaud and Weber 1997). Articles presented practices that allowed students to learn to "do fieldwork". They showed the importance of a reflexivity that is itself to be acquired during the exercise and that the teacher can transmit. All the experiences presented, such as field placements, quantitative or qualitative collective surveys, underscored the advantages of a direct, repeated and long pedagogical relationship with the students, which is in direct opposition to the reduction of the volume of hours in the curriculum, the problems of financing specific pedagogical devices such as placements, or the desire to deploy distance learning courses.

A final point common to the interventions showed how and to what extent sociology can be its own resource for teaching sociology and for reflecting on how it is done. Unsurprisingly, sociologists do not leave behind their sociological knowledge about teaching or students when they teach. Whether it concerns the transformation of the university, the diversification of student populations, the social construction of academic failure, the specificity of knowledge or the position of the written word within scholarly cultures, this knowledge guides teaching practice, from the construction of courses to their realization, including the evaluation of student productions. In particular, the discipline arms sociologists to think about the work of appropriation of the transmitted knowledge in its complexity. Considering the university as well as the students in all the diversity of training, knowledge, study conditions, previous socializations, intellectual and practical habits, etc. thus offers three ways of going beyond the current discourse. The first is to break with the representation of a generic student, which is the one from which the Bologna directives and teacher training programs reason. The second is to take a reflexive look at how to make one's teaching practices as effective and as non-inequitable as possible. The third is to remain aware of the multilevel material effects on teaching and learning conditions, ranging from the layout and furniture of a classroom to tuition fees, remuneration, employment of teachers and student life: not everything is a matter of teacher goodwill in student "success".

Ultimately, the discipline is equipped to distance itself from and/or dialogue with the theories coming from neighboring disciplines (economics, political science, educational sciences, psychology, linguistics, etc.), and thus the explicit or implicit theories that make up the common discursive fund on "higher education pedagogy". It is therefore very difficult to take at face value and to impose the categories of perception and action promoted by this discourse. And in particular one of them, whose particularity is the defusing in advance of any conflictual exchange which is necessary and indispensable to any scientific practice. For this amounts to asking lecturers and researchers *not* to mobilize one of the most structuring and fundamental practices of the construction of scientific knowledge, namely the radical questioning, deconstruction and reconstruction of any knowledge, know-how, theory and concept likely to be mobilized. In other words, it consists of asking them to suspend the critical and constructive dimensions of thought, which are the guarantee of mastery and control of the theoretical and conceptual tools used, which lets (others) think and speak.

6.5. Conclusion

In 2012, the journal *Education et sociétés* published an issue entitled "*vers une mise en ordre cognitive*" (Towards a cognitive ordering) which followed a colloquium on "the sociology of education and the recomposition of the state at a time of globalization and European construction". In the introduction to the issue Jean-Louis Derouet drew up the state of play of social science disciplines, whose critical dimension was in crisis, in the face of an order "whose installation was based at least in part on the criticisms that they had formulated in the 1970s: the denunciation of the Leviathan

State and of bureaucracy, calls for the recognition of the actors' capacities for initiative, the taking into account of differences, etc". He stated that these disciplines were then "embarrassed to question this order that took up many of their conclusions and sometimes their concepts, even if they noted that it prolonged, and even often aggravated, the forms of domination of the old [...]". This introduction was meant to announce a "new period of criticism [...] based on a permanent interplay between participation in the new networks of knowledge production and the ability to analyze their functioning" (Derouet 2012).

The announcement was optimistic. The theme of "higher education pedagogy", resituated in a socio-history of higher education showing the masked influence of politics, underlines all the difficulties in escaping from a particularly pervasive common discursive background. Lecturers and researchers are caught up in a cognitive and practical framework that draws on different sources, including scientific theories and concepts. They are sometimes called upon to take on expert roles and to mobilize widely to change teaching practices. No doubt, depending on the degree of proximity to the social sciences, the very possibility of installing a critical space to analyze one's teaching practices differently varies greatly. It turns out, however, that such a space is more necessary than ever to give oneself the means to (re)think one's practices in a universe that is not merely a "paraphrase" of reality, nor a pre-formatting of the problem and the solutions. It is then the very possibility of reintroducing history and conflict, and thus the social realm, into a discourse that has confiscated it, and more broadly of "presenting an alternative project" (Cussó 2008) that is raised.

6.6. References

Beaud, S. and Weber, F. (1997). *Guide de l'enquête de terrain*. La Découverte, Paris.

Béjean, S. and Monthubert, B. (2015). Pour une société apprenante. Propositions pour une stratégie nationale de l'enseignement supérieur. Report, Comité pour la Stratégie Nationale de l'Enseignement Supérieur [Online]. Available at: https://www.enseignementsup-recherche.gouv.fr/pid30540/strategie-nationale-de-l-enseignement-superieur-stranes.html [Accessed 12 July 2020].

Bertrand, C. (2014). Soutenir la transformation pédagogique dans l'enseignement supérieur. Rapport à la demande de Madame S. Bonnafous, Directrice générale pour l'enseignement supérieur et l'insertion professionnelle [Online]. Available at: https://www.enseignementsup-recherche.gouv.fr/cid82478/soutenir-la-transformation-pedagogique-dans-l-enseignement-superieur.html [Accessed 12 July 2020].

Bourdieu, P. and Passeron, J.-C. (1964). *Les Héritiers. Les étudiants et la culture.* Minuit, Paris.

Croché, S. (2006). Qui pilote le processus de Bologne ? *Éducation et sociétés*, 2(18), 203–217 [Online]. Available at: https://www.cairn.info/revue-education-et-societes-2006-2-page-203.htm [Accessed 30 June 2020].

Cussó, R. (2008). Quand la Commission européenne promeut la société de la connaissance. *Mots. Les langages du politique*, 88, 39–52 [Online]. Available at: https://journals.openedition.org/mots/14263 [Accessed 30 June 2020].

Cussó, R. and Gobin, C. (2008). Du discours politique au discours expert : le changement politique mis hors débat ? *Mots. Les langages du politique*, 88, 5–11 [Online]. Available at: http://journals.openedition.org/mots/14203 [Accessed 30 June 2020].

Dakowska, D. (2017). What (ever) works. Les organisations internationales et les usages de "bonnes pratiques" dans l'enseignement supérieur. *Critique internationale*, 4(77), 81–102 [Online]. Available at: https://www.cairn.info/revue-critique-internationale-2017-4-page-81.htm [Accessed 27 May 2021].

De Ketele, J.-M. (2010). La pédagogie universitaire : un courant en plein développement. *Revue Française de Pédagogie*, 172, 5–13 [Online]. Available at: http://journals.openedition.org/rfp/2168 [Accessed 27 May 2021].

Derouet, J.-L. (2012). L'Europe : une mise en ordre cognitive ? Présentation. *Éducation et sociétés*, 1(29), 5–10.

Filâtre, D. (2017). Réformer le premier cycle de l'enseignement supérieur et améliorer la réussite des étudiants. Rapport général [Online]. Available at: https://cache.media.enseignementsup-recherche.gouv.fr/file/concertation/26/6/RAPPORT_GENERAL_Reformer_le_premier_cycle_de_l_enseignement_superieur_et_amerliorer_la_reussite_des_etudiants_835266.pdf [Accessed 13 July 2020].

Garcia, S. (2008). L'expert et le profane : qui est juge de la qualité universitaire ? *Genèses*, 1(70), 66–87 [Online]. Available at: https://www.cairn.info/revue-geneses-2008-1-page-66.htm [Accessed 27 May 2021].

Jounin, N. (2014). *Voyage de classes. Des étudiants de Seine-Saint-Denis enquêtent dans les beaux quartiers.* La Découverte, Paris.

Lahire, B. (1999). *L'invention de l'"illettrisme". Rhétorique publique, éthique et stigmates.* La Découverte, Paris.

Monte, M. and Rémi-Giraud, S. (2013). Les réformes de l'enseignement supérieur et la recherche. Mots, discours et représentations. *Mots. Les langages du politique*, 102 [Online]. Available at: https://journals.openedition.org/mots/21244 [Accessed 12 July 2020].

Ravinet, P. (2011). Comment fixe-t-on les objectifs d'une politique publique ? Le cas du Processus de Bologne, ou processus de construction d'un Espace européen d'enseignement supérieur. In *Sociologie de l'action organisée. Nouvelles études de cas*, Barthélémy-Stern F. (ed.). De Boeck Supérieur Editeur, Louvain-la-Neuve.

Recherche et Formation (2011). Former les universitaires à la pédagogie. *Recherche et formation*, 67, 9–121.

Recherche et Formation (2014). La posture d'accompagnement dans l'enseignement supérieur. *Recherche et Formation*, 77, 9–100.

Rege-Colet, N. and Romainville, M. (2006). *La pratique enseignante en mutation à l'université*. De Boeck Supérieur, Brussels.

Revue des Sciences de l'Education (2008). La recherche sur la pédagogie de l'enseignement supérieur. Où en sommes-nous ? *Revue des Sciences de l'Education*, 3, 529–728.

Revue Française de Pédagogie (2010). La pédagogie universitaire : un courant en plein développement. *Revue Française de Pédagogie*, 172, 5–76.

Revue Internationale d'éducation de Sèvres (2019). La pédagogie universitaire. *Revue Internationale d'éducation de Sèvres*, 80, 49–134.

Socio-Logos (2019). Enseigner la sociologie dans le supérieur. *Socio-Logos*, 14 [Online]. Available at: https://journals.openedition.org/socio-logos/3286 [Accessed 12 July 202].

Stavrou, S. (2013). Des discours politiques au discours de l'évaluation. Autour de la réforme des formations universitaires. *Mots. Les langages du politique*, 102 [Online]. Available at: https://journals.openedition.org/mots/21357 [Accessed 12 July 2020].

Tralongo, S., Court, M., Kakpo, S. (2019). Dire plutôt que laisser dire. Analyser en sociologue ses pratiques d'enseignement. Introduction au dossier. *Socio-Logos*, 14 [Online]. Available at: https://journals.openedition.org/socio-logos/4144 [Accessed 13 July 2020].

6.7. Appendices

6.7.1. *Appendix A: the program for the day (June 27, 2016)*

Schedule	Speakers and title
Morning	Stéphanie Tralongo, "Introduction"
	Romuald Bodin, Mathias Millet and Emilie Saunier, "Teaching practices in the HSS captured in comparison with other disciplinary sectors"
	Charles Soulié, "Family trees as introductory tools to sociology: a Franco-Brazilian experience"
	Sandrine Garcia, "Completion of the research master's degree for students with low academic resources"
	Yvan Bruneau and Nancy Venel, "The field placement: teaching through practice, creating another student/teacher work space"
	Beatrice de Gasquet, "Direct observation as an application exercise for a sociology course"
	Stéphane Vaquero, "Can we 'spill the beans'? Training in the mobilization of disciplinary knowledge in a research process"
Afternoon	Hélène Stevens, "Unfolding the social. Review of a practice of teaching sociology through self-socioanalysis"
	Audrey Boulin, Séverine Chauvel and Anne-Claudine Oller, "Tutoring in the first year of higher education: trial and error around a project"
	Sophie Denave, "Training students in the social sciences through the implementation of empirical surveys"
	Irène Pereira, "Training elementary teachers through sociological research: using qualitative inquiry methods to improve classroom practices"
	Léa Dousson, Mélanie Guillaume, Simon Kéchichian, Claire Piluso, Stéphanie Tralongo, "The workshop 'Teaching social sciences in higher education'. Feedback"

Table 6.1. *June 27, 2016 Study Day "Social sciences, knowledge and practices to and for teaching"*[10]

---

[10] This study day took place in French. All conference titles have been translated into English for ease of comprehension.

6.7.2. Appendix B: the 2017 program

Schedule	Speakers and title
November 9	Stéphanie Tralongo, "Introduction to the study days"
	Session 1: Teaching the fundamentals of sociology
	Delphine Serre "Building and delivering a thematic course without an associated seminar: what paths are there between lectures and inductive pedagogy?"
	Pierre Blavier, Samuel Coavoux, Anton Perdoncin, The teaching of quantitative sociology in France: an overview
	Speaker: Martine Court
	Session 2: Teaching inquiry through inquiry (1)
	Abigail Bourguignon and Julie Maurice, "Getting students' hands dirty: a reflexive look at teaching qualitative inquiry methods in a grande école"
	Sandrine Nicourd, "Teaching in a professional master's program: collective inquiry as a research approach"
	Speaker: Sylvia Faure
	Session 3: Students at work
	Gaële Henri-Panabière, "Investigating one's students and reflecting on one's practices: the case of a 'quantified participant observation'"
	Etienne Guillaud and Juliette Mengneau, "Learning the sociological gaze through comics. Feedback on a unique educational experience"
	Speaker: Frédéric Rasera
November 10	Stéphane Beaud, "The field is not that easy". Critical reflections on field teaching in sociology"
	Speaker: Sandrine Garcia
	Session 4: Teaching inquiry through inquiry (2)
	Stéphane Bonnéry, "Initiating sociological research in an undergraduate course in educational sciences in a popular university: issues, advantages and limits of an experience"
	Corinne Davault, Anaïs Leblon: Learning reflexivity through the field
	Speaker: Sophie Denave
	Session 5: Self-analysis exercises
	Séverine Kakpo and Claire Lemêtre, "Self-socioanalysis: a tool at the service of university democratization? Critical feedback on an educational experience"
	Anna Mesclon, Frédérique Letourneux, Daniel Veron and Juliette Mengneau, "Teaching sociology as a sociologist: feedback on an experience of initiation to sociology through self-socio-analysis"
	Speaker: Charles Soulié

	Session 6: Teaching sociology in professional training
	Marianne Woolven, "Elements of sociology for speech and language therapists and senior school administrators. Which 'theory' for which 'fields'?"
	Xavier Pons, "Teaching the sociology of public action to education professionals or how to re-enchant the social world"
	Speaker: Stéphane Bonnéry

Table 6.2. *Study days of November 9 and 10, 2017, Lyon*[11]

---

11 These study days took place in French. All conference titles have been translated into English for ease of comprehension.

7

Transmitting Knowledge in the First Year of University: A Sociology of Work Perspective

7.1. Introduction

Since the 1960s, the transmission of knowledge in the university institution has been the subject of several types of sociological research. The founding work of Bourdieu and Passeron approaches it from the cultural angle and draws attention to the inequalities that this transmission contributes to reproduce between students (Bourdieu and Passeron 1964). This has been the central issue in the sociology of higher education for the past 50 years (Beaud 2003; Millet 2003; Orange 2013). For its part, the sociology of science is interested in the formation and circulation of knowledge in higher education, but rather from a research perspective (Latour and Woolgar 1979; Becher 1989; Latour 2005; Vinck 2007). For the past 20 years, the pedagogical practices of higher education teachers have also been the subject of studies conducted by higher education sociologists (Boyer et al. 2002; Faure et al. 2005; Bourgin 2011; Millet et al. 2018), who have sought to show the disciplinary variations of these practices.

In this chapter, I shall use a sociology of interactionist work to analyze the pedagogical work of higher education teachers (course preparation and classroom teaching). In a field survey of the first year of university undergraduate studies (L1), I sought to identify not only the variations but also the regularities of this pedagogical work, setting aside any normative

Chapter written by Marie DAVID.

objective, that is, without seeking to identify good or bad pedagogical practices.

Mobilizing the sociology of interactionist work consists of observing and analyzing the ways in which teachers work, their working conditions, the evolution of the institution[1] in which they work and the interactions between them and with students, in order to understand what they contribute to producing: transmitted knowledge. My approach is part of the Chicago sociological tradition (Chapoulie 2001) in which researchers are interested in the study of work and professions by paying attention to the context of the work, the institutions in which it takes place, and the interactions between professionals and with users (Hughes 1996; Becker 1997). These studies have made it possible to draw up a list of general propositions for the study of a wide variety of forms of work: all work is collective; this collective dimension must be taken into account in the analysis; work is based on a division of labor, between workers in the same category and with those in other occupations, which is based on collective moral judgements. Applied to the case of the work of higher education teachers, this approach implies looking at how these staff in the university institution act, according to the way they define the situation (Thomas 2009) and how they anticipate and interpret the actions of others, particularly colleagues and students.

The Chicago interactionist tradition also relies on a method of survey, direct observation and an inductive type of data analysis. Here, the field survey was conducted in the first half of the 2010s, in a multidisciplinary university in western France. It took place within the university's science and sociology training and research units (UFRs). I observed teaching sessions (lectures, tutorials and practical work) in sociology, physics and chemistry, for groups of L1 students (Table 7.1). These observations were completed by interviews[2] with the teachers and students with whom I

---

1 For interactionist sociology, institutions, such as schools, hospitals or prisons are the product of collective actions, that is, they are the result at a given moment of the past actions of different actors (state, staff, users, etc.), but the norms that constitute them are always susceptible to renegotiation by these actors (Hughes 1996).

2 The interviews are secondary to direct observations: they aim to confirm or refute hypotheses formulated from the observations and to obtain information on aspects of the work that cannot be directly observed (such as homework). The interview guides are constructed from the observation categories constructed from the field data: for example, for teachers, the allocation of teaching services, the preparation of sessions, class work, evaluations, student work and the definition of academic discipline.

followed the lessons. I also collected and analyzed documents (course preparations, course and tutorial handouts, students' notebooks, training models and syllabi, etc.). Finally, I directly observed pedagogical meetings, informal discussions between teachers and students, as well as their work in the university library.

	Number of sessions observed	Number of hours of observation	Type of session	Interviews	
				Teachers	Students
Sociology	12	24	Mainly tutorials/ lectures	13	7
Physics	8	10	Mainly integrated courses and practical work	4	5
Chemistry	7	10	Mainly integrated courses and practical work	2	

Table 7.1. *Observed teaching sessions and recorded interviews*

The inductive approach aims to produce a "grounded theory" (Glaser and Strauss 2010) in the facts and relationships observed, that is, to produce concepts from the data collected in the field of investigation, and not the other way around. In this methodological framework, researchers go into the field with general questions but without seeking to confirm pre-existing theories. The theory is produced as the investigation progresses, through a back-and-forth process between the collection of field data (observations, interviews, situational statements, documents) and the progressive construction of analytical categories to account for them. In other words, the first direct observations make it possible to formulate more precise questions, to identify regularities (or exceptional cases) and to construct hypotheses that will be put to the test during the rest of the survey (according to the sequential analysis model, Becker 2006).

In this chapter, I shall present two findings from this investigation of pedagogical work in higher education. First, I shall highlight the fact that the teaching of the three disciplines conforms to teaching conventions, which are partly disciplinary. These conventions concern the ways of teaching (pedagogical conventions) and the ways of presenting knowledge, which correspond to logics specific to teaching: they do not therefore necessarily correspond to conventions in research.

I shall also show how teachers mark up the important knowledge transmitted in class and distinguish it from secondary knowledge, to frame the learning work by their students.

7.2. Conventions in content and teaching methods

Sociological observation of teaching work allows us to identify regularities, either disciplinary or common to the different disciplines[3]. In this section, I shall highlight the regularities that concern the pedagogical methods and the formatting of the knowledge transmitted, while emphasizing the disciplinary variations observed.

7.2.1. *Educational conventions*

Observations made in the first year in physics, chemistry and sociology show that the pedagogical form of teaching is very similar across these three disciplines. The ways of teaching, although they vary between teachers, groups of students or disciplines, follow a common pattern:

– The teacher leads the lesson: he/she indicates when the lesson starts, decides on the different stages, distributes the floor and indicates the tasks to be carried out.

– The teacher brings knowledge, writes on the board, explains and clarifies. Students say things, but they must be validated (and sometimes transformed) by the teacher.

– The teacher defines what should be remembered and noted down.

– The students' tasks are to listen, answer the teacher's questions (although this is not mandatory), ask questions if necessary and write in their notebooks.

– An exercise is carried out, which is a component of the course.

This corresponds to what is usually called a "dialogued course". It is a course in which much of the time is devoted to speeches, that of the teacher

---

3 It is, moreover, common with the general high school form of schooling (David 2015).

(mainly) and of several students. When students say something audible to the whole group, it is either in response to a request from the teacher or to ask a question. Classes can be thought of as dialogues, with the teacher on one side, and the students on the other side, who speak less, if at all. This is a broad definition of a dialogued lecture, including times in the lecture when the teacher speaks alone for a few minutes, as long as the teacher explicitly expects the students to intervene after this exposure time.

This "dialogical" form of lecture is not a free discussion: it is always the teacher who organizes and controls the discussion. The teacher is not the only one to ask questions, but the students' questions do not have the same status. The teacher asks questions to which he/she knows the answer, to teach something, while the students ask questions to learn and understand. The teacher's questions, or their elicitations (Mehan 1979), thus serve to convey knowledge or to make students convey it. This is an indirect form of knowledge enunciation, in contrast to the so-called "lecture". Generally, the teacher does not specify how the students are supposed to answer the questions: should it be with their personal extra-academic knowledge (the "knowledge of experience" (Deauvieau 2009, p. 84), with the help of the previous years' course, or at random?

The dialogical lecture is also not an exchange between the teacher and all the students, but only a few students. In my observations, the number of students participating in the exchanges varies from two to more than half the group. This implies that for a whole section of students who do not participate, the dialogical lecture is ultimately a lecture in which it is others who state the knowledge.

The recurrent observation of this pedagogical form in the different sessions, disciplines and groups suggests that the dialogic lesson is a pedagogical convention. I mobilize the concept of convention in the sense defined by Becker (1988). Conventions are ways of doing things that are habitual for people placed together in the same situation. In order to carry out an activity – for example, teaching knowledge to young adults – there are generally multiple possible ways of doing things, but individuals generally do things the way they are used to doing them, the way others usually do them, and the way things have been done before. This does not mean that there is no room for maneuver and that nothing ever changes. Acting conventionally is often the easiest way to do things, because others (in this case, colleagues and students) expect you to do things that way and because the rooms, schedules, and materials are designed for that kind of use.

The dialogical lesson is a convention insofar as it is a form shared by sociology, chemistry and physics teachers, known to all concerned, which does not need to be made explicit to be understood. It is not compulsory to teach in this way, nor is it necessarily the best way to teach, but at the time of the survey, this is how all the teachers observed were teaching (with variations, see below). Pedagogical conventions are not valid at all times and in all places. As Héry (2007) shows in relation to the spread of "active methods" in school education, they are the result of a historical process.

According to the disciplines, variants of the dialogued course have been observed. In physics and chemistry, in L1 (undergraduate year one), one of its variations consists of the dialogued resolution of calculative exercises. Here is a noteworthy example.

CHEMISTRY COURSE IN L1. The teacher has presented several formulas since the beginning of the course and dictated definitions. She refers the students to the first exercise of the chapter from the handout. She writes "Exercise 1" on the board and then says to the students, "I am listening". She waits for the students to solve the exercise live, orally. For the first questions, which correspond to the course that has just been given, several students answer at the same time (four or five at a time): why do we write the composition of atoms in a certain way? What do we get when we add up the number of protons and the number of neutrons (the number of nucleons)? The exercise then involves counting the number of nucleons for different examples. The teacher then takes turns questioning the students sitting in the room.

Part of the course is devoted to solving exercises, either prepared in advance by the students or not. Very rarely, a student solves the exercise alone (orally or on the board), or the teacher gives the correction alone; in most of the situations observed, the solution is collective, that is, the teacher addresses all the students to obtain partial answers to the questions of the exercise. I have observed many situations where the student at the blackboard is simply a scribe who writes down the answers of the other students that have been validated by the teacher, or even writes under the dictation of the teacher.

In sociology, a variant of the dialogical course consists of the organization of oral presentations by the students. The teacher gives a topic to a small group in advance. The group prepares the presentation outside of class time, and then presents it to the entire student body. In the sessions observed, the presentation quickly reverts to a dialogue-based lecture.

SOCIOLOGY OF INSTITUTIONS COURSE IN L1. It is Arthur and Kamal's turn to present their paper. They were given an excerpt of a few pages from Michael Pollak's The Concentration Experience. Arthur talks about the depersonalization and repersonalization of deportees, and how this happens. The teacher interrupted him after 2 minutes: "It is not the Jews who lose their personality, it is the institution that makes them lose it". Arthur replied that he was going to get round to explaining that, and the teacher apologized. He continued by talking about desocialization and then resocialization. He brings up the question in the text: "Why didn't the Jews leave before the deportation?" The teacher interrupts to explain the question. She then asks Arthur to continue. He explains the concepts of exit, voice and loyalty in order to analyze the behavior of Jews threatened with deportation. The teacher asks him to clarify this. He answers, then she gives examples herself. She speaks alone for 3 minutes, then gives the floor back to Arthur, who speaks for another minute.

Then it is Kamal's turn to speak. He speaks for almost 5 minutes without being interrupted, after which the teacher asks, "Do you see any similarities with Goffman's total institution?" Arthur begins to respond, making assumptions (because he has not read Goffman's text, which he does not tell the teacher). The teacher adds, "The similarity is primarily structural. In both spaces, there is hierarchy among the recluses". She continues to ask questions of Arthur and Kamal, who after three questions are unable to answer: the teacher then speaks alone for 5 minutes. She then asks the boys if they have anything to add. Kamal talks about the cessation of menstruation and erections in the concentration camps. The teacher takes up the speech and rephrases it, talking about the effect of the total institution on people's bodies.

In these two types of variants of the dialogued course, we find the main characteristics (see above): even if some students participate, it is the teacher who brings the knowledge, by stating it or validating it; it is the teacher who leads the session, who speaks the most and who indicates what is important to retain.

The dialogued course is presented by the teachers surveyed as a personal way of teaching, linked to a pedagogical preference. Marc (chemistry teacher) indicates that he "really likes the interactivity". Chantal (sociology teacher) considers that "there is a nice side", even if the dialogued classes, which she gives in lecture theatre, are more tiring. Bertrand (sociology teacher) considers that this type of course is "more productive", and Rania (chemistry teacher) believes that it allows her "to check who is following or not".

But that alone does not explain why it is a convention. This form is used as a group management tool, to ensure that all students are working. It is also a convenient and inexpensive way to ensure that students are intellectually active, as language activity is seen as a tangible sign of intellectual activity (Deauvieau 2007), which is a form of "constructivist illusion" (Mousseau and Pouettre 1999). L1 students, coming from high school, are used to this (David 2017b), so it is easier to teach them this way rather than confront them with other ways of teaching. In this way, students participate in the development and dissemination of pedagogical conventions.

However, the lecture has not disappeared from undergraduate teaching (Altet 1994; Boyer et al. 2002; Duguet 2014). It remains the conventional form of lecture hall courses[4], which is notably linked to material constraints (David 2015): larger number of students and organization of space in the lecture hall.

7.2.2. Conventions concerning the presentation of knowledge

The knowledge taught at the university is formatted and technicalized, presented in the form of written texts or equations, tables and diagrams. They consist of statements, using vocabulary, abbreviations or signs. This formatting varies according to the discipline.

Observations of teaching sessions in physics and chemistry show that student mastery of the conventional form of presenting knowledge is crucial. Teachers spend a lot of time teaching conventional ways of solving exercises and transmitting standardized language. Thus, learning a subject is first and foremost learning the form of this knowledge: this is what counts the most,

---

4 At the time of the survey, these lecture theatre courses were a small part of L1 courses in the UFRs surveyed, which explains why they are not detailed here.

what teachers insist on and what will allow students to pass the exams (which does not guarantee that the learning intended by the teachers has been achieved).

In class or at home, the work that the students have to do most often consists of solving exercises by calculation. These can be in the form of texts, diagrams or directly mathematical equations. The expected solution is of a computational type and, more rarely, is based on a diagram. Students are expected to be aware of this requirement, as teachers do not accept that they make a written response, without mathematical demonstration, to a problem posed. This does not mean that it is impossible in physics or chemistry to write one's answers in French, but that the standard of production of exercises in the studies assumes mathematical answers (possibly followed by a written sentence of answer)[5].

SECOND LECTURE-SEMINAR SESSION OF L1 ON STATICS (PHYSICS). After a recap of the lecture, the teacher projects the first exercise on the board. The statement indicates a basis and a force with its components; the instruction is to show that the vectors form an orthonormal basis of the plane. The teacher reads the statement and asks the students how to solve it. One boy replies, "we use orthonormal vectors". The teacher says that this is correct, but that we must be careful with the vocabulary: "it is a normed vector, its norm is equal to 1". He writes on the board what must be demonstrated by transforming the statement into mathematical symbols. Several exercises follow, solved on the board by the teacher with suggestions from the students. After half an hour, the teacher says: "Don't despair, the mechanics will come in a little while. This is not a math class; we're doing a warm-up lap. The mechanics will come soon".

During the physics sessions, students learn that the main issue is knowing how to use mathematics to answer questions. Some of the exercises could be solved otherwise, but that would not be an acceptable answer. Many physics courses thus look, to the layman, like math courses.

Chemistry knowledge is very often presented in the form of diagrams. Students must be able to understand an exercise statement in the form of a

---

[5] The way in which the use of the problem and the exercise using mathematics developed in physics in the 19th century is presented in Hulin (1992).

diagram, or to transform it into a diagram, or to answer with a diagram. The latter is a symbolized way of representing an object of study.

FIELD NOTES ON THE SCIENCES UFR. Here is, for example, an excerpt from an L1 chemistry exercise found in the survey: "Represent these molecules in structural formula, locate the polarized bonds and indicate the partial charges (δ+ and δ-) on the atoms participating in these bonds. [...] TO: CH_3–CH_2–Cl". The expression "CH_3–CH_2–Cl" represents a molecule in a schematic way.

In physics, teachers also use diagrams to explain knowledge or exercise statements. Diagrams are conventional ways of representing objects of study. The work of the students consists of learning these representations (how one usually represents a force, a vector, a bond between molecules, an electron, etc.) and knowing how to manipulate them. They must also learn standard procedures for writing their answers. The teachers insist that the students must know and respect these procedures.

L1 CHEMISTRY CLASS. In the previous session, the teacher presented a method for solving a type of exercise to study molecules. She gave the students exercises to do for this session. Before correcting them, she reminds them of the procedure to follow. One must determine in succession: "1. main function; 2. main chain radical; 3. number the main chain; 4. unsaturations; 5. substituents; 6. names". She then insists that students who come to correct the exercises on the board follow all these steps explicitly. She indicates that on the exam, their answer will not be accepted if they do not.

A month later, the teacher corrects on the board an exercise that the students had to prepare. Wilfried, a student, prepared it at home, but with a different method than the one used by the teacher. He explains how he did it; his method gave him the same result, but with more steps, and a slightly different process. The teacher tells him that he should not do it that way and that it is not the expected method. She concludes by saying: "I don't like this method". I don't understand whether Wilfried's method is scientifically correct or not, but the teacher's response makes it clear to everyone that there is only one acceptable way to do the exercise.

STATICS COURSE IN L1. The teacher announces: "We are going to write our first statics problem, and I am going to give you the framework of writing". He writes on the board, saying that he is going to write "clearly". He writes a protocol for solving the exercise. It is a question of first carrying out a "physical balance sheet" and then transforming it into a mathematical problem.

For each type of exercise studied in L1, there are protocols for solving them that are presented by the teachers and that must be followed to the letter by the students. Teachers agree that there are other ways of solving problems, but which they believe are more complicated, or less common. Learning the protocol is a simple and reliable way to successfully complete the tasks expected on the exam.

INTERVIEW WITH RANIA, LECTURER IN CHEMISTRY: "[what is important] is the development of reasoning. [...] It's a methodology for solving a type of problem. And here, typically, in aqueous solutions, we always reason in the same way. We look at what we introduce as a solution, then we look at the species that are likely to react, we write down this reaction, we make a progress table, and then we use this progress table. And here again, there is a methodology, either the action is balanced and there is a certain type of reasoning, or it is total, we look for the limiting reagent, which is another reasoning. And with this methodology, whatever your system is, you will always get there. If you don't have this methodology, whatever the system, you'll never get there".

The conventions also concern the way results are presented. Answers in physics and chemistry, in exercises and evaluations, must, according to the teachers surveyed, be written in French: a complete sentence is expected. Precise rules concerning the units used and rounding are given, which the students must learn.

In sociology, students must also learn to handle the conventions of formatting knowledge. These conventions include the ways in which knowledge is presented in writing. Teachers expect students to write organized paragraphs, according to the argumentative model of the essay. Precise formal codes are required and are the object of specific transmission, notably during the methodology sessions. Unless specifically instructed, other modes of writing are not permitted: use of abbreviations, unwritten presentations (list in the form of dashes, for example).

However, the knowledge taught in physics and chemistry is clearly more formalized and codified than in sociology. This corresponds to the differences in the degree of codification of the research disciplines, which Millet (2003) attributes to three main elements: the epistemological status of knowledge (the existence or not of widely recognized laws), the logics of knowledge (in particular, the fact that knowledge is recognized as being already there or under construction) and the intellectual traditions (tending more toward the literary tradition for sociology).

The formal conventions of teaching also contain a specific language, that of physics, chemistry or sociology in teaching, which includes the vocabulary used, the mathematical language for solving exercises and the diagrams. The conventional language in university teaching includes the disciplinary idioms, which first-year students must learn. In the teaching sessions of the three disciplines surveyed, the importance that L1 teachers attach to the use of the specific vocabulary of their discipline is clear. They very frequently rephrase students' contributions using disciplinary idioms.

OBSERVATION NOTES DURING A SEMINAR ON THE SOCIOLOGY OF INSTITUTIONS, OCTOBER 2013. The assignment focuses on the study of an excerpt from a text by Suaud (1976). Four students present the paper they prepared on this text. The teacher (a lecturer in sociology) has them complete their presentation by asking questions of the four students and then of the entire seminar group about the text. She rephrases each student's answer by changing the vocabulary used. For example, she says, "There is one element that you glossed over quickly, and that is the internship. What are the minor seminarians cut off from, and how?" Students offer several answers, including the time of other young men. One student says they do not have the same vacations. The teacher rephrases the answer by indicating that there is a "time desynchronization". A little later, she asks what the minor seminarians are to the institution. The students do not respond. The teacher herself responds that "they are the clientele of the minor seminary; you have to use the course to answer". For the teacher, it is imperative that the students learn the terms "clientele" and "temporal desynchronization" and reuse them if the opportunity arises.

The importance attached by the teachers surveyed to the precise terms of the vocabulary of the disciplines may nevertheless have the effect of diverting their attention, and that of the students, from mastering the concepts that are targeted. Mobilizing idioms does not necessarily imply an understanding the phenomenon or concept designated by the word. According to Bautier (2006), the form of the dialogical course tends to reinforce this focus of the teacher and students on vocabulary to the detriment of meaning.

7.2.3. Conventions specific to teaching

Teachers' insistence on conventional ways of presenting knowledge and on standardized procedures for solving exercises could lead one to believe that these conventions are linked to the nature of disciplinary knowledge and that it is not possible to present it otherwise. This would imply that all teachers transmit knowledge in physics, chemistry and sociology in the same way and that there are no variations from one level of teaching to another or from one university to another. This is not the case. Formal conventions on disciplinary knowledge are partly based on local agreements between teachers (David 2019). Some conventions differ between high schools and universities.

Different conventions coexist in teaching (between teaching levels and research specialties). There are competing ways of notating notions, of schematizing and of symbolizing. In theory, all of them are equally valid, if the criterion of validity is conformity to academic knowledge. But this poses problems for teaching and evaluation: students can be disconcerted by the variations between teachers and can be put in difficulty at the time of common exams.

INTERVIEW WITH RANIA, LECTURER IN CHEMISTRY. She explains to me that by modifying the course handout for L1, she tried to standardize the way of teaching chemistry in L1 with some colleagues.

"The ultimate goal is that all students leaving the first semester of the core curriculum have a basic, common vocabulary for chemistry. And in fact, because of historical relationships, in chemistry even researchers do not speak with the same vocabulary to describe the same thing, because it depends a little bit on the history of each sub-discipline of chemistry [...]. We wanted to make a continuity with that by establishing a single common vocabulary for chemistry, at least at the beginning".

In the reported situation, the chemistry teachers appealed to an external standard (outside the academic institution and research) to decide between the different possible ways of writing chemistry: they relied on the programs of preparatory classes.

The conventions used are indeed teaching conventions and not research conventions: if the notations, the ways of writing, the diagrams, etc. are sometimes the same as in some research articles, this is not always the case. The conventions used in teaching are mainly valid in this context. Moreover, research specialties do not always help to decide between different ways of grading. Research in the sciences, particularly in physics, is more internationalized than in sociology, which implies broad theoretical but also practical agreements (on the formalization of results, for example), but intra-disciplinary variations (between research specialties) remain important.

These results echo those of Caussarieu and Tiberghien (2017), who studied how uncertainty in physical measurements is taught in higher education. They show that uncertainty is a major teaching issue, but that uncertainty as it is taught has neither the same meaning nor always the same notation as in physics research.

In sociology, the theoretical analyses to which the teachers refer offer a much wider range of formatting of knowledge than in physics and chemistry. Paradoxically, in the UFR of the survey, this theoretical diversity is not automatically reflected in the teaching: the modes of presentation and transcription of the knowledge taught are relatively more homogeneous than the research knowledge in sociology. This can be explained by the organization of teaching work (David 2017a): the lack of time to prepare their courses and the fact that they have to teach knowledge that they are not specialists in lead sociology teachers to fabricate their courses from that of their colleagues. This produces a certain standardization of the knowledge taught and its relative autonomy from academic knowledge.

The teaching conventions observed during the survey, which concern the shaping of knowledge, therefore appear to be partly contingent and local, which shows their variability from one level of teaching to another or from one team to another, but also the possible variations with the shaping of knowledge in the research work. They are the result of provisional agreements and adjustments within the teaching teams.

7.2.4. *The role of common evaluations*

In the survey, it appears that the content and forms of teaching are more standardized in the science faculty than in the sociology faculty. This is due in particular to the existence of prescriptive course documents and common evaluations. In the sociology department, common teaching documents exist in the form of "collections" of sociological texts, which are used in courses and in class. Most of the time, these collections are drawn up by one teacher on his or her own behalf, more rarely by two or three teachers together. They are then distributed to other teachers of the same course or tutorial, who use them to prepare their teaching more easily. There is thus a non-institutionalized circulation of sociological collections in the UFR, which are adapted by each user teacher and transmitted from one year to the next. This produces a flexible standardization of teaching content.

But this standardization is not imperative: nothing obliges the teachers to use the common documents and some do not have access to them (because they do not ask for it or are not offered it). Above all, no exam is strictly common to several teachers of the same course, tutorial or practical work in this UFR, so the teachers have the freedom to teach or not to teach the same thing. In the survey, some sociology teachers prepare evaluation subjects together, but voluntarily, without solicitation or administrative control. No one then comes to check whether the subjects or examination conditions were the same and the correction of papers is not shared.

On the contrary, when common assessments are institutionalized, this produces a strong and prescriptive homogenization of the taught content.

EXTRACT FROM THE FIELD NOTES ON THE SCIENCES UFR. The students of L1 sciences are subjected to common evaluations (continuous control and partial exams at the end of the semester) for most of their courses. In physics and chemistry, the subjects are prepared by a small group of teachers who are in charge of the course that year. They are based on the course material (or "handouts"). They have to take into account the views of other teachers in the same course, especially if they have a different way of approaching a particular concept or law, or a different opinion on the degree of requirement for students (which is reflected in the complexity of the exercises and their degree of formalization). Disagreements are expressed about the content of the evaluation topics and the marking schemes.

Common assessments for the same teaching define expectations for students in terms of knowledge and form. These expectations become conventions when teachers transpose them into their teaching. The content taught is then strongly standardized by the evaluation subjects.

The designers of the subjects also take into account the exercises given in previous years, which are circulated among students in the form of "annals". These allow students who obtain them to anticipate teachers' expectations for the evaluation. They also help to define an evaluation standard: if the subjects turned out to be very different from those in the annals, it is likely that students would protest. This is especially true since it is the most studious students who use the exams: to radically change the type of assessment is to risk alienating these students.

In the sciences, the teaching conventions that are developed and adjusted from year to year are transcribed in the course handouts, which in the survey are generally written by the same authors as the evaluation designers. The handout is used by all the teachers in the survey for two main reasons: it simplifies the work of preparing the sessions and it also serves as a reference for making common topics. In other words, the knowledge selected in the document, its formal presentation and the exercise resolution procedures indicated correspond to the conventions that will be used in the assessments.

There is no formal obligation for a teacher to use a handout, to follow it in order, or to complete the exercises in the handout. The knowledge presented can be worked on in a different way, and it is possible to work on other knowledge. But observation shows that two categories of people limit the possibilities of variation in teaching: colleagues and students. Colleagues criticize teachers who do not follow the handout to the letter; they put pressure on them to fall in line; they can also turn to the department head. The students, on the other hand, check with their peers in other groups to see if they are being taught in a similar way. They compare the rate of progress in the handout, the number of exercises completed, the degree of detail given (e.g. in correcting exercises). If they observe variations between groups, they raise concerns with the teacher.

INTERVIEW WITH PASCAL, LECTURER IN PHYSICS. Interviewer: and could you say: "in my course I don't do the exercises belonging to the course, I do others..."?

Pascal: maybe I could... It depends. My experience, having worked in different teams, is that in some, with certain colleagues, we force ourselves to do at least such and such an exercise, so that we know that all the students have at least seen this kind of prompt. And so, we can give the test something like that, or something similar, etc. Because, you know, there is the discourse with the students, who say "ah with us, he skipped this exercise, and this exercise is exactly the one that came up on the day of the exam", well, you see, there is sometimes this kind of feedback that you get from the students, who are very... hyper academic, and say "I didn't have the same thing as the group next to me". Moreover, there is the student pressure, which perhaps makes you reluctant to engage in this approach of coming up with different exercises.

These repeated pressures from students and colleagues in the sciences make it difficult not to conform to collectively prescribed knowledge when there are common assessments. In sociology, on the other hand, students have little concern about comparing lessons across groups because assessment is dependent on their teacher alone.

All in all, the observation and analysis of the work of university science and sociology teachers brings to light teaching conventions that are in part common to all three disciplines: this is the case of the dialogical course in all small group teaching. There are disciplinary variations of these conventions. The practical and material organization of teaching, as well as disciplinary traditions, can lead to a strong standardization of teaching, in particular when evaluations are common. This depends both on locally negotiated modalities and on the internal homogeneity of academic disciplines, between countries and research specialties (David 2019). Let us now turn our attention to another common dimension of teaching work at the undergraduate level: the way in which important knowledge is defined.

7.3. Knowledge markers

The volume and scope of knowledge taught in a course are very coherent, if we transcribe all the content stated by the teachers and what is projected or given to read.

It would likely be impossible for a student to retain all the knowledge taught in 1 year. Students and their teachers know this. The former as well as the latter are then focused on defining the knowledge that it is necessary to retain. On the other hand, the other knowledge is secondary or accessory.

Sociologically observing the work of students and teachers at the university allows us to identify what knowledge is essential to them, how they delimit and identify it. In this section, we will see how undergraduate teachers place oral and written markers for their students to identify important knowledge and how, for the same reason, they seek to control student notetaking.

7.3.1. *The work of delimiting important knowledge*

In preparing courses, presenting knowledge and evaluating students, the teachers surveyed sort out the "good" and "bad" knowledge, in other words, that which is useful and that which is less useful. In this way, they delimit the knowledge to be learned by the students: to mark each important piece of knowledge, they delimit or "tag" it, either in written form or orally, explicitly or more implicitly.

This marking work is observed during the teaching sessions. To ensure that the students will identify the important knowledge without error, they constantly give indications. In all the courses observed in the three disciplines, I noted the use of expressions such as: "this is important", "this is the course, this is what you need to know", "remember these equations", "if you have a sentence to remember..." or equivalents.

COURSE OF MECHANICS IN L1. The session is about sliding. The teacher solves exercises, by questioning students from time to time, then completes the course. After 1 hour, he asks them if they have understood, in light of the continuous assessment which will take place the following week. A student asks a question, the teacher answers by recalling the course in three sentences and by making a diagram on the board: "That is the sliding criterion. This is the only criterion you have to know, or learn, for slippage. Every time you have a question about slippage, this is it".

The "important" marker punctuates a sequence that varies in length, from a few minutes to a whole session, with explanations, developments, exercises or activities. The marker indicates what the students should remember but does not summarize everything that has been worked on. It draws a line between what is important and everything else, which therefore becomes unimportant. The non-important is, according to the teachers, what the students need to understand the course: the demonstrations, the examples, the developments and the exercises.

L1 SOCIOLOGY, ANTHROPOLOGY CLASS IN A LECTURE THEATRE. The teacher talks about the 12 prohibitions of the Bible. He specifies: "Don't write them down! Try to identify the main prohibitions". Before reading the 12 prohibitions and detailing them, he insists: "do not write them down".

Some respondents defend the idea that in the first year, the main thing is that students learn essential knowledge, even if they do not yet understand it. This position is more frequently defended in chemistry and physics than in sociology. It is particularly supported by those who perform a significant portion of their service in L1 (David 2017a).

These teachers do not think that L1 courses are of no value for understanding knowledge, but they consider that students in the first years cannot understand all the knowledge that is presented, which leads them to insist on the fact that one must first learn knowledge, before trying to understand it.

MECHANICS COURSE IN L1. The teacher projects on the board a diagram on the displacements of objects. He presents the notations of displacements. He draws the attention of the students to the questions of writing: it is necessary to first write the forces, then the movements, and not the other way around.

A student asks if there are mathematical reasons for this way of writing. The teacher replied, "Exactly, but you will see that in the second or third year. Just remember that the notation for forces is the first column, while moments are the second column".

There is thus a reduction both in the scope of knowledge and in its difficulty. There are indeed situations where teachers answer students' questions that go beyond what they had planned to present. But in this case, the explanation is accompanied by a clarification: "just remember that..." or "we won't ask you". On the other hand, placing knowledge markers allows teachers who wish to do so to talk about something other than what is in the program of study. They expand on examples or anecdotes while indicating that it is off topic or optional.

When students participate orally in the course, they do not do the work of marking up knowledge themselves. For example, in sociology lectures, students present things that the teachers consider important and others that are anecdotal without distinction. For this reason, students' interventions are almost systematically retranslated by the teachers. Far from repeating what they have said, teachers transform them to delimit the important knowledge: they change the terms used to use the conventional concepts or words of the discipline instead, they summarize by putting aside what seems to them to be incidental, and sometimes they even completely transform the meaning of the students' words to translate them into what should be retained from the course.

The teachers surveyed also place written markers: on the board, in slide shows, or in course handouts.

CHEMISTRY COURSE IN L1. The teacher begins by reminding the students of the course: she draws their attention to a page in the chemistry handout that summarizes "the essentials". The course delivered during the previous session is much more extensive than the page in question, but according to the teacher it summarizes what should be retained. She then corrects with the students the exercises that they had to prepare at home. This takes 20 minutes, after which she points to a chart in the handout: "so you have a chart that summarizes what I just said here that you need to know".

This represents a sharp reduction in knowledge: the students who prepared the exercises spent anywhere from a few minutes to an hour on them, followed by more than 20 minutes of class work, but what counts in the end is a brief table. In the L1 science handouts, boxes, summary sheets or tables explicitly tell students what they need to remember from the course.

The written markers reinforce the indications given orally. Several procedures are used to indicate important knowledge in writing and visibly distinguish it from other knowledge: putting it in bold, highlighting it and using titles such as "summary" or "essential". The slide shows used in class contribute to this tagging of important knowledge: apart from the diagrams or tables that are discussed during the session, few words and sentences are included. The teachers who use them say that they put down the "most important" things, and that is how the students interpret them.

7.3.2. *Note-taking, a collective activity of teachers and students*

7.3.2.1. *Teachers' supervision of notetaking*

The teacher's tagging of the knowledge taught also takes place as students take notes. In the L1 courses observed, the teachers expect their students to produce a written trace of the teaching, whether on paper or, increasingly frequently, digitally. However, this written trace is one of the main supports from which students will work after the course and will learn the knowledge, notably to prepare for the exams.

Delineating important knowledge therefore also means getting students to take note of it, as this increases the likelihood that they will learn it. Important knowledge is what needs to be graded, and conversely what is graded is what is designated as important.

The first-year survey shows that students' notetaking is supervised by their teachers. However, there are variations in this control work, from the least supervised (very few explicit indications) to the most supervised (course entirely dictated or written on the board):

– The teacher dictates the entire course.

– The teacher dictates part of the lesson: what seems most important, summaries, important sentences, definitions and theorems. He writes down some sentences as well as formulas and equations. However, he lets the students write down extra things, such as examples or explanations.

– The teacher gives many written and oral indications on what to write down, but without really dictating: he repeats several times the important sentences and puts many tags to indicate that it is necessary to write down ("note this down, it's important"). Among these teachers, some have the students write texts themselves, but then dictate them to the whole class to avoid the possibility that some students have jotted down a false or incomplete synthesis.

– The teacher is not overtly concerned with the students' notetaking: he or she does not give explicit guidance on this subject. This last situation is the one most rarely encountered during the survey.

Cases 2 and 3 (partially dictated course/many indications) are the most frequently observed[6], which echo other research on pedagogical modalities in higher education. Duguet's (2014) survey shows that, even in lecture halls, dictated lecture practices are common. Very few teachers do not bother to guide students' notetaking, at the very least by repeating important sentences several times; many clearly frame notetaking (Bourgin 2011). Contrary to a widespread idea, most L1 teachers do not let their students identify the knowledge to be noted on their own but guide them strongly.

Variations appear between disciplines (Duguet 2014): in my survey, the case of the "partly dictated lecture" is the most frequently encountered in physics and chemistry; teachers write or project on the board all the formulas, equations, developments, diagrams and sometimes definitions; they dictate some definitions. In addition, they give oral explanations and examples that the students can write down. In sociology, even if there are fully dictated courses in seminars, the most frequent case is that of numerous oral and written indications (case 3).

The L1 teachers surveyed state, in interviews or in open discussions, that they seek to control notetaking because they feel that students do not know how to do it. This, they say, is the result of year after year of adjusting to students' work. In checking students' notebooks, or correcting their papers, they found that notetaking was incomplete or poorly focused. The following interview excerpt expresses a widely shared view among experienced teachers.

INTERVIEW WITH A LECTURER IN PHYSICS. "I've noticed over the years that, well, maybe it's a mistake on my part, but [the students] don't know how to take notes, etc., and so I really write down everything I want them to have written down. I mean, whatever I think would be useful for them to have written down if they ever go back and read their notes… So, when I realize that I'm saying a sentence and I say to myself, "Oh, this is actually quite important", […] I write it down. You see, […] it wasn't necessarily like that in my day, but I realized that if I didn't […] I'd go through the rows, I'd

---

6 The small number of teachers surveyed makes it impossible to quantify these results. Counting the number of cases encountered is therefore of little interest. It does, however, make it possible to verify whether the situation corresponds to the results of quantitative surveys on the same phenomenon (which is the case here) and, above all, to orient the subsequent fieldwork to understand the motives of the actors: in this case, what leads them to frame the note-taking.

see nothing about the content... And I do it [...] because otherwise I think that the students, they don't know how to take the... They wouldn't know how to recover, let's say, the information that I've given them".

7.3.2.2. *Students take note of "what is important"*

Students are also concerned with identifying what is important among the body of knowledge provided and taking note of it. They will thus adjust to the teacher's framework.

During my investigation, I systematically observed what students wrote in their notebooks, and I regularly read and compared these notes to see what variations there were between students. The result is this: there is very little variation between notebooks from one student to the next.

Whenever teachers give directions on what to write down, students copy the designated content into their notebooks. Thus, the same phrases and formulas are found on the documents of students in the same group. What the teachers designate as important is indeed found in the students' written record. Moreover, what teachers do not label as important is rarely noted: developments or explanations, developed examples.

By participating in classes with the students, I learned along with them how to spot what each teacher may or may not test them on. One of the things you have to learn at the beginning of the semester is to recognize the signs of what to write in your notebook. Some signs are quite explicit, so they are easy to spot: when the teacher says, "write this down now", "I'm dictating", "this is important, you have to write it down", "I'm giving the definition, write it down, it could always be useful". But most often, the signs are implicit. The teacher who dictates his lesson slows down the flow, raises his voice a little and repeats exactly the same sentences several times.

Although the notetaking of students in the same group is very similar, students talk about it in two different ways. The first category of students is minimalist: these are the ones who say they only write the essentials.

INTERVIEW WITH MORGANE, STUDENT IN L1 OF SOCIOLOGY. "I write down what I find most important.

Interviewer: How do you know what is most important?

Morgane: Well... I don't know, when I listen to him, I get a sense of what is important, or, I don't know, if he's telling his life story, I know it's not important".

The second category is maximalist: these students say they try to write down everything the teacher says.

OBSERVATION NOTES DURING A SOCIOLOGY CLASS IN A LECTURE HALL. During a break in a sociology lecture, I talk with Emma, sitting next to me. She tells me that she tries to write down as much as possible of what the teacher says, and then she will synthesize it at home (by making cards). She does not intend to learn everything. She thinks that the teacher says a lot of things, but that not everything is important. He gives too many details.

These two categories, minimalist and maximalist, have been identified in other surveys (Frickey and Primon 2002), which show, among other things, that the quantity of written notes is not a good indicator of student success or seriousness.

There is an important difference in student notetaking between tutorials on the one hand, and lecture theatre-based lectures on the other: sociology students[7] who note down the essentials in tutorials say that they note "everything" or "as much as possible in lectures".

GARANCE, STUDENT OF L1 OF SOCIOLOGY. "In fact, I write down the ideas that I have understood, the main ideas that I have understood, and then there are times when I write down everything to the letter. That is to say, I really write down the whole sentence, but it's rare, because you can't do that all the time either. But in general, it's more the ideas that I understood. I listen and then I write down quickly. [...] In lectures, in general, I take notes of everything, because I don't have the time to just take the ideas and transcribe. [Since] the relationship with the teacher is less direct, I prefer to take everything down and then I rework it, make index cards, and all that".

My observations and the students' comments have led me to compare the two categories that appeared at first glance: there are not necessarily clear-cut differences between maximalists and minimalists. The maximalists can be deferred minimalists: they too sort out what is important and what is secondary, but after the course. Second, it cannot be said that minimalists are

---

7 There were no lecture courses in L1 science during the survey period.

more autonomous than maximalists, since they all give priority to what the teacher designates as important: the sorting of minimalists is modeled on that of the teacher.

7.4. Conclusion

What can we see with the help of a sociology of the work of transmitting knowledge at the university, that is, by observing the practices of first-year teachers? The interest of this approach is not to focus on the result of the work (the effectiveness or not of the teaching[8]) but rather to focus on the daily practices of working with knowledge, on the meaning that the teachers give to them and on the way in which these practices adjust to the students. This approach makes it possible to identify certain regularities in pedagogical work.

The ways of teaching are partly shared in L1, regardless of the discipline and regardless of the teacher. This means that the variations are circumscribed within a common conventional practice, that of the dialogic lesson. The variations that have been observed are linked to disciplinary traditions and to local habits. They do not seem to be linked to the requirements of disciplinary knowledge itself, as shown by the differences between teaching conventions and research conventions.

Wanting to adapt to the level of their students also leads university teachers to supervise student work and to delimit, among the knowledge transmitted, that which they consider most important. This is reflected in the concept of "tagging", a process by which teachers indicate essential knowledge and distinguish it from other knowledge transmitted. This practice not only affects student learning, but also the knowledge itself: markers tend to reduce the amount of knowledge actually learned.

These observations also show that, contrary to a widely held idea, teaching practices in L1 have changed significantly with the massification of university education in the 21st century. Concern for student understanding and success has led teachers to be concerned about their teaching practices (Fave-Bonnet 1993) and to seek to adapt them to new students (Soulié 2002). Teacher training in higher education would therefore benefit from a

---

[8] The main question, then, is not "do teachers work well?" but rather "how do they work?".

complete and multidisciplinary inventory of existing practices, to which sociology can contribute, rather than from preconceived ideas about practices that are supposedly unchanged.

7.5. References

Altet, M. (1994). Le cours magistral universitaire : un discours scientifico-pédagogique sans articulation enseignement-apprentissage. *Recherche et formation*, 15, 35–44.

Bautier, E. (2006). Le rôle des pratiques des maîtres dans les difficultés scolaires des élèves. *Recherche et formation*, 51, 105–118.

Beaud, S. (2003). *80% au bac... et après ? Les enfants de la démocratisation scolaire*. La Découverte, Paris.

Becher, T. (1989). *Academic Tribes and Territories: Intellectual Enquiry and the Cultures of Disciplines*. Open University Press, Buckingham.

Becker, H.S. (1988). *Les mondes de l'art*. Flammarion, Paris

Becker, H.S. (1997). Les variations dans la relation pédagogique selon l'origine sociale des élèves. In *Les sociologues de l'éducation américains et britanniques*, Forquin, J.-C. (ed.). De Boeck, Brussels.

Becker, H.S. (2006). *Le travail sociologique. Méthode et substance*. Academic Press, Fribourg.

Bourdieu, P. and Passeron, J.-C. (1964). *Les héritiers. Les étudiants et la culture*. Les Éditions de Minuit, Paris.

Bourgin, J. (2011). Les pratiques d'enseignement dans l'université de masse : les premiers cycles universitaires se scolarisent-ils ? *Sociologie du travail*, 53(1), 93–108.

Boyer, R., Coridian, C., Erlich, V., Fijalkow, Y., Primon, J.-L., Soulié, C. (2002). *Pratiques enseignantes et pratiques étudiantes du cours magistral en premier cycle universitaire*. Institut national de recherche pédagogique, Paris.

Caussarieu, A. and Tiberghien, A. (2017). When and why are the values of physical quantities expressed with uncertainties? A case study of a physics undergraduate laboratory course. *Int. J. Sci. Math. Educ.*, 15, 997–1015.

Chapoulie, J.-M. (2001). *La tradition sociologique de Chicago. 1892–1961*. Le Seuil, Paris.

David, M. (2015). Les savoirs des formes de scolarisation. Comparaison entre le lycée et la première année de licence. *Revue française de pédagogie*, 193, 25–40.

David, M. (2017a). La division du travail enseignant et ses effets sur les savoirs enseignés. *Recherches en éducation*, 30, 50–62.

David, M. (2017b). Les savoirs comme construction collective. Enquête au lycée général et en première année à l'université. PhD Thesis, Université de Nantes, Nantes.

David, M. (2019). Le travail collectif de définition des savoirs par les enseignants de physique, de chimie et de sociologie à l'université. *Revue d'anthropologie des connaissances*, 13(1), 195–224.

Deauvieau, J. (2007). Observer et comprendre les pratiques enseignantes. *Sociologie du travail*, 49(1), 100–118.

Deauvieau, J. (2009). *Enseigner dans le secondaire. Les nouveaux professeurs face aux difficultés du métier*. La Dispute, Paris.

Duguet, A. (2014). Les pratiques pédagogiques en première année universitaire : description et analyse de leurs implications sur la scolarité des étudiants. PhD Thesis, Université de Bourgogne, Dijon.

Faure, S., Millet, M., Soulié, C. (2005). Enquête exploratoire sur le travail des enseignants-chercheurs. Vers un bouleversement de la "table des valeurs académiques" ? [Online]. Available at: https://halshs.archives-ouvertes.fr/halshs-00602398/document [Accessed 18 March 2021].

Fave-Bonnet, M.-F. (1993). *Les Enseignants-chercheurs physiciens*. Institut national de recherche pédagogique, Paris.

Frickey, A. and Primon, J.-L. (2002). Les manières sexuées d'étudier en première année d'université. *Sociétés contemporaines*, 48(4), 63–85.

Glaser, B.G. and Strauss, A. (2010). *La découverte de la théorie ancrée. Stratégies pour la recherche qualitative*. Armand Colin, Paris.

Héry, É. (2007). *Les pratiques pédagogiques dans l'enseignement secondaire au 20e siècle*. L'Harmattan, Paris.

Hughes, E.C. (1996). *Le regard sociologique. Essais choisis*. École des hautes études en science sociales, Paris.

Hulin, N. (1992). Le problème de physique aux XIXème et XXème siècles. Forme, rôle et objectifs. *Histoire de l'éducation*, 54, 39–58.

Latour, B. (2005). *La science en action. Introduction à la sociologie des sciences*. La Découverte, Paris.

Latour, B. and Woolgar, S. (1979). *La vie de laboratoire. La production des faits scientifiques*. La Découverte, Paris.

Mehan, H. (1979). *Learning Lessons: Social Organisation in the Classroom.* Harvard University Press, Cambridge and London.

Millet, M. (2003). *Les étudiants et le travail universitaire : étude sociologique.* Presses Universitaires de Lyon, Lyon.

Millet, M., Bodin, R., Saunier, E. (2018). Entre triple contrainte et ancrage disciplinaire. Pratiques et conditions d'enseignement à l'Université. *Cahiers de la recherche sur l'éducation et les savoirs*, 17, 143–167.

Mousseau, M.-J. and Pouettre, G. (1999). Histoire-géographie, sciences économiques et sociales. In *Un transfert de connaissances des résultats d'une recherche à la définition de contenus de formation en didactique*, Colomb, J. (ed.). Institut national de recherche pédagogique, Paris.

Orange, S. (2013). *L'autre enseignement supérieur. Les BTS et la gestion des aspirations scolaires.* Presses universitaires de France, Paris.

Soulié, C. (2002). L'adaptation aux "nouveaux publics" de l'enseignement supérieur : auto-analyse d'une pratique d'enseignement magistral en sociologie. *Sociétés contemporaines*, 48(4), 11–39.

Suaud, C. (1976). Splendeur et misère d'un petit séminaire. *Actes de la recherche en sciences sociales*, 4, 66–90.

Thomas, W.I. (2009). Définir la situation. In *L'école de Chicago. Naissance de l'écologie urbaine*, Grafmeyer, Y., Joseph, I. (eds). Flammarion, Paris.

Vinck, D. (2007). *Sciences et société.* Armand Colin, Paris.

8

Postface: Synthesis and Perspectives

Our postface takes up the main points presented in our closing conference of the scientific day held at the ESPÉ[1] of the University of Rouen Normandy on April 1, 2019 entitled: *"La pédagogie universitaire : un terrain pour les recherches en didactique des disciplines[2]"* (*Laboratoire de Didactique André Revuz [LDAR];* André Revuz Didactics Laboratory) and ESPÉ of the Académie de Rouen in collaboration with the laboratory of the *centre interdisciplinaire de recherche normand en éducation et formation* (CIRNEF; Normandy interdisciplinary research center in education and training). The content of this conference, which offered a synthesis of the researchers' communications, was enriched by the reading of the contributions of the authors of the book entitled *"Les recherches en pédagogie universitaire : vers une approche disciplinairement située ? Les enseignants-chercheurs en sciences au prisme de leurs formations et de leurs pratiques"*. Before beginning an analysis of the chapters that make up the book, we feel it is important to recall the origins of the co-organization of the scientific day by researchers from the LDAR and the CIRNEF that gave rise to this book. The members of these two research units got to know each other during a meeting organized at the ESPÉ. This meeting was driven by a common desire to share the results of research on the practices of higher education teachers conducted by members of the two laboratories, which was reinforced by the organization of a partnership event. This event, which

---

Chapter written by Emmanuelle ANNOOT.

1 *Ecole Supérieure du Professorat et de l'Education*. A French school for the training of future teachers.
2 University pedagogy: a field for research in disciplinary didactics.

is the subject of this publication, brought together an audience of practitioners and researchers from different disciplines. The number of views of the conferences filmed on the CIRNEF laboratory website confirmed its great success.

In the field of academic pedagogy research, publications in education and training sciences are widely represented (De Ketele 2010; Lameul and Loisy 2014; Annoot 2017). In this volume, researchers from different disciplines speak out to produce knowledge. A discipline "constitutes a communication network producing a constellation of discourses, guaranteed by venues of publications, scientific events and associative groupings. The discipline is also the institution that transmits the knowledge developed, and thus trains, initiates and socializes the professionals working within it" (von Hofstetter and Schneuwly 2002, p. 6). The research results presented in this book can inform the designers of the training of higher education professionals who are lecturers and researchers. The originality of this book lies in its interdisciplinary approach. Indeed, "the internal decompartmentalization of the social sciences reveals all the intellectual benefits that result from the capacity of scientific training and approaches to free themselves from disciplinary pillars, which result rather from the effects of traditions than from methodical imperatives" (Commaille and Thibault 2014, pp. 55–56). The other particularity of this book is that it takes on the complexity of a research subject, the practices of lecturers and researchers, which are studied as "a fabric (complexus: that which is woven together) of heterogeneous constituents inseparably associated" (Morin 1990, p. 121). This is a demanding scientific approach that deserves to be praised.

This book focuses on research in university pedagogy, that is, on "the practices of teaching, learning and evaluation and, therefore, on research in this area" (Annoot and Fave-Bonnet 2004; Adangnikou 2008). In a book on collaborative practices, we have defined the term *practices* as "what lecturers and researchers do when they are teaching students face to face or remotely, but also preparing lectures, designing the course with teaching aids, maintaining a climate conducive to learning, supervising students' work, and working with peers formally in groups or informally". (Annoot 2020a, p. 138). Interest in pedagogy in higher education is certainly on the rise. Indeed, witnessing the recommendations of public policies for the improvement of teaching practices (Bertrand 2014) relayed by institutions, Tralongo (Chapter 6 in this book) deconstructs the discourse on the promotion of university pedagogy made by administrators: "The challenge is then to show that the recent deployment of a discourse of promoting 'university pedagogy' or 'higher education pedagogy' matched with devices and practices circumscribes within a narrow socio-cognitive framework the space of the thinkable within which to consider its practices and transformations". The project that led to the writing of this book is not to provide answers to a goal of transforming practices carried by these public policies, but to understand the way in which lecturers and researchers develop in the environment of their work as they go about their activity (Wittorski 2007). The ambition of such a project is to be commended, but its realization could have been perilous. Indeed, Leininger-Frézal (Chapter 2 in this book) considers how to "develop a pedagogical training offer for beginner and/or experienced higher education teachers". The author observes that "including the discipline in the proposed training courses was a point of tension between the various stakeholders in the training of higher education teachers". She identifies two conditions for thinking "of training in higher education in terms of disciplinary culture":

– making "training in higher education an end and not a means" (i.e. "subject him or her [the teacher] to standards that are exogenous");

– creating "networks of 'smugglers'", "practitioners and researchers of the teaching of their discipline" in higher education.

The book responds to these expectations by adopting an interdisciplinary approach to the field of research on university pedagogy, which is certainly partly based on the practices of lecturers and researchers in institutions, but which is made up of theoretical frameworks and methodological approaches that are robust and approved by different scientific communities.

The synthesis of the book is presented around four themes, which cut across all the contributions. First, we give some contextual and theoretical references on university pedagogy, which designates both a field of research and a field of practice. Second, we specify the relations between these fields by introducing the notion of expertise. Thirdly, we identify what a disciplinary approach to university pedagogy is. Finally, we question the links between the professional identity of academics and disciplinary specificities before presenting our conclusion.

8.1. University pedagogy: fields of research and fields of practice

Research on teaching practices in the field of university pedagogy or, more precisely, the expertise of researchers built on the results of their work is on the rise. "Discourses and practices on 'higher education pedagogy' in France date back to the last thirty years" (Tralongo, Chapter 6 in this book). Based on a consultation of the *Francis* database between 2006 and 2018, Leininger-Frézal (Chapter 2 in this book) shows that, "The discipline has become an entry point for research conducted on pedagogical practices and learning in higher education. These results need to be put into perspective. The number of articles published in 10 years is low. We are talking about one to two articles per year". However, the author emphasizes that "The subject matter is central to describing, analyzing and understanding teaching practices in higher education" and insists on the importance of encouraging new approaches. These fields of research in university pedagogy linked to fields of practice have developed considerably since the autonomy of universities in France, with particular attention being paid to the engineering of training and the attractiveness of institutions for both students and higher education teachers. This is why the use of the term "university pedagogy" sometimes refers to scientific issues and sometimes to professional issues. How can a field of practice feed a field of research? Jean-Marie Barbier (2013) sets out a series of conditions, including the need to transform problems of action into problems of knowledge (Barbier 2013, p. 13). This book is situated in this perspective. The research presented in this book echoes the burning issues for universities, notably those of teaching quality and student success. Based on proven theoretical frameworks and argued methodological choices, it presents research results in university pedagogy on teaching practices. The success of research findings in this area should not be equated with prescriptions. Tralongo (Chapter 6 in this book) pays particular attention to "discourses on 'higher education pedagogy'" and notes that "discussion of 'higher education pedagogy' evokes a series of topics that always seem to go together: it centers about change, why it is necessary, and how to implement it". However, beyond a possible adaptation to institutional recommendations, a diversity of factors produces the pedagogical activities of higher education teachers. The systemic approach initiated by Jean-Marie De Ketele (2010) to define university pedagogy assumes this complexity:

If, in the beginning, the emphasis was placed on pedagogical activities within universities (teaching activities and, later, learning activities), it soon became clear that these could hardly be studied in isolation, so important was the interplay with other components [...] We can identify the following components: at the center, the pedagogical activities (teaching and learning); upstream, the curriculum; downstream, the results of the pedagogical activities; across the board, the internal context factors (academic and student environment) and the external context factors (political, social, cultural, economic) (De Ketele 2010, p. 5).

In conclusion, the field of research on university pedagogy is consistent with current French public policies that value the pedagogical dimension of the teaching and research profession. Several measures illustrate these political orientations: the constitution of competency frameworks for higher education teachers, the creation of leaves of absence for pedagogical innovation based on the model of research leave, the development of university pedagogical services and the introduction of new forms of management focusing on the professional development of higher education teachers, in particular the mandatory training of new teachers. These measures are sometimes the subject of research. For example, the report published by the French Institute of Education on university pedagogy services (UPS) entitled *"Etat des lieux de la formation et de l'accompagnement des enseignants du supérieur"* (Cosnefroy 2015) or Sacha Kiffer's thesis (2016): *"La construction des compétences d'enseignement des enseignants-chercheurs novices de l'université en France"*. However, this field of research cannot be confused with fields of practice. This proximity of the two fields sometimes confers a dual role on academics as both researchers and experts. This point deserves particular attention.

8.2. Research and expertise

In higher education institutions, the expression by practitioners of a demand for expertise in the field of university pedagogy is concomitant with measures aimed at transforming their practices. We provide a few examples of reforms that call for these changes: the reorganization of bachelor's degrees with the *Plan réussite en licence* (success plan for bachelor's degrees) that began in 2007, then the application of the law on the "Orientation and success of students" (ORE), the generalization of the hybridization of training courses on digital work spaces and the development of various forms of tutoring. The recruitment of instructional designers working alongside higher education teachers and the extension of university pedagogical services constituted as a network throughout the country (Annoot 2016) are one way of responding to these new needs. The connection between these measures and the field specific to our object of study, the practices of lecturers and researchers, has led us to clarify the relationship between research and expertise in higher education (Annoot and De Ketele 2021): "In expertise, we are in an ethic of partnership to co-construct; in research, we are in an ethic of scientific collaboration between researchers: upstream, researchers have produced provisionally validated knowledge; the object currently under study is seen from several angles, which can lead to teamwork by several researchers (an increasingly strong trend); downstream, peers will validate (provisionally) or invalidate (always also provisionally) the scientific production. In expertise, it is a process of institutional legitimization; in research, a process of scientific validation" (Annoot and De Ketele 2021, p. 235). Research may correspond to a commission from public authorities to ultimately produce expertise. "These requests resemble a sort of injunction to the education and training sciences to prove their "usefulness" and to produce knowledge that can 'enlighten' public action" (Paivandi 2021, p. 6). The research produced by academics on practices can lead to an expertise that modifies them under certain conditions. Tralongo (Chapter 6 in this book) illustrates the experience of this dual role by taking the example of lecturers and researchers in the social sciences: "Lecturers and researchers are caught up in a cognitive and practical framework that draws on different sources, including scientific theories and concepts. They are sometimes called upon to take on the role of experts and to mobilize widely to change teaching practices". If this demand for expertise is sometimes supported by the public authorities, it can also be produced on the initiative of researchers recognized by the scientific communities of the academic world in the humanities and social sciences who are situated: "in a certain idea of science, as a project of elucidation of man, society and the world, without distinction of order or dignity, starting from a common demand for method, criticism and progress, in the service of a common ambition of knowledge but also of social utility" (Commaille and Thibault, 2014 p. 14). The scientific day and the book whose synthesis we are writing were born of the sole initiative of researchers supported by the institution in which they practice their profession. The authors of the chapters that are expressed are teachers and are directly concerned by the results of their own research. The meeting between researchers and practitioners has sometimes been made possible in university teaching services: "University pedagogy services base their training on the results of research. They sometimes develop research projects. The research carried out is often action research aimed at improving the practices of higher education teachers" (Leininger-Frézal Chapter 2 in this book). In short, if the chapters gathered here produce knowledge on teaching practices, they will be able to document them if researchers implement the conditions for their transfer. The design of the two-volume book published by Berthiaume and Rege Colet (2013) illustrates the dual approach of research and expertise and provides an example of how research findings can be transferred to practitioners. While drawing on the content of scientific works identified in a solid bibliography, the book written by the two researchers is aimed at both practitioners teaching in higher education, educational advisors, and students in the process of becoming professional in the field. The representatives of various academic disciplines who wrote the book assume the role of experts by making scientific research results available to the greatest number of people, by identifying situations that raise questions among practitioners, and by using vocabulary that is accessible to the general public in the chapters. Among them, those who declare themselves to belong to the education and training sciences community are largely represented. The question of disciplines is not central to this book, and yet the ways of teaching in lecture halls, or of using digital resources in supervised work or in hybrid training, for example, can be situated in disciplines. The writing of specialized manuals in different fields of science could be an objective in order to link two often separated components of the higher education teaching profession: discipline and pedagogy.

8.3. A disciplinary approach to university pedagogy

Among the scientific productions in the field of higher education pedagogy, the book written by a diverse range of authors links two research realms that have often been separate in the academic sphere of the French National Council of Universities: *Conseil National des Universités* (CNU), research on disciplines in different sections (e.g. English studies, physical, human, economic and regional geography, sociology, mathematics) and research in education and training sciences in the group entitled "multidisciplinary". Thanks to its interdisciplinary approach, the book explores the question of knowledge taught at the university with the contribution of researchers belonging to different scientific communities, which is innovative: "The regular meeting of research communities on higher education issues [...] in order to move towards interdisciplinarity is fundamental, as is the promotion of the results of their joint work" (ifé 2016, p. 12). It seems, however, that the question of the place of the scientific specialization of lecturers and researchers at the university in pedagogical practices is rarely addressed in contemporary research. How can this be explained? If the conceptions of science have varied with the history of universities, a legacy persists through the attraction for a model of training through research that has given a special status to teachers in the modern university: "Professors teach a general culture – *Bildung* – that presides over the formation of the mind and prepares for freedom. Gradually, they teach their scientific specialty [...] The student is introduced to science through this observation of the intelligence producing knowledge" (Dupont et al. 2014, p. 4).

In the 20th century, from the 1990s onward, the increase in the number of students, particularly those engaged in undergraduate studies, raised the question of how to adapt the organization of university education. In France, research on students dominated and gave rise to publications by sociologists, notably those of the French Student Life Observatory: *Observatoire de la vie étudiante* (Gruel et al. 2009). Twenty years after the European harmonization of degrees, publications on the pedagogical practices of academics and their effects have multiplied in education sciences, information and communication sciences, in particular (Annoot 2017). This research is itself part of different academic traditions in different countries. In the field of educational sciences, for example, Denis Berthiaume points out that pedagogy, that is, the psychological dimension of the relationship between teacher and learner, is more on the side of "Anglophone literature" while didactics, that is, the knowledge taught and the knowledge learned, is on the Francophone side. Denis Berthiaume (Chapter 1 in this book) shows that "The two intellectual traditions began to come together in the 1990s when English-speaking university pedagogy began to focus on "disciplinary specificity" (Becher 1994; Hativa and Marincovich 1995) and, at the same time, the French-speaking world of higher education began to question "university pedagogy", that is, the conditions of study and the future of university graduates (Dupont and Ossandon 1994)". He supports the rapprochement between these two distinct intellectual traditions oriented toward university didactics and pedagogy by defining the concept of "disciplinary pedagogical knowledge" developed below. In France, the success of undergraduate students has been the horizon of public policies for several decades (Annoot 2017), and particular attention has been paid to pedagogy associated with the quality of training and then the professional development of lecturers and researchers (Paivandi and Younès 2019). In order to respond to the demands for transformations in practices called for by public authorities, we hypothesize that in France research on higher education pedagogy that theoretically addresses all disciplines has been more widely disseminated than research on university didactics that is not universal in nature. The MOOC "Training to teach in higher education" which "aims to support the training and support of teachers, lecturers and researchers and doctoral students in higher education in their knowledge of learning processes and in their teaching and evaluation practices" piloted by the Ministry of Higher Education, Research and Innovation is an example. This type of resource, which relies on the expertise of a team of researchers, can be mobilized for the training of beginners in institutions, for example, without disciplinary distinction. However, the use of the MOOC does not exclude the joint organization of collective sessions on the analysis of the practices of these beginners who take note of these disciplinary specificities. In an institution where the question of free knowledge and the independence of the researcher have been founding principles of university education, the question of what knowledge is taught at the university is more relevant than ever. David (Chapter 7 in this book) shows that "The knowledge taught at the university is formatted and technicalized, presented in the form of written texts or equations, tables and diagrams. They consist of statements, using vocabulary, abbreviations or signs. This formatting varies according to the discipline". The book demonstrates that the specific disciplinary characteristics of lecturers and researchers influence their practices. The term "discipline" itself has different meanings, depending on whether, according to Bridoux et al. (Chapter 4 in this book), it has an institutional meaning or whether it is part of an epistemological reflection in which disciplines and subdisciplines can be discussed. The forms of articulation between teaching and research, for example, vary according to disciplinary specificities, sometimes with points of convergence between disciplines. Grenier-Boley (2019) studies what he calls the imprint of the research discipline in the teaching practices of lecturers and researchers. For example, Gueudet (2017) highlights the relevance of considering, in the context of a mathematician's teaching work, the role and place of resources from research in the design of resources for teaching.

David (Chapter 7 in this book) made observations in the first year in physics, chemistry and sociology, and found that the pedagogical form of teaching was very similar in these three disciplines, with the use of the "dialogued course", a convention shared by the teachers. "According to the discipline, variants of the dialogued course have been observed": dialogued resolution of calculation exercises (physics, chemistry in undergraduate first year) and organization of oral presentations by the students (sociology in undergraduate first year).

Scientific rigor therefore calls for the construction of a model for the explanation of the pedagogical practices of lecturers and researchers that links disciplines and university pedagogy in a systemic approach defined by De Ketele (2010). Based on this heritage, Denis Berthiaume (Chapter 1 in this book) develops the concept of disciplinary pedagogical knowledge that "allows the teacher to help the learner by focusing on both the knowledge taught and the psychological processes underlying their relationship. Thus, we find ourselves drawing from both elements of didactics and elements of pedagogy". The operationalization of this concept clarifies the way in which "pedagogical activities" placed at the center of De Ketele's (2010) schema are constructed by making explicit the relationship between pedagogical knowledge and taught knowledge. The disciplinary pedagogical knowledge defined by Denis Berthiaume has three dimensions:

– the teacher's pedagogical knowledge base (the teacher's goals and objectives, knowledge, and beliefs);

– disciplinary specificity (the epistemological structure of the discipline and the socio-cultural representations of the teachers of this discipline);

– the teacher's personal epistemology.

This disciplinarily situated definition of university pedagogy illustrates the "particularities of the knowledge of teaching at the university, which stems from the conditions of access to the teaching function and the professional identity of teachers with their allegiance to the discipline" (Rege Colet and Berthiaume 2009, p. 138). Yet, we can ask ourselves what, beyond these specificities, is common to lecturers and researchers regardless of the discipline they teach, which contributes to the construction of their professional identity.

8.4. The professional identity of lecturers and researchers and their practices

How can we define the professional identity of an academic who is both a researcher and a teacher? The hypothesis according to which the scientific discipline of lecturers and researchers and the research dimension of their profession would drive their relationship to teaching has been put forward by members of the Laboratoire de Didactique André Revuz (EA 4434 LDAR). Bridoux et al. (Chapter 4 in this book) use the concept of professional identity to enter these pedagogical territories through an empirical study of four disciplines (chemistry, geography, mathematics, physics). The authors identify the institutional or tacit norms assigned to the profession and recognized as such, the qualities deemed necessary to practice the profession and the values. Bridoux et al. (Chapter 4 in this book) identify constants in terms of values that transcend these disciplines: "to transmit a taste for the discipline while showing their own pleasure to students. Thus, they share the same qualities: to make students autonomous by putting them in a position to pursue the discovery of the content on their own, and to make students experience an approach of questioning and problem solving close to the activity of a researcher". David (Chapter 7 in this book) uses an interactionist theoretical framework to study the profession of higher education teaching by focusing on the study of work and professions and by paying attention to the context of the work, the institutions in which it takes place, and the interactions between professionals and with users (Hughes 1996; Becker 1997). Previous experiences influence the practices of these teachers in higher education; the role of the agrégation (civil service competitive examination in France), for example, is evoked as a model of training among physicists but also previous experiences of teaching or transmission in the broadest sense; experience as a sports coach in sciences and techniques of physical activities and sports (STAPS), for example as an instructor of leisure centers in education and training sciences, is a role where active methods are implemented (Etienne et al. 2018). Kiffer and Wittorski (Chapter 3 in this book) "approach the issue of lecturer and researcher training from the perspective of the professionalization of higher education". University teaching is different from secondary school teaching. No program is imposed, although the French High Council for the Evaluation of Research and Higher Education (*haut conseil de l'évaluation de la recherche et de l'enseignement supérieur*, HCERES) and the institutions issue guidelines for the accreditation campaigns for courses leading to the awarding of diplomas to students. Pedagogical recommendations are also linked to programs structuring the reform of university studies, particularly at the undergraduate level. Academics have certain beliefs about student learning, possess a pedagogical knowledge base and implement pedagogical practices to teach or get students to learn. The knowledge to be taught is drawn from the discipline, the main reference for identity. Sabra (Chapter 5 in this book) insists on the function of analyzing resources in order to understand the teaching done by academics: "We can say that considering the resources of a university professor in general and those resulting from research in particular opens up avenues for better understanding the relationship between the two types of activity (teaching and research)". Kiffer and Wittorski (Chapter 3 in this book) state that the "recognition of informal learning practices, which are overwhelmingly what novice academics do according this research, could contribute to the overall improvement of their pedagogical training in their early career". They emphasize the role of peers: "The results show that learning by observation-imitation is a practice present among all novice academics, regardless of their profiles". Our work on academics just starting out, which led to the same findings, asked us about "the conditions of empowerment of these beginners to elaborate their own pedagogical choices in a framework that is nevertheless constrained" (Millet and Annoot 2017, p. 11). These different research results, the professionalization of the profession, the modalities of design and choice of resources for teaching, the place of informality and the role of peers constitute a corpus for developing an approach to the professional development of lecturers and researchers.

8.5. Conclusion

To conclude, I will specify the two main contributions of this book. Reading it has led me to question the aims of university education and, more broadly, the relationship between science and society. "The essence of man [...] is defined by a human heritage, transmitted by education and increased by each generation" (Charlot 2017, p. 21). A researcher who is imbued with a disciplinary culture derived from this heritage forges their relationship to the world and contributes to the production of knowledge. Openness to a diversity of disciplines seems to be a priority for the intellectual training of students in a society undergoing profound changes. For such training to be possible, it seems important to look at the conditions in which this learning takes place. Thus, in a conception of public policy that relies exclusively on a closer relationship between the university and the world of work, the academic disciplines are not equal (Annoot 2020b). Let us give an example by citing the work of Christophe Point (2020), who points out that one of the consequences of this conception of training is the formulation of criticisms of ancient knowledge deemed of little use (archaeology, history or literature, for example), even though it is part of human heritage (Point 2020, para. 13).

The second contribution of this book is that it helps to define more precisely the practices of lecturers and researchers.

A generic formula is often used to qualify this mission inherited from a university tradition: *training through research*. However, this formula seems reductive because it does not explicitly refer to disciplinary cultures in the sense of the epistemology of the disciplines and the diversity of practices exercised in the different fields. The book addresses this issue and reveals the multiple ways in which links can be made between teaching content and teacher practices and between practices and research results. It reminds us that the relationships established with students and peers also guide the practices of higher education teachers. In summary, this book defines the profession of lecturers and researchers as a human profession (Bodergat and Buznic-Bourgeacq 2015), its activity being addressed to others (Piot 2009) in a knowledge society, which explains why disciplines cannot be neglected in university pedagogy research.

8.6. References

Adangnikou, N. (2008). Peut-on parler de recherche en pédagogie universitaire, aujourd'hui, en France ? *Revue des sciences de l'éducation*, 34(3), 601–621.

Annoot, E. (2016). Débat sur la pédagogie universitaire à l'heure de l'internationalisation et de la professionnalisation des formations supérieures en France. *Revue Education comparée*, 15, 19–38.

Annoot, E. (2017). La recherche en pédagogie universitaire en France [Online]. Available at: http://cache.media.enseignementsup-recherche.gouv.fr/file/2017/42/0/Volume_2_16_avril_2017_753420.pdf [Accessed 9 September 2021].

Annoot, E. (2020a). La place de la collaboration entre pairs dans l'entrée dans le métier d'enseignant-chercheur. In *L'observation des pratiques collaboratives dans les métiers de l'interaction humaine. Des pratiques pluri-adressées*, Mérini, C., Marcel, J.F., Piot, T. (eds). Presses universitaires de Rouen et du Havre, Mont Saint Aignan.

Annoot, E. (2020b). Un enseignement supérieur juste est-il possible ? [Online]. Available at: https://journals.openedition.org/edso/13442 [Accessed 9 September 2021].

Annoot, E. and De Ketele, J.-M. (2021). *Recherche ou expertise en enseignement supérieur : des postures et des identités à construire.* Éditions Academia, Louvain-La-Neuve.

Annoot, E. and Fave-Bonnet, M.F. (2004). *Pratiques pédagogiques dans l'enseignement supérieur : enseigner, apprendre, évaluer.* L'Harmattan, Paris.

Barbier, J.-M. (2013). Un nouvel enjeu pour la recherche en formation : entrer par l'activité [Online]. Available at: https://www.cairn.info/revue-savoirs-2013-3-page-9.htm#pa2 [Accessed 9 September 2021].

Becher, T. (1994). The significance of disciplinary differences. *Stud. High. Educ.*, 19, 151–161.

Becker, H.S. (1997). Les variations dans la relation pédagogique selon l'origine sociale des élèves. In *Les sociologues de l'éducation américains et britanniques,* Forquin, J.C. (ed.). De Boeck, Brussels.

Berthiaume, D. and Rege Colet, N. (eds) (2013). *La pédagogie de l'enseignement supérieur : repères théoriques et applications pratiques, Tome 1 : Enseigner au supérieur.* Peter Lang, Bern.

Bertrand, C. (2014). Soutenir la transformation pédagogique dans l'enseignement supérieur. Report requested by Madame Simone Bonnafous, Directrice générale pour l'enseignement supérieur et l'insertion professionnelle. Ministère de l'éducation nationale, de l'enseignement supérieur et de la recherche, Paris.

Bodergat, J.-Y. and Buznic-Bourgeacq, P. (2015). *Des professionnalités sous tension. Quelles reconstructions dans les métiers de l'humain ?* De Boeck, Brussels.

Charlot, B. (2017). Formes et enjeux des recherches en éducation et formation. *Les Sciences de l'éducation – Pour l'Ère nouvelle,* 50(1–2), 17–30.

Commaille, J. and Thibault, F. (2014). *Des sciences dans la Science.* Alliance Athéna, Paris.

Cosnefroy, L. (ed.) (2015). Etat des lieux de la formation et de l'accompagnement des enseignants du supérieur [Online]. Available at: http://ife.ens-lyon.fr/ife/recherche/enseignement-superieur/enseigner-et-apprendre-dans-l2019enseignement-superieur/rapports-et-etudes/etat-des-lieux-de-la-formation-et-de-l2019accompagnement-des-enseignants-du-supe301rieu [Accessed 9 September 2021]

De Ketele, J.-M. (2010). La pédagogie universitaire : un courant en plein développement. *Revue française de pédagogie,* 172, 5–13.

Dupont, P. and Ossandon, M. (1994). *La pédagogie universitaire*. Presses Universitaires de France, Paris.

Dupont, S., Meert, G., Galand, B., Nils, F. (2014). Comment expliquer le dépôt différé du mémoire de fin d'études [Online]. Available at: hal-00976884. [Accessed 9 September 2021].

Etienne, R., Annoot, E., Biaudet, P. (2018). Les enseignants-chercheurs débutants en France : l'urgence de la pédagogie. In *La formation entre universitarisation et professionnalisation. Tensions et perspectives dans des métiers de l'interaction humaine*, Adé, D., Piot, T. (eds). PURH, Rouen.

Grenier-Boley, N. (2019). *La recherche en mathématiques : une ressource pour les didacticiens ?* HDR, Université de Paris Diderot (Paris 7) Sorbonne Paris Cité, Paris.

Gruel, L., Galland, O., Houzel, G. (eds) (2009). *Les étudiants en France : histoire et sociologie d'une nouvelle jeunesse*. Presses Universitaires de Rennes, Rennes.

Gueudet, G. (2017). University teachers' resources systems and documents. *Int. J. Res. Undergrad. Math. Educ.*, 3(1), 198–224.

Hativa, N. and Marincovich, M. (1995). *Disciplinary Differences in Teaching and Learning: Implications for Practice*. Jossey-Bass, SF.

von Hofstetter, R. and Schneuwly, B. (2002). Introduction. Émergence et développement des sciences de l'éducation : enjeux et questions vives. In *Science(s) de l'éducation, 19e–20e siècles. Entre champs professionnels et champs disciplinaires / Erziehungswissenschaft(en), 19–20. Jahrhundert. Zwischen Profession und Disziplin*, von Hofstetter, R., Schneuwly, B. (eds). Peter Lang, Bern.

Hughes, E.C. (1996). *Le regard sociologique. Essais choisis*. École des hautes études en science sociales, Paris.

ifé (2016). Conférence de consensus : Réussite et échec dans l'enseignement supérieur : quels éclairages de la recherche ? Synthèse du rapport du jury [Online]. Available at: http://ife.ens-lyon.fr/ife/recherche/enseignement-superieur/enseigner-et-apprendre-dans-l2019enseignementsuperieur/seminaire-de-consensus/reussite-et-echec-dans-lenseignement-superieur-1/reussite-et-echec-danslenseignement-superieur [Accessed September 2021].

Kiffer, S. (2016). *La construction des compétences d'enseignement des enseignants-chercheurs novices de l'université en France*. Université de Strasbourg, Strasbourg.

Lameul, G. and Loisy, C. (2014). *La pédagogie universitaire à l'heure du numérique, questionnement et éclairage de la recherche.* De Boeck, Brussels.

Millet, C. and Annoot, E. (2017). Devenir enseignant-chercheur à l'heure de l'autonomie des universités. Une recherche sur les représentations du métier chez les doctorants [Online], Available at: http://journals.openedition.org/questionsvives/2547 [Accessed 9 September 2021].

Morin, E. (1990). *Introduction à la pensée complexe.* Le Seuil, Paris.

Piot, T. (2009). Quels indicateurs pour mesurer le développement professionnel dans les métiers adressés à autrui ? [Online] Available at: https://doi.org/10.4000/questionsvives.622 [Accessed 9 September 2021].

Point, C. (2020). Hospitalité épistémique et pédagogie universitaire : l'égalité et ses problèmes [Online]. Available at: http://journals.openedition.org/edso/13112 [Accessed 9 September 2021].

Paivandi, S. (2021). Préface. In *Recherche ou expertise en enseignement supérieur : des postures et des identités à construire.* Annoot, E., De Ketele, J.-M. (eds). Éditions Academia, Louvain-La-Neuve.

Paivandi, S. and Younès, N. (2019). *A l'épreuve d'enseigner à l'Université. L'enquête en France.* Peter Lang, Bern.

Rege Colet, N. and Berthiaume, D. (2009). Savoir ou être ? Savoirs et identités professionnels chez les enseignants universitaires. In *Savoirs en (trans)formation. Au cœur des professions de l'enseignement et de la formation,* von Hofstetter, R., Schneuwly B. (eds). Editions De Boeck, Brussels.

Wittorski, R. (2007). *Professionnalisation et développement professionnel.* L'Harmattan, Paris.

List of Authors

Emmanuelle ANNOOT
Université de Rouen Normandie
Centre Interdisciplinaire de
Recherche Normand en Education et
Formation (EA 7454)
France

Denis BERTHIAUME
Université de l'Ontario français
Canada

Stéphanie BRIDOUX
Université de Mons
Belgium
and
Laboratoire de Didactique André
Revuz (EA 5434)
Université de Paris,
Université Paris-Est Créteil,
CY Cergy Paris Université,
Université de Lille,
Université de Rouen Normandie
France

Marie DAVID
Université de Nantes
Centre Nantais de Sociologie
(UMR 6025)
France

Martine DE VLEESCHOUWER
Université de Namur
Belgium

Nicolas GRENIER-BOLEY
Normandie Université
and
Université de Rouen
and
Laboratoire de Didactique André
Revuz (EA 5434)
Université de Paris,
Université Paris-Est Créteil,
CY Cergy Paris Université,
Université de Lille,
Université de Rouen Normandie
France

Cécile DE HOSSON
Université de Paris
and
Laboratoire de Didactique André
Revuz (EA 5434)
Université de Paris,
Université Paris-Est Créteil,
CY Cergy Paris Université,
Université de Lille,
Université de Rouen Normandie
France

Rita KHANFOUR-ARMALÉ
CY Cergy Paris Université
and
Laboratoire de Didactique André
Revuz (EA 5434)
Université de Paris,
Université Paris-Est Créteil,
CY Cergy Paris Université,
Université de Lille,
Université de Rouen Normandie
France

Sacha KIFFER
Université Rennes 2
Centre de Recherche sur l'Education
les Apprentissages et la Didactique
(EA 3875)
France

Nathalie LEBRUN
Université de Lille
and
Laboratoire de Didactique André
Revuz (EA 5434)
Université de Paris,
Université Paris-Est Créteil,
CY Cergy Paris Université,
Université de Lille,
Université de Rouen Normandie
France

Caroline LEININGER-FRÉZAL
Université de Paris
and
Laboratoire de Didactique André
Revuz (EA 5434)
Université de Paris,
Université Paris-Est Créteil,
CY Cergy Paris Université,
Université de Lille,
Université de Rouen Normandie
France

Zoé MESNIL
Université de Paris
and
Laboratoire de Didactique André
Revuz (EA 5434)
Université de Paris,
Université Paris-Est Créteil,
CY Cergy Paris Université,
Université de Lille,
Université de Rouen Normandie
France

Céline NIHOUL
Université de Mons
Belgium
and
Laboratoire de Didactique André
Revuz (EA 5434)
Université de Paris,
Université Paris-Est Créteil,
CY Cergy Paris Université,
Université de Lille,
Université de Rouen Normandie
France

Hussein SABRA
Université de Reims
Champagne-Ardenne
Centre d'Etudes et de Recherches sur
les Emplois et les
Professionnalisations (EA 4692)
France

Stéphanie TRALONGO
Centre Max Weber (UMR 5283)
Université Lumière Lyon 2
France

Richard WITTORSKI
Université de Rouen Normandie
Centre Interdisciplinaire de
Recherche Normand en Education et
Formation (EA 7454)
France

Index

A, B, C

academics, 47–52, 54, 55, 57–60, 62–64
assessment, 177–180
Bologna Process, 144, 148, 149, 156
chemistry, 73–75, 77–79, 82, 84, 85, 87, 91–94, 97, 98, 100, 101
convention, 165–168, 170, 173–176, 178, 179, 187
common discursive fund, 140, 141, 143, 146, 150, 152, 154, 156

D, E

DAD (Documentational Approach to Didactics, 110, 116–118, 122, 131
dialogued course, 166, 168–170
didactics (*see also* disciplinary), 30, 31, 38, 43
direct observation, 164, 165
disciplinary (*see also* pedagogical)
  culture, 72, 74, 75, 77, 79
  didactics, 73, 75, 102
  specificity, 4, 5, 7, 8, 10–19

disciplines (*see also* epistemology), 5, 6, 8, 10, 12, 13, 17, 27, 29–40, 42–44, 62, 71–75, 77, 78, 81, 82, 84, 85, 87, 89, 92, 94, 97–100, 102, 111, 113, 114, 120, 140, 153, 154, 156, 164–168, 170, 174, 175, 179, 180, 182, 184, 187, 191, 192, 197, 199–203
  didactics of, 6, 10, 73, 75, 110, 113, 115, 191
epistemology, 10, 15–18, 30, 40, 79, 84, 85, 88, 96–98, 101, 115, 120, 200, 203
  of disciplines, 72, 73, 75, 77, 79, 82, 84, 85, 88, 93, 96–98, 100–102
  personal, 15–18
evaluation, 15, 19, 29, 34, 49, 50, 60, 72, 76, 91, 96–98, 115, 141, 155, 175, 177, 178, 192, 199, 201

G, H

geography, 73–75, 77–79, 82–87, 89–92, 95, 97, 98, 100, 101
high school, 166, 170, 175

higher education (*see also* pedagogy), 3–5, 10–12, 15–18, 27–29, 31–34, 36–43, 47, 48, 50–52, 54, 55, 71, 73, 90, 101, 109, 111, 132, 139–157, 160, 163–165, 176, 184, 191–195, 197, 198, 201, 203
  teacher, 3, 5, 7–12, 14–19, 28–33, 39, 40, 42, 43
  training in, 27, 29, 40, 43, 144, 187, 193

K, L

knowledge (*see also* pedagogical), 3–12, 14–19, 30, 31, 36, 38, 40, 41, 49, 50, 56, 60, 62, 71–73, 75, 77, 78, 80, 81, 85, 86, 88–90, 94, 95, 97, 99–101, 109, 111, 112, 114, 118–121, 128, 129, 131, 148, 150, 153–157, 160, 163–167, 169–176, 178–185, 187, 192, 194, 196–198, 200, 202, 203
  economy, 151
learning, 3–10, 12, 13, 15–17, 30, 33–41, 47, 48, 51, 52, 54–64, 73, 74, 80, 86, 87, 99, 102, 110, 115, 116, 127, 145, 155, 156, 161, 166, 170, 172, 173, 187, 192, 194, 195, 199, 202
lecturer, 16, 29–31, 39, 47, 61, 75, 89, 143, 146, 147, 173–175, 178, 184, 201
  new, 28, 31
lecturers and researchers (LR), 71–77, 79, 81–102, 105
  norms linked to, 75, 100, 101
  qualities linked to, 75–77, 100, 101
  tensions linked to, 81, 92, 97–101
  values linked to, 72, 73, 75, 76, 78, 79, 81, 82, 84–88, 91, 98–101

M, N, P

mathematics, 73–75, 77, 78, 80–84, 86, 87, 89, 92, 94, 95, 97, 99–101
  teaching practices, 109, 113–119, 123, 127, 129, 132
note-taking, 183, 184
pedagogical
  development, 47, 51
  disciplinary knowledge, 7, 9–11, 14–19
  knowledge, 4, 5, 8–12, 14–19
  practices, 19, 35, 71, 73, 74, 98, 100, 101, 153, 163, 164, 194, 198, 200, 202
  training, 28, 30, 32, 40
pedagogy
  higher education, 4, 48, 50–52, 54, 55, 140–148, 152–154, 156, 157
  university, 3, 4, 7, 8, 11, 18, 33, 34, 38, 39, 41, 42
physics, 73–75, 77, 78, 81–85, 87, 88, 91–94, 97, 99–101
profession, 48–52, 57
professional
  development, 8–10, 18, 19, 40, 42, 71, 142, 145, 195, 199, 202
  identity, 44, 71, 74–76, 100, 101, 114, 193, 200, 201
learning
  development of, 48, 51
professionalization, 47, 48, 50, 54, 149, 151, 201, 202

R, S, T, U

research (*see also* teaching and research)
  activity, 109–115, 121–124, 127, 129–132

resources, 9, 11, 29, 31–33, 39, 48, 52, 54, 56, 60, 109, 110, 113, 115–118, 120–127, 129–132, 140, 145, 160, 197, 199, 202
  pivotal, 121, 122, 124, 125, 127, 129, 130, 131
  research, 116, 119, 126, 127, 130
  system, 119, 122
scheme, 117, 118, 121, 124, 131, 132
scholarship of teaching and learning (SoTL), 38, 39, 42, 102
science didactics, 113
skills, 6–9, 15–19, 28, 47, 48, 50, 53, 54, 56, 62, 63, 91–93, 97, 120, 142
socio-historical reflexivity, 139
sociology
  of education, 9, 156
  teaching practices, 139, 140, 152–155
student, 6, 14, 29, 33, 34, 36, 42, 48, 52, 60, 83, 90, 92, 96, 97, 99, 101, 113, 115, 119, 128, 145, 146, 155, 160, 163–175, 177–187, 194, 195, 198, 202
  difficulties, 76, 79, 92–94, 97–100

teacher, 163–187
teaching (*see also* sociology *and* teaching and research), 3–13, 15, 16, 19
  practices (*see also* mathematics), 71, 72, 74, 76, 86, 87, 99, 100, 102
  resources for, 109, 113, 116, 117, 119, 121, 122
  training, 27–44, 47, 51, 54, 55
teaching and research
  relationship between, 110, 111, 113–117, 119, 120, 130–132
university (*see also* pegagogy), 27, 28, 30–34, 36–43, 163–165, 170, 174, 175, 179, 180, 187
  pedagogy, 4, 7, 8, 11, 18, 33, 34, 38, 39, 41, 42, 100, 101, 139–141, 151, 191–195, 197, 198, 200, 203

Other titles from

in

Innovations in Learning Sciences

2022

BISAULT Joël, LE BOURGEOIS Roselyne, THÉMINES Jean-François,
LE MENTEC Mickaël, CHAUVET-CHANOINE Céline
Objects to Learn About and Objects for Learning 1: Which Teaching Practices for Which Issues?
(Education Set – Volume 10)

BISAULT Joël, LE BOURGEOIS Roselyne, THÉMINES Jean-François,
LE MENTEC Mickaël, CHAUVET-CHANOINE Céline
Objects to Learn About and Objects for Learning 2: Which Teaching Practices for Which Issues?
(Education Set – Volume 11)

DAVERNE-BAILLY Carole, WITTORSKI Richard
Research Methodology in Education and Training: Postures, Practices and Forms
(Education Set – Volume 12)

HAGÈGE Hélène
Secular Mediation-Based Ethics of Responsibility (MBER) Program: Wise Intentions, Consciousness and Reflexivities
(Education Set – Volume 13)

2021

BUZNIC-BOURGEACQ Pablo
Devolution and Autonomy in Education
(Education Set – Volume 9)

SLIMANI Melki
Towards a Political Education Through Environmental Issues
(Education Set – Volume 8)

2020

BOUISSOU-BÉNAVAIL Christine
Educational Studies in the Light of the Feminine: Empowerment and Transformation
(Education Set – Volume 6)

CHAMPOLLION Pierre
Territorialization of Education: Trend or Necessity
(Education Set – Volume 5)

PÉLISSIER Chrysta
Support in Education

2019

BRIANÇON Muriel
The Meaning of Otherness in Education: Stakes, Forms, Process, Thoughts and Transfers
(Education Set – Volume 3)

HAGÈGE Hélène
Education for Responsibility
(Education Set – Volume 4)

RINAUDO Jean-Luc
Telepresence in Training

2018

BARTHES Angela, CHAMPOLLION Pierre, ALPE Yves
Evolutions of the Complex Relationship Between Education and Territories
(Education Set – Volume 1)

LARINI Michel, BARTHES Angela
Quantitative and Statistical Data in Education:
From Data Collection to Data Processing
(Education Set – Volume 2)

2015

POMEROL Jean-Charles, EPELBOIN Yves, THOURY Claire
MOOCs: Design, Use and Business Models

Printed and bound by CPI Group (UK) Ltd, Croydon, CR0 4YY